The Word for Teaching is Learning

The Word for Teaching is Learning

Language and Learning Today
Essays for James Britton

Edited by Martin Lightfoot and Nancy Martin
in association with the National Association for the Teaching of English

Heinemann Educational Books
London
BOYNTON/COOK PUBLISHERS
PORTSMOUTH, NH

8755.

HEINEMANN EDUCATIONAL BOOKS LTD
Halley Court, Jordan Hill
Oxford OX2 8EJ

Boynton/Cook Publishers
A Division of
Heinemann Educational Books, Inc.
70 Court Street, Portsmouth, NH 03801

Oxford   London   Edinburgh
Melbourne   Sydney   Auckland
Singapore   Madrid   Ibadan
Nairobi   Gaborone   Harare
Kingston   Portsmouth NH

© National Association for the Teaching of English

First published in 1988

Cover design by Linde Hardaker

HEB/UK ISBN 435 10090 4

HEB/Inc ISBN 0 86709 237 8

Library of Congress Cataloging-in-Publication Data

The Word for teaching is learning.

Bibliography: p.
Includes index.
1. English language – Study and teaching (Secondary)
2. Language arts (Secondary)   3. Britton, James, N.
I. Britton, James N.   II. Lightfoot, Martin.
III. Martin, Nancy (Nancy C.)   IV. National Association
for the Teaching of English.
LB1631.W64   1988   428′.007′12   88–5069
ISBN   0–86709–237–8

Typeset by Fakenham Photosetting Ltd.
Printed in Great Britain by
Biddles Ltd., Guildford, Surrey

Contents

Introduction
Nancy Martin

The teaching of English is still at the centre of public debate about education. In this book we have been concerned to review where English teachers stand in relation to language and learning. The contexts of British teachers' work have changed somewhat, and some critiques of theory and practice have been offered, and rebutted or accepted in part, but the central theoretical structure based on the role of language development in learning remains.

While the first three essays mount a programme for the future, the other pieces are items on an agenda – new items or ones which amend existing items. Thus the focus is on those aspects of English teaching which are particularly relevant in the current social and political context. The book may be seen as a kind of map with certain areas clearly defined, and others be taken as starting points for possible directions awaiting the definition which research and practice has yet to give. Certain ideas recur; they appear as arguments, or as side notes or comments attached to examples of practice. This introduction attempts to show how these ideas relate to each other and to the theoretical framework of the book; and it develops more fully some of those which are only glanced at as part of another focus. We also draw attention to the critiques – which illustrate the way in which intellectual structures are revised and maintained.

Informing the whole book is a realization of the way in which language enters into learning from the very beginning – from the first reciprocal exchanges between mothers and infants to the development of mature writers. The way children learn their mother tongue is a potential model for all learning and is in process of being institutionalized as the interactive model of learning begins to take hold. We now have a concept of English teaching and learning which applies to all learners – the spectrum of abilities. But we have not forgotten the individual histories which lie behind the theories. The contributors, while they locate changes in the broad context of theoretical ideas, also locate them in a texture of personal views, vignettes of classroom events and documentations of work with children.

Vygotsky hypothesized long ago that shared social behaviour was the origin of individual consciousness. He said:

An interpersonal process is transformed into an intra-personal one. Every function in the child's personal development appears twice, first on the social level and later on the individual level ... All the higher functions originate as actual relations between human individuals [Vygotsky, 1978].

Now, some fifty years later, with teachers' attention focused on how children learn, we can see the gradual elaboration of his ideas in practice as we follow the patient documentations of social learning contained in Part Two.

And there is a corollary. In coming to understand how children learn language, we have come to understand that this is also the way of much other learning. In taking part in rule-governed behaviour – a meeting, a party, group discussion, dramatic improvisation, and so on – a newcomer picks up the implied rules by responding to the behaviour of others and quickly internalizes them. Becoming literate operates in a similar way. We learn what stories are by reading and telling and writing them; similarly with other genres. There is, of course, the alternative, traditional mode by which teachers analyse the rules and then teach them as procedures or models. In Part One Douglas Barnes describes and assesses the advantages and disadvantages of both ways of learning and argues for a model which draws on both but which has social interaction at the centre.

If we look now at the less well-defined areas of our map, we find one of the recurring themes is what might be called aesthetic experience. This thread is pervasive. As one reads the group of articles in Part Two about children writing stories of their lives and reading stories of other lives, something seems to be emerging which asserts the primacy of the meaning of the stories in their hold on the children. Can this be seen as the beginning of an aesthetic response or is it just the mysterious control of the narrative thread unwinding? A child's response to a story is not usually thought of as the aesthetic response; we tend to see this as the product of education and developing later, if at all. Yet, if Vygotsky (1978) is right, feeling and subordination to voluntarily created 'rules' are the means by which children move – in play – from the world of objects into the world of ideas. He suggests that play is the realization in play form of tendencies that cannot be immediately realized in the real world – for instance, the change from a child wanting its mother to wanting to be the mother. He goes on to say that children's imaginative play *teaches them new desires*. Whatever the word for 'desire' means in Russian, in English it is a word connoting power and passion. In their play world children's new desires can be realized, but only by fulfilling the rules of behaviour they make for their imagined persona. Vygotsky suggests the source of the strength of this alternative world lies in the 'rules' children set for themselves, guiding them to follow the form of the imagined narrative – to be in feeling and action the fictitious 'I' which carries the new desires. He says that children's relation to reality is radically altered at this point; the structure of their perceptions has altered.

What is interesting to us in Vygotsky's ideas is that he locates the change in the realms of feeling and of form – new desires guided and enforced by self-created rules of the game. But he does not leave the matter there. He asks how, in play, a child floats from one object to another, from one action to another, and suggests that this is accomplished by 'movement in the field of meaning which subordinates all real objects and actions to itself. Behaviour is not bound by the immediate perceptual field; in play, movement in the field of meaning predominates.' This does, indeed, begin to look like a transitional form of the aesthetic experience.

The imagined world of ideas is a world of possibilities, and we can see the emerging possibilities at work in the accounts of children following the picture story in the articles by Henrietta Dombey and Margaret Meek. Similar 'rules' operate in reading and listening as in play: our feelings guide us through the narrative patterns of the characters and events in the possible worlds encountered, though in this case the 'rules' are willingly accepted rather than self-created. We see this response to imagined worlds as the beginning of the aesthetic response, but call it transitional because of the absence of conscious reflection. Day-dreaming is also the creation of an alternative world of ideas. It occupies much of the lives of adults as well as children, but is usually seen as different from the imagined world of art – though D. W. Harding places it in the spectrum of spectator-role activity.

In this context the work of Labov and Waletsky (1967) on oral narratives is illuminating as a gloss on the role of reflection. They analysed the clause structure of a great many oral narratives and found the clauses to be of two sorts, undisplaceable and displaceable. The undisplaceable ones were narrative clauses; the displaceable ones were evaluative of the events narrated. The authors concluded that 'if we found narrative without evaluative clauses (or implied such) they read as empty or pointless narratives.' They therefore deduced two functions within narrative, referential and evaluative. Perhaps we might conclude that while children's earliest entry into imagined situations in play is characterized by feeling and guided by the demands of form, evaluative comments come later as children's language develops in the course of talking their way through picture story books, for instance, and in advancing towards independent reading and writing stories. In a later essay in the book Peter Medway argues that what lies at the centre of the lives of innumerable students is a quest for aesthetic experience (he is here referring to music), and in aesthetic experience he sees the perception of formal elements. 'Maybe,' he says, 'it will be through the *pleasure* of the text and not the *lessons* of the text that our students may best be brought into motivated engagement with reading and writing.' To literature teachers this may seem old hat. They have always been trying to help students towards such perceptions, but Medway's point is that thousands of students are already experiencing this in music, and anyway the point is in the pleasure not the analysis.

Intention is perhaps the haziest area in our map. It is a difficult topic, obviously central to learning, yet is seldom referred to in curriculum guides or treatises on teaching methodology; even attempts to document learning, to catch it on the wing, are more concerned to identify it than to explain the place of intention in these learning events. Clearly it is a major aspect of speech. Psycholinguists, for instance, have explored the part it plays in utterance and have shown that, while it directs what is said, people have great difficulty when asked to repeat exactly what they have just said. This can only be explained by the absence of their guiding intention in the repetition situation. It is now the listener's intention that they should repeat their utterance. At an altogether different level, if one looks at the extent to which student intention is allowed for in ordinary classroom work, it is often found to be minimal. Teachers plan and decide, and most people think they should, so the implications of students' intentions for learning are seldom a serious consideration in the planning of school work. This is not only a matter of control, though control enters into it. It is primarily the mode of socialization that our culture has pursued. Moreover, an aim to develop the autonomy of young persons and ethnic minority groups posits a threat to established institutions; yet we also claim to want to aim to develop independence and creativity, of which individual intentions are the source and the power. A telling illustration is the widespread practice of teachers who see the setting of written assignments as their particular role. Teachers find it hard to escape from the belief that it is they who should be the source of topics for writing. Cracks in this view are beginning to appear, but they tend to have arisen more in the field of writing, because people are coming to understand more of its nature, than in the field of learning as a whole. There is no comprehensive view of the role of student intention in the picture of learning presented by a school curriculum.

Courtney Cazden concludes her account of children learning with an adult by the question: 'Is what seems to be happening what is happening? Issues of control and intention need to be further explored.' In this way she pinpoints the process of research: the solution of a problem raises new problems; the process of revision and extension is a continuing one.

The need to extend and revise theory in practice is taken up in one way or another by many of the writers – important if a new orthodoxy is not to develop. For example, Peter Medway offers a critique of the present state of our theory and practice of English teaching. He thinks we are caught in a superficial literary model for writing and would like to see a broader aim. Learning English should be a means of learning about the world, but this posits an unresolved problem in that there appears to be a contradiction between the socially engaged English that he advocates and the importance most of us intuitively ascribe to literature. He notes the widespread 'quest for aesthetic experience' which is a driving force in the lives of young people, and suggests an alternative model for English teaching which would bring into play the ludic possibilities of 'doing things with words' and reunify English around the notion of 'textuality'.

Another extension to theory comes from Tony Burgess, who writes about cultural and linguistic diversity. He thinks we may be paying too high a price by trying to develop a 'single perspective – a common developing vision of English teaching'. 'Consensus', he says, 'may finish by excluding or trimming divergent, critical opinions arising from people with different histories, different interests and demands'. He wants to see openness – a recognition of diversity as a principle within an integrated theory of language development.

Criticisms from linguists need to be attended to because any theory based on language development must include ideas derived from linguistics. David Crystal, who himself works with children, is critical of the research base on which Britton's theory of mother tongue teaching depends and argues that teachers should have more knowledge of linguistic forms to balance the place they give to language functions. The trouble is that Crystal's arguments come from within an academic discipline, whereas education, of which English is a part, is compounded of many disciplines.

James Britton acknowledges the need for certain kinds of linguistic knowledge to be part of the equipment of English teachers, and the course in linguistics and English teaching he and Michael Halliday set up between University College and the London Institute of Education marked this recognition. But differences in conceptions of research and its methodology remain. As David Crystal pointed out in *Child Language, Learning and Linguistics* (1987), first published in the same year as Britton's research into the development of writing abilities, (1976) no systematic account of language functions has yet been developed. He argues that 'to propound views about language functions in advance of the needed research is hazardous. . . . We need systematic knowledge of language functions and their accompanying forms. If we don't balance these dimensions of linguistic knowledge there is no way to control the theoretical position, and facts and hypotheses give way to opinions and feelings.' The problem cannot be addressed in Crystal's terms. According to Britton:

Teachers are pragmatists in a field drawing from many disciplines. They have to be theorisers too, but their theorising stops at a point nearer the phenomena than does a linguist or a psychologist whose theories have a bearing on education but are developed within other specific disciplines. Teachers have to beg questions because week in and week out they are committed to fostering children's efforts to read and write. Both methods of enquiry, both levels of theorising are necessary since they fulfil distinguishable and complementary purposes. . . . Teachers cannot afford the fragmentation of their fields of concern that result from articulation upwards into the frames of reference of a number of disciplines [Britton, 1977].

We would therefore argue that a researcher in education needs to explore the field of his/her special interest and work from what is there, knowing that results may well be temporary or open to amendment as research from adjacent disciplines becomes available. In the pragmatic situations of teaching much educational research has been useful to teachers. Britton's is a case in point. His model of language use has helped teachers to think in a different way about language and has given them a theoretical hold on their own practice. Further, it resonates with categories based on philosophy and literary criticisms in the field of literary studies (Rosenblatt, 1978) – an important part of their work as English teachers, but not part of the discipline of linguistics.

An introduction to a book so much influenced by James Britton's thinking would be incomplete without some attempt to look at his particular relationship to the book. It is not only a matter of identifying his most influential or original ideas, but something much more difficult and intangible. One can pinpoint certain ideas and perceive how they have affected people's thinking and practice, but a large part of his influence is other than this. In Part One Gordon Pradl writes about the need for a teacher to be a special kind of listener, that is, he needs to attend with all his heart and mind to the person he is attempting to teach. This is the kind of attention we see in action in Part Two, in the essays about work with young children; it is this kind of listening (or attention) to what people (adults as well as children) do and say which is James Britton's distinctive mode. But he listens also to the voices of his own inner experience as a writer and poet. He once remarked: 'If you mess about with words you may become a poet. If you start with an idea you probably won't'. It is the kind of remark which short-circuits the smooth flow of assumptions we live with. Such insights crop up in conversation, as he listens to tapes of children talking and in his professional writing. A sense of the human voice – of the continuing conversation which is the stuff of our lives – is at the centre of his thinking. His writings weave continual variations on the themes of intentionality, speech and the social nature of learning, themselves variations on one

theme. His belief that poems have a voice in the physical sense led him to
investigate the nature of poetic language and its relation to speech.

A consideration of his theoretical writing leads one to see that he handles
theory differently from many other theorists. He does not engage in the
traditional polemic mode, that of overcoming an adversarial notion before
advancing one's own (note here the metaphors of battle). Britton works in
another way. He is a great synthesizer. His usual procedure is to begin with
the general statement of an idea he wants to develop; then he draws on work
by other researchers which bears on his topic and constructs a kind of
narrative of quotations which becomes his argument. Then he restates and
develops his own thesis as an extension of the argument. In this way he
synthesizes other people's work into the pattern he is developing. He has a
profound sense that the confrontations of argument merely serve to en-
trench people more firmly in the positions they have already taken up. It
may be that his synthesizing, narrative mode enables his ideas to move
quickly into people's personal experience and lodge there.

However, in the long run it is not only the way his influence has made
itself felt but the ideas themselves which have effected changed; we want to
draw attention to those which seem to us the most far-reaching in their
effect.

While it seems likely that knowledge of language development in learning would have made its way, piecemeal, into concepts of English teaching
as the result of studies in other disciplines, it was James Britton's *Language
and Learning* (1970), written by a teacher of English for teachers of English,
and still in print, which made those ideas from other sources accessible. But
it did more than this. It included the central ideas from the research which
he was then developing at the London Institute. It is the view of learning
arrived at in the course of the research which lies at the heart of his
subsequent work; and it is these ideas which have been the chief source of
his influence abroad and at home. A single research project does not often
have such widespread impact. It is as if the ideas chime with the knowledge
which teachers intuitively possess from their day-to-day contact with
learners.

One of his most influential and, in some ways, controversial ideas may be
found in his attempts to distinguish between literary and non-literary
discourse – a matter which has occupied scholars over many years. His
starting point, as we might expect, was writing (mostly unpublished) by
non-professionals, by children in school and students in college which took
forms clearly related to literary forms. His view was that any study of the
psychology of writing should seek both to relate these art-like writings to

literary works of art and to distinguish between them. In 'The spectator role and the beginning of writing' (Britton, 1982b), he describes the history of his development of the notion of the spectator role as the distinguishing feature of literary discourse and the effect of his encounter at the Dartmouth Anglo-American seminar with D. W. Harding, who introduced him to his (Harding's) earlier publications in this field. Both Harding and Britton were members of the study group concerned with response to literature, and the final report of this group, prepared by Harding, includes this comment:

It is impossible to separate response to literature sharply from response to other stories, films or TV plays, or from children's own personal writing or spoken narrative. In all of these the student contemplates represented events in the role of a spectator, not for the sake of active intervention.

What this theory of the spectator role does is to put all imaginative, or art-like 'verbal objects' on one spectrum of function, so we have to see children's storytelling and writing as part of the same creative activity which finds expression in developed art products. Britton also explains that the formal elements, together with the overall vision, are the justifying distinction between the art-like products of children and the creations of mature writers. A number of critics misinterpreted this analysis as equating the 'creative' writing of children and students with 'literature', and thereby removing literature from its traditional place at the centre of the English curriculum. Other English teachers, however, perceived that Britton's and Harding's notion of a spectator role, operating from an informal anecdote in speech to published work by a mature writer, gave a spectrum of poetic discourse on which the writing of all students could be placed. Rather than diminish the centrality of literature in the English curriculum, it empha-sized and extended it.

Another influential idea coming out of the writing research is the notion of 'expressive' language as one of a set of three language functions. Britton describes expressive language as reflecting the contours of a speaker's thought and feeling, and suggests that it is likely to be the mode in which the first tentative approaches to new learning are made. This has proved a liberating idea for teachers. Recognizing the value of a child's nearest-to-hand language not only as an aspect of cognition but also as the first step in getting into the more formal language of education has allowed teachers to accept, indeed, to encourage, a kind of utterance which depends on rela-tionships of trust. This is the nature of good conversation, and classroom discourse based on it has a new potential for learning. Peter Medway once compared the implications of the acceptance and encouragement of expressive language in classrooms with the implications of translating the Bible into the vernacular.

It seems fitting to conclude this introduction with James Britton's words. He is writing about the way in which ideas work in people and how they must constantly be remade. In, 'A note on teaching, research and development' (1982b) he says:

It is the continual reformulation of what we know in the light of what we perceive that matters; and the hardening of what we know into a formula that we apply ready made instead of reformulating – that is the danger. Thus, our most powerful ideas are relatively general, relatively unformulated starting points from which we constantly reformulate.

And again:

Development is a two-way process; the practitioner does not merely *apply*; he must reformulate from the general starting points supplied by the research and arrive at new ends – new not only to him, but new in the sense that they are not a part of the research findings, being a discovery of a different order. The value of the research lies in supplying the starting point for many such discoveries; the value of each discovery is limited to the successful solution of this particular problem at this particular time; but the power of the teacher to make this journey and make it again – there above all lies the value of the whole enterprise.

Part One   Teaching the Mother Tongue as a Model for Education

It is hard to speak about learning without metaphor, though learning is perhaps too complex to do otherwise. What one makes of outward events is an inward thing (all symbolic worlds are inward), but learning (education) is also essentially interactive – in part shared – its inwardness transmitted or acted upon in some way. The passage from outward event to inward construct and out again transformed by the interactive situation defies description and often can only be recognized obliquely. These complexities involve other complexities, a nexus of things which are themselves indeterminate. As teachers, we intervene in the varied, ongoing patterns of behaviours and relationships of our students. It is this intervention which is specially complex because one is never quite sure what one is intervening in. Ecologists have taught us this. Learning and the human relationships of its context are inextricable. What do metaphors do in this situation? They pinpoint some bit of the complex enterprise and define a small part of it by some recognizable comparison, but leave the rest indeterminate or wrongfully bounded by the limits of the metaphor.

In the first essay in this section Courtney Cazden strikes out with a metaphor which is becoming current – social interaction as scaffold which self-destructs (a metaphor of our time indeed). She uses it to express the power of the shift from the traditional view of the teacher as a provider of information, as an instructor of how to do things and a selective reinforcer of children's attempts towards one in which the child shares responsibility for producing a complete performance with an adult. The child does what he or she can and the adult does the rest, gradually increasing the expectation of how much of the full performance the child can be responsible for. The experimental work with children which she describes represents a reinvigoration of Vygotsky's ideas which people had insufficiently explored the first time round. This shift towards social interaction runs through the book and is the main new dimension. It was foreshadowed in James Britton's *Language and Learning* (1970), but was not applied and documented in the practice of teachers, and therefore remained a largely unexplored area. Now the balance is being righted. Courtney Cazden's accounts of situations which reflect this shared responsibility mark this change in action, but she goes on to explore the limits of the scaffold metaphor. She asks whether such a scaffolding of adult support helps children to learn strategies as well as items? And does it raise dilemmas of intention and control? 'Who's building whose building?' she asks.

In the second essay Douglas Barnes examines the contemporary view of the curriculum as a purveyor of knowledge and distinguishes and describes the characteristics of knowledge gained from schooling and from experience outside school. He points out the contradictoriness of the central authority's demands for *both* traditional academic programmes *and* for a shift to a curriculum which is more directly related to the world of work. These official policies, he says, would lead to an unthinking pursuit of technique or a simplistic transmission model of knowledge. What is needed, he argues, is a 'critical curriculum' which will involve learners in judgement, deliberation and choice. They should have access to the grounds of knowledge and thus understand that it is a human construct perpetually open to participation and revision. Here, as in other essays, we can see the new educator at work – knowledge no less than language is a cooperative social enterprise. Though discussion lies at the heart of Douglas Barnes's ideas about critical teaching and learning, his field is the curriculum as a whole rather than English teaching. His essay draws on a wide range of sources from the UK, Canada, Australia and the USA – many of them from sociology – and although his immediate context is the current position in the UK, his notion of a critical curriculum takes account of relevant studies in all four countries.

Gordon Pradl, writing about listening in the third of these articles, looks at talk from a somewhat different perspective. In earlier work English teachers have tended to focus on the value to the speaker of talking; Gordon Pradl explores the complex roles of the listener in helping the speaker to find his own agenda, of being aware not only of what is said, but also of the speaker's intentions and sense of self-worth, and to be protective towards all these. All this is part of a changing view of reciprocal talk. 'We used to see it', he says, 'as a major step in the achievement of separation and individuation; the present view asserts that the opposite is equally true. . . . Every word learned is a by-product of uniting two mentalities ... a forging of shared meaning.' At one level he is concerned to lay bare the complex, unstated social rules which govern our communications with others; at another level he attempts to describe the phenomenon of inner listening, of feeling the necessary correspondence between our words and our intentions where the guiding and caring presence of others – real or imagined – can help to draw out the words from us.

Social Interaction as Scaffold: The Power and Limits of a Metaphor[1]
Courtney Cazden

Questions about the social context of learning are being asked more widely now than they were when Britton published *Language and Learning* in 1970. But they are still not easy to answer. We are immediately in the midst of the difficult area of relationships between thought and language, or 'thinking and speech' as the title of Vygotsky's (1962) book should be translated. The change from thought to thinking and from language to speech is more than a quibble about the correct translation from the Russian. The shift in each case is to the more dynamic term: from thought as a product to thinking as a mental activity, and from language as a symbolic system to speech as the use of language in social interaction.

Correction of the title of Vygotsky's well-known book in recent writings (Emerson, 1981; Wertsch, 1985; Kozulin, 1987)[2] is itself symptomatic of an important intellectual shift in psychological conceptions of language. When *Thought and Language* was first published in English in 1962, by MIT Press and with an introduction by the Harvard psychologist Jerome Bruner, the impact of the MIT linguist Noam Chomsky's work was already strong. But by the mid-1980s, that work – while still respected – is now a smaller part of a larger picture.

In thinking about educational issues within this larger picture, I have found it useful to separate social interaction between learners and an 'expert' (usually the teacher) from social interaction among peers. I will focus here on the former, while in a later chapter Branscombe and Taylor focus on talk among peers.

Near the end of a lengthy review of recent theories of cognition and instruction, Resnick[3] writes about changes in how cognitive psychologists view learning, particularly its relationship to the social context:

Traditional views of the way in which social interaction affects learning focus on the adult as provider of new information, as a modeler of correct performance, and as a selective reinforcer of children's tries at producing the performance.... a different view of social processes in learning is attracting increased attention among cognitive psychologists interested in the development of general cognitive competence. The Soviet psychologist Vygotsky (1978) has argued that cognition begins in social situations in which a child shares responsibility for producing a complete performance with an adult. The child does what he or she can, the adult the rest. In this way, practise on components occurs in the context of the full performance. In naturally occurring interactions of this kind, the adult will gradually increase expectations of how much of the full performance the child can be responsible for [1985, pp. 178–9].

The metaphorical term 'scaffold' introduced by Bruner and his colleagues (e.g. Wood, Bruner and Ross, 1976), has come to be applied to social interactions of this kind. A familiar picture may clarify both the concept and the pervasiveness of its exemplars: imagine a picture of an adult holding the hand of a very young toddler with the caption: 'Everyone needs a helping hand.' Exactly as Resnick says, the child does what he or she can and the adult does the rest; the child's practice occurs in the context of a full performance; and the adult's help is gradually withdrawn as the child's competence grows – from holding two hands to just one, then to offering only a finger, then withdrawing that a few inches – leaving the child walking alone but with help available if needed when the going gets rough.

I will explore both the power and the limits of this metaphor. In doing so I consider only scaffolds that include dialogue. But, as Fischer and Bullock (1984) point out in a review of post-Piagetian views of development, scaffolds also include help that is designed by an expert, such as good computer software, even if the learner works alone at the moment of use.

Scaffolds at Home

A great deal of spontaneous interaction with young children can be conceptualized in these terms. Even before the toddler tries to walk, there is assistance to infants trying (at least as some mothers believe) to communicate. Snow (1977) describes how hard mothers work to achieve a 'conversation' despite the inadequacies of their three- to eighteen-month-old conversational partners. At first they accept burps, yawns and coughs, as well as laughs and coos (but not arm waving or head movements), as the baby's turn. They fill in for the babies by asking and answering their own questions and by phrasing questions so that a minimal response can be treated as a reply. When, by about seven months, the babies become considerably more active partners, the mothers no longer accept all the baby's vocalizations, only vocalic and consonantal babbles. As the mother raises the ante, the child's development proceeds.

Another example comes from Wertsch's analysis of a mother guiding her child through the task of copying a jigsaw puzzle from a model. The task has three steps:

Step 1: Consult the model to determine the identity and location of the piece needed next.

Step 2: Select the piece identified in Step 1 from the pieces pile.
Step 3: Add the pieces selected in Step 2 to the copy object in accordance with its
location in the model [1984, p. 10].

Here is a description of three episodes of interaction between a mother and
her two-and-a-half-year-old child as they worked through the pieces of a
single puzzle.

The first two episodes began with the child asking where a piece was to go and the
mother responding by directing the child's attention to the model puzzle. In both
these episodes, the child's original question led to a response by the mother which,
in turn, led to the child's response of consulting the model. All of these 'moves' or
'turns' were part of external, interpsychological functioning. The third episode
began quite differently. First, the child did not produce a fully expanded question
about where a piece should go. Second, and more importantly, her gaze to the model
puzzle was not a response to an adult's directive. Rather than relying on an adult to
provide a regulative communication, she carried this out independently using
egocentric and inner speech. That is, in the case of some of the strategic steps
required here, there was a transition from external social functioning to external and
internal individual functioning [Wertsch and Stone, 1985, pp. 175–6].

Then there are the early language games, such as Peekaboo, which share
four features: a restricted format, clear and repetitive structure, positions
for appropriate vocalizations and reversible role relationships (Ratner and
Bruner, 1978). Similar to Peekaboo in its early versions, but open to the
development of greater complexity, is picture-book reading, also first
analysed by Bruner and colleagues in these terms. In the family described
by Ninio and Bruner (1978), for example, book reading in the child's
second year typically had a four-part sequence:

an attentional vocative, such as 'Look'.
a query, such as 'What's that?'
a label, such as 'It's an X.'
if the child has provided the label, a feedback utterance, such as 'Yes, that's an X.'

As with Peekaboo, as the child's development proceeds, he or she takes over
more and more of the script.[4]
    In all these examples of early interactional games, the mother can and
does enact the entire script herself at the beginning, but the child gradually
assumes an increasingly active role. Variations in the games over time are
critical. The adult so structures the game that the child can be a successful
participant from the beginning; then, as the child's competence grows, the
game changes so that there is always something new to be learned and tried
out, including taking over what was the adult's role. Bruner's terms 'scaffold' has become a common caption for the adult's role in these games, but

it is a good name only if we remember that this is a very special kind of scaffold – one that self-destructs gradually as the need lessens and the child's competence grows.

Scaffolds in School

Figure 1 shows the basic structure of all learning environments which fit the scaffold metaphor. The author (in Pearson and Gallagher (1983)), suggests, as did Resnick, that the model can be applied generally to education. Most instructional examples come from the language arts, but there seems no reason why some teaching sequences in other areas of the curriculum could not be conceptualized in the same terms.

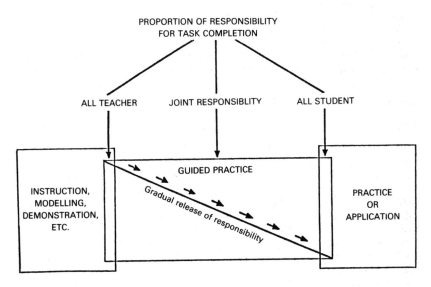

Figure 1

Because of problems inherent in fine-tuning instruction to a group of children at the same time, it is easier to find instruction fitting this model in teachers' interactions with individual students. Consider, as an example, what happens when a primary teacher taught a nine year old, third-grade child, Leola, how to do a verbal puzzle so that she could later teach it to several of her peers (Cazden *et al.*, 1979). Here are the first two items of the task in completed form, a sequential analysis of the task and an edited version (minus repetitions, self-corrections, etc.) of the interaction by which the teacher (T) talked Leola through the first two items (much as the mothers observed by Wertsch talked their younger children through the jigsaw puzzle):

1. new   1. y   2. told   3. me

2. no

3. off   You   told   me

1. Read the word in list on the left: *new*
2. Think of its opposite: *old*
3. Spell the opposite: O-L-D
4. Find the set of letters with the corresponding number and cross out the letters that spell the opposite
5. Copy letters that are left in spaces below: Y-O-U
6. Read these letters as a word: *you*

(After all ten items are finished, the remaining words together made a funny caption for the cartoon that accompanied the task.)

Teacher's instructions to Leola

Item 1

Teacher	Leola
OK, now number 1 here says 'new'	
What's the opposite of 'new'?	'Old.'
OK, how would you spell 'old'?	O-L-D
OK, in the letters that are on this paper, cross out the letters you just used for spelling 'old'.	L. does it.
Good. What word is left?	Y-O-U.
What does it spell?	'You'.
OK, and down here you'll write 'you'.	

Item 2

Teacher	Leola
OK, now number 2 here says –	'No'.
'No'. What's the opposite of 'no'?	'Yes'.
OK, how do you spell 'yes'?	Y-E-S.
All right, now what are you going –	L. crosses out the letters Y-E-S.
	'Told'.

Evidence that such aid can indeed be gradually withdrawn, and that Leola did learn to do the task independently, can be seen in a comparison of the teacher's instructions for the first and second items. For the second item, T repeated the first three parts, but then a much vaguer and incomplete question, 'Now what are you going –', was sufficient, and Leola took off on her own.

The best-documented instruction designed on the scaffold model is called 'reciprocal teaching'. In 1981 Palincsar and Brown initiated a series of studies designed to improve reading comprehension through instruction in four cognitive strategies: predicting, generating questions, summarizing and clarifying. The format they devised is a 'dialogue between teacher and students in which participants take turns assuming the role of teacher.' They worked first with remedial teachers and their junior-high students and have since extended and evaluated the model with other grades and teachers. Basically,

When classroom teachers are introduced to reciprocal teaching, it is within the framework of scaffolded instruction. That is to say, the teachers are told that the purpose of this instructional program is to guide students from the acquisition to independent application of the four strategies for the purpose of enhancing comprehension. They are instructed that this transfer of responsibility means that they will engage in different teaching strategies over the course of instruction. They initially provide explanation coupled with modeling, then fade out the modeling and function more in the role of a coach providing corrective feedback and encouragement, promote self-evaluation, and reintroduce explanation and modeling as appropriate. The teachers are also told that the rate at which this transfer occurs will vary among their students, but no matter how slow the rate, each learner must always be challenged at his or her level of competence [Palincsar, 1986, p. 78; see also Brown and Palincsar, in press.]

The Reading Recovery Programme, carefully designed by Marie Clay and colleagues in New Zealand (Clay, 1985) and now used throughout that country, could also be analysed in scaffold terms.

In current discussions the term 'scaffold' is often linked with Vygotsky's construct of 'zone of proximal development' (1962, pp. 103–4). Scaffold refers to the temporary and adjustable help. If, in fact, the learner takes over more and more responsiblity for the task at hand, as shown in the central rectangle of Figure 1, then we can infer, retrospectively, that the help was, in effect as well as intent, well timed and well tuned, and that the learner was functioning in his or her zone of proximal development, doing at first with help what she could very soon do alone.

Documentation of instructional scaffolds for older students is harder to find. For example, when students have a hard time reading a text of a certain difficulty level, the frequent instructional remedy is to give those students as easier book. But, as my colleague Dennie Wolf, points out (personal communication) that further deprives the students of the possibility of incorporating the more difficult syntax and vocabulary into their mental language system and may only make them fall farther behind. Could we instead, she asks, keep the more difficult texts but give more instructional support in the form of what Vygotsky's descendants in Moscow call 'graduated aids' (Cazden, 1979), perhaps of the kind suggested in reciprocal teaching?

Or consider the common instructional practice of singling out isolated vocabulary words for attention prior to assigning a text in which they will appear. While such a vocabulary lesson may ease the reading of a particular text, it does not help students learn a strategy they can use independently for reading through unfamilar words (as readers have to do all their lives). Would it not be better, Wolf asks, and again more in keeping with Vygotsky's ideas, to teach such strategies directly, in the context of reading the whole text (comments in class, Bread Loaf School of English, 27 July 1987)?

Three Issues

In thinking about the generalizability of the scaffold metaphor, three issues need to be considered: the difference between learning a strategy and learning an item, the process of internalization, and dilemmas of intention and control.

Learning a Strategy *vs* Learning an Item

There is a critical difference between helping a child somehow get a particular answer and helping a child gain some conceptual understanding from which answers to similar questions can be constructed alone at a future time. Consider the following sequence:

T: What's four times three?
S: Eigh-
T: What is two times four?
S: Eight
T: Mm, three times four?
S: Nine, ten, eleven, twelve.
T: So what's three times four?
S: Twelve.

The teacher may hope that from such a sequence students will learn something about the relationship of addition to multiplication. But they may only learn the pattern of a verbal sequence in which 'so' introduces a question that has the same answer as the preceding question. This pattern, complete with the particular connector, 'so', seems to be common at all grade levels. It gets the right answer into the air and thus helps the teacher 'get through' the lesson. But, as Swedish researcher Lundgren points out, 'The language used establishes a pattern of communication which gives the illusion that learning is actually occurring' (1977, p. 202, from which the example above is adapted.)

The important task for the teacher is to listen for evidence that learning of more than the pattern itself has taken place. Here is another example from a preschool classroom observed by preschool educator Kathryn McGeorge (personal communication, 1984):

S: There's a fly in here [in the classroom].
T: Why did the fly come inside?
S: I don't know.
T: Why did the mice [in the story that we just read] come inside?
S: Because it was cold.
T: So why do you think the *fly* might have come inside?
S: Because *he* was cold.

In this case, the child's emphasis on 'he', tying it to 'fly' in the preceding teacher's utterance, seems to indicate understanding of the substantive relationship between the two animals that the teacher was hoping to suggest. But we still have to ask whether the child has learned the strategy implicit in this interchange: in trying to think of reasons for an action by an unfamiliar agent, try to bring to mind similar and more familiar actions from other contexts – from first-hand experience or from books.

Clay defines 'strategy' as 'mental activities initiated by the child to get messages from a text' (1985, p. 14). I would add, 'or to construct messages in a text'. Such strategies, not particular items of knowledge or skill, are the most important objectives of education if we truly seek to help learners become, in Clay's felicitous words, 'self-improving systems'.

The Process of Internalization

It is important not to have a mechanical conception of the process of internalization whereby overt social interaction (speaking and listening) becomes transformed into covert mental processes (thinking). About reciprocal teaching, Resnick points out that 'The automatic nature of many reading comprehension processes, the speed at which reading proceeds, and its sequential nature make it implausible that in the normal course of skilled reading people actually pose questions or create summaries for themselves' (Resnick, 1985, p. 177).

In research on mathematics instruction Resnick and her colleagues have distinguished between algorithms that are taught and more mature algorithms (that is, closer to what experts do) that the learners somehow figure out for themselves. For example, Resnick and her colleagues found that children who were instructed in one addition algorithm invented a more mature one for themselves. To add 3 and 4, they were instructed to count the two groups together: 1, 2, 3 – 4, 5, 6, 7. They then invented the strategy of starting with the larger number, whether it is first or second, and incrementing by the smaller: 4 – 5, 6, 7 (Groen and Resnick, 1977). There is evidence against any simple version of internalization as covert imitation. In A. N. Leont'ev's words;

The process of internalization is not *transferal* of all external activity to a pre-existing internal 'plane of consciousness'; it is the process in which this internal plane is *formed* [Leont'ev, 1981, p. 57, emphasis in the original; see discussion by Wertsch and Stone, 1985].

In teaching, therefore, we should not assume a one-to-one relationship between the components of mature performance and the ingredients of the most effective instruction. As with children's language development, the models provided are samples to learn from, not examples to learn.

Dilemmas of Intention and Control

The last issue is the most difficult, a dilemma (Berlak and Berlak, 1981) for which no resolution is appropriate for all teaching: whose intentions – teacher's or student's – should take precedence in a particular interaction? Questions must be asked about conceptions of knowledge and education implicit in scaffold-like structures. How one judges their pedagogical value depends on the content of particular instructional sequences and on one's educational philosophy.

Consider one more example, this time from a typical interaction between a teacher and a primary-school child during 'Sharing Time' (or 'News'). Mindy has volunteered to report an out-of-school experience, and the teacher is collaborating with Mindy by her comments and questions:

Mindy: When I was in day camp/we made these candles//
T: You made them?
Mindy: And I – I tried with different colours/ with both of them but
    /one just came out/this one just came out blue/
    and I don't know/what this colour is//
T: That's neat-o//Tell the kids how you do it from the very start/   Pretend we
    don't know a thing about candles//
    OK//What did you do first?//What did you use?//
    Flour?//
Mindy: There's some hot wax/some real hot wax/
    that you/just take a string/and tie a knot in it//
    and dip the string in the wax//
T: What makes it have a shape?//
Mindy You just shape it//

T: Oh you shaped it with your hand//mm//
Mindy: But you have/first you have to stick it into the wax/
   and then water/and then keep doing that until it gets to the
   size you want it//
T: OK//who knows what the string is for?// . . .

This student – teacher dialogue can be interpreted positively as a kind of interactional scaffold by which the teacher helps Mindy put into words a more explicit and precise description of her experience in making candles, a description that is more 'literate' in assuming (in the teacher's words) 'that we don't know a thing about candles'. In her analysis of this dialogue Michaels shows how the teacher's questions are both well timed and well tuned:

Most of Mrs Jones's questions occur when Mindy pauses after a low falling tone. Such pauses indicate some kind of closure. Hence Mrs Jones's questions occur at the end of a complete unit and are not seen as interruption. Furthermore, her questions descend from general to specific, until a level is reached at which Mindy can and does respond appropriately. Lastly, the teacher's responses and clarifications build on Mindy's contributions [1981, p. 433].

Through such interactions, sharers are encouraged to be more clear and precise and put more information into words, instead of relying on shared background knowledge (here, about candle making) or visual contextual cues (the candles Mindy is holding) to communicate part of the intended message. If teachers see Sharing Time as an opportunity for young children not only to share out-of-school experiences with the whole class, but also to construct an oral text that is as similar as possible to a written composition, then Sharing Time can be, as Michaels calls it, an 'oral preparation for literacy'.

But another interpretation should be considered. When I presented Mindy's Sharing Time turn at a National Council of Teachers of English (NCTE) conference, several teachers felt that Mrs Jones had, in their words, 'appropriated' the child's text for her own teaching purposes and forced the development of the narrative in particular ways. Mindy started talking about colours, they pointed out, but the teacher shifted the talk to materials.

In response to another presentation of this same dialogue, Searle repeated the NCTE teachers' concerns and linked them to the wider dilemma of intentions and control:

Cazden suggested and demonstrated intervention in young children's show-and-tell sessions to help the children learn to speak in focused, extended narrative. In Cazden's examples, however, the children's understanding, valuing, and excitement of the personal experiences were negated as the children were led to report the experience in an appropriate form. Applebee and Langer (1983) advocate 'instructional scaffolding' and provide examples in which teachers scaffold students' science experiment reports by providing a sheet of questions which outline the required steps. Undoubtedly, these outlines help the students report the experiment more completely, but do they really help them learn the purposes and nature of scientific writing? Why, for example, are the students performing and reporting the experiment? Whose intentions are being honored in the report [1984, p. 481]?

These are important questions. They are most obviously important when student and teacher are discussing the student's construction of his or her own text – whether an oral text as in Sharing Time or a written text as during writing conferences at any level of school or college (Michaels, in press). But the same questions should be asked about instruction whose objective is the interpretation of texts written by others. Searle acknowledges, as I do, the usefulness of the scaffolding metaphor, but asks the question at the heart of all teaching dilemmas: at any instructional moment, 'Who's building whose building?'

Even when instruction can be shown to be effective as means, that fact alone does not make it worthy as ends. Questions of value remain to be argued and answered by teachers and researchers alike.

Notes

1. This paper is adapted from *Classroom Discourse: The Language of Teaching and Learning*, Heinemann, 1987.
2. The title in Russian is *Myshlenie i Rech*. Kozulin gives the translation as *Thought and Speech* (1987, p. lvii). Wertsch explains: 'Russian clearly distinguishes between thought (*mysl'*) and thinking (*myshlenie*) and between language (*yazyk*) and speech (*rech'*)' (1985, p. 234, n. 8). Emerson is even more emphatic that 'A more precise translation of the work's title ... would be *Thinking and Speech*: the thinking is specifically a process and not a product, and the language is uttered' (1981, p. 37. n. 6).
3. Resnick is one of the foremost educational psychologists in the United States: he was president of the American Educational Research Association in 1987 and is a founding editor of the journal *Cognition and Instruction*.
4. Cochran-Smith (1983, 1984) gives the richest description of how reading to young children can mediate between children and texts, in the direction of both 'world to words' and 'words to world'.

Knowledge as Action
Douglas Barnes

A Challenge to the Academic Curriculum

In both industrialized and developing countries two apparently contradictory policies for school curricula face each other. One policy seeks to make schooling more responsive to what are seen as economic realities; the other policy seeks to preserve a curriculum based upon traditional academic 'subjects'. The Conservative government of Britain has pursued both these policies concurrently through different agencies. Through the Manpower Services Commission the government embarked upon an explicit criticism of traditional academic schooling; recommendations of 'practical learning', relevance to 'the real world of work' and learning through 'cooperative work, problem-solving, doing and talking' appeared in official documents, and the Technical and Vocational Educational Initiative (TVEI) was set up in order to offer to fourteen- to eighteen-year-olds the option of less academic courses. Four years later the Secretary of State for Education proposed a bill in Parliament to limit the curriculum to conventional academic subjects, though with technology added. The criticisms of the traditional academic curriculum used to justify TVEI are based upon the assertion that there is a mismatch between what is offered to pupils in the curriculum and their needs in our society. The national curriculum seems to be intended, on the contrary, to make it impossible for schools to deal with matters that do not fall within the framework of existing subjects. This seems likely to exclude many issues of direct relevance to the young and particularly to ban from classrooms any controversial and value-laden issues.

In discussing the implications for secondary-school curricula of such apparently contradictory policies – and not for Britain alone – it is useful to consider what we require of children in school. In what way do the social, behavioural and cognitive demands of schooling match the demands of the world outside school in which young people are already participants? We should certainly not be considering only the 'real world of work' of official documents: there are other real worlds in which citizens need to be competent. Is the epistemology that is embedded in our curriculum a reasonable match for the understanding and competences on which young people's future lives will be based? There are many different kinds of knowledge to be found both inside and outside schools; is it justifiable to generalize about the one or the other?

Educational Knowledge and Knowledge for Action

It is a commonplace of writing about school knowledge that it is radically different from the knowledge used and valued outside education systems. School knowledge is typically described as generalized, theoretical and explicit rather than particular, applied and implicit; as descriptive, analytical and passive rather than engaged or oriented towards action (Young, 1971; Saunders, 1982); expressed in writing rather than orally (Young, 1971); and distant from children's everyday cultural realities. School work requires the young to grapple with tasks which they themselves have not formulated and which may have little relevance to what they believed to be their concerns (Neisser, 1976; Wagner and Steinberg, 1986; Young, 1971). Demands for academic intelligence begin early: talk in the nursery school deals with a narrower range of topics than talk at home and is so dominated by adults that children are unable to play an active part. It fails to engage with the real world because teachers pursue their educational aims without regard to children's perspectives and priorities (Tizard and Hughes, 1984). Classroom discourse is believed to be different from much of the discourse young people take part in during their lives: children must learn to 'answer the question', that is, to look for an answer that conforms to the teacher's unstated expectations (Edwards and Mercer, 1986). School tasks are well defined – there are unambiguous criteria for successful conclusion – all the necessary information is provided and there is a single right answer (Wagner and Steinberg, 1986). Children learn that in school they must not use their existing knowledge of the world but pretend that only the information 'given' by the teacher is valid, so that they have to ignore many of the considerations that influence us in our everyday lives in favour of solving idealized logical problems posed by the teacher. (In the familiar question about men digging holes, did we ever ask ourselves whether they all worked equally hard?) This faces them with the task of internalizing sets of unfamiliar social norms; success in doing so is a crucial part of academic 'intelligence' and school success (Edwards and Mercer, 1987; Hammersley, 1974).

Many commentators refer to the wide gulf between decontextualized school knowledge and the knowledge that the children bring to school with them (Olson, 1977, quoted by Edwards and Maybin, 1987). Schutz and

Luckman (1973, quoted by Soloman, 1983) distinguish 'life-world structures' from 'symbolic universes'. 'Life-world structures are those pictures of the world that we live by; according to Schutz and Luckman, they are based on loose typifications yet are strong because they are shared with other people. 'Symbolic universes' refers to school subjects which are kept separate from everyday life. It is important to realize that the life-world structures are upheld because they have a function: the school pupils who refused to accept their biology teacher's assertion that human beings are animals were influenced by the fact that for most of our everyday purposes it is more useful to emphasize the difference than the similarity (Hills, 1983). Moreover there seems to be a value judgement implicit in the shift from 'structures' to 'universes' which deserves to be unpacked. 'Children come to school with a practical conception of reality only to encounter a theoretical conception of reality' (Edwards and Maybin, 1987). Schooling substitutes decontextualized logic for the purpose-driven thinking which binds our normal behaviour to the here and now. Their home lives offer children from different families very different levels of assistance in the task of bridging this cultural gulf, which may be one of the most difficult demands that school lays upon the young.

It is important to understand what constitutes this task. Meaning does not lie in words but in the cultural competences which we bring to the words. Joining in the cultural life of a group (such as that of a classroom) is not merely a matter of being able to manage the expected patterns of interaction; we need appropriate knowledge. 'Children who fail in school are those who operate with ways of meaning different from those of schooling (Christie, 1985). What is meant is not inherent in the words spoken; the words have to be reconstituted as meaning by the hearers on the basis of whatever cultural competences they can bring to the task. Behind every utterance lies 'the unspoken backcloth of meaning' (Edwards and Furlong, 1978). When education is seen as 'the induction of learners into 'preferred discourses' or 'genres' (Whitty, 1985; Christie, 1985), what is being referred to is not just linguistic forms or even patterns of social exchange. To take part in lessons requires 'sharing general epistemological frameworks, pragmatic and communicative assumptions and purposes, particular knowledge and experience' (Edwards and Mercer, 1986, 1987). Those students who in a public examination in English language wrote about a pop music idol in the language of a favourite magazine had seriously misread the tacit meaning of the task.

There are other ways in which school curricula differ radically from the competences required in everyday living. It is a normal part of teachers' work to give exercises to their students; typically they prescribe a rule and then set tasks which are intended to exemplify that rule. Very often what is demanded of the pupil is that he or she should operate a routine procedure, in some subjects even an algorithm, which does not always necessitate the student having much grasp of when this procedure is appropriate or how it is related to the principle that the teacher has enunciated. Traditional 'academic' pedagogy rests upon the hope that through rehearsing the procedures the pupil will eventually gain access to the principle, but since a procedure does not necessarily imply its own justification, this often happens very slowly and only for a minority of students.

It is in response to this that it is now commonly recommended that students be given 'problems' to solve, but even the word 'problem' is ambiguous. A good problem would require more than the application of a routine procedure and would be different enough from any example already discussed in class to require choice and reinterpretation by the student. Perhaps some transformation would be required; perhaps it would be necessary for the pupil to construe the terms of the problem and then decide what model or procedure was most appropriate as a basis for solving it. Some cases would need one treatment and some another, thus requiring the learner to have enough understanding of underlying principles to choose from a repertoire of models and methods. This would already have been built up by experience with other similar and dissimilar problems. These steps would perhaps lead to better textbook problems but would not make them like problem-solving in everyday life. In pursuing everyday goals, such as organizing a family trip, we are at the very same time deciding what we want, gathering information, considering possibilities for action and trying things out: there is no clear logical sequence. In real-life problems the choice of method is often far from clear. This is true even of technical problems: can I fasten this spring under tension using a hammer and a staple or should I use a screw hook? If the spring is too taut for either, I must look still further for a method. How much more true this is of interpersonal projects. I wish to influence a colleague and so embark on persuasion or bargaining, yet I modify and redirect these according to the response I receive. Of course, sometimes we know exactly what to do, but we usually call these 'tasks' rather than 'problems'. In real life we struggle at one and the same time to determine what should count as success and what methods are worth trying. The goal itself is often open to redefinition: one is often 'responding appropriately in terms of one's long-range and short-range goals, given the actual facts of the situation as one discovers them' (Neisser, 1976). Constructing the problem and the criteria that shall determine what constitutes success are as much part of the problem solving as working through to a solution.

There is no qualitative difference between thinking in an academic and an everyday context; the characteristics of everyday reasoning arise from the interaction of the actor's goals and the perceived possibilities and constraints of the situation (Lave, Murtaugh and de la Roche, 1984). What may differ is the value loading of problems met in and out of the classroom; understanding the diets of animals in a biology textbook is a different matter from understanding the needs of a pet, not because the principles involved are different but because the new ideas are brought into a different relationship with what the learner already knows. Feeling and values play an essential role in action-oriented uses of intelligence, since in the real world intellectual performance involves satisfying one's own motives (Neisser, 1976). It is true that there are occasions outside school when we find ourselves constrained to follow purposes not our own, as, for example, at work, which offers us money or other extrinsic inducements to accept others' goals. Do these occasions justify an education which requires young people to demonstrate their willingness to pursue goals whose value they are not in a position to appreciate? It is not an easy question to answer. Central to critiques of schooling, whatever political perspectives they come from, is its frequent failure to coopt the learners' purposes.

We must ask ourselves whether we are using an accurate account of academic schooling. If we compare it with the work of outstanding teachers, or perhaps of most teachers in their more inventive moments, the picture of abstract theorizing seems something of a caricature. Teaching large groups of youthful conscripts under pressure of time and for tests designed by others often does push teachers in that direction, however, even against their will. Moreover, there is considerable divergency in the traditional curriculum, which has never been simply a matter of transmitting 'objective knowledge'. Much of the curriculum has always been heavily value-laden, as witness the kinds of history or literature commonly taught or the older emphasis upon 'character building' and the more recent one of 'personal and social education'. Nor has traditional education been concerned only with cognition: skills and motor activities have always played a part, not only in physical education and in craft but also, for example, in the academic subjects in the form of the teaching of handwriting or laboratory skills. Some teachers of geography, English, history, religious education, social studies and even science have made it their business to deal overtly with moral and social issues. However carefully teachers avoid overt indoctrination, it is impossible to teach any of these subjects without implying some perspective and making some choices which will be implicitly value-laden. The British Government's attempt to banish values from the curriculum is in danger of becoming an attempt to banish all values except their own.

The Need for Disembedded Thought

To formulate a case for a 'practical' curriculum implies some denigration of the traditional one, so it is necessary to review some arguments that can be adduced in support of an 'academic' curriculum. How far is the distance of schooling from everyday life essential to its effectiveness? Can it be that some of the characteristics for which schooling is criticized – the generalizing tendency of school knowledge, its separation from the effects of action, the manner in which it requires children to assimilate alien cultural norms – are essential to its value to our society? Should schools try to break down the barriers and become like the world outside or would that be to destroy their particular value?

Some commentators see the particular contribution of schooling to our culture to be the enabling of pupils to disembed their thinking from the here-and-now shared experience (Edwards and Maybin, 1987). Maturation in our education is sometimes associated with the ability to transcend the here and now (Bruner, 1966; Tough, 1979). Those who take this view sometimes refer to research on cognitive styles which has claimed to identify 'field-independent' persons whose judgements and actions depend more upon internalized interpretive frameworks and patterns of values than upon the judgement of people about them and who will succeed better at disembedded logical-perceptual tasks (Witkin et al., 1977). It is probable that the classroom dialogues of teachers with pupils generate the ability to marshal decontextualized logical arguments in written or spoken form (Scribner and Cole, 1981, quoted by Edwards and Maybin, 1987). Walkerdine (1982) shows how an infants teacher moves her pupils thinking from the individual case to the generalization potentially implicit in a numerical statement.

Other writers stress the importance of literacy rather than schooling itself, as a medium of learning out of context (Olson and Bruner, 1974). Street (1984), however, argues persuasively that ways of thinking and the uses of literacy are alike generated by the patterns of life in the community, and that those who attribute to literacy the ability to shape people's lives are ignoring its diversity and misrepresenting its nature. It can be argued that it is precisely an education in decontextualized thinking that is at a premium in a highly complex technological society such as ours, with its differentiated productive skills and its high valuation of technical innovation divorced from the immediate needs of the technologist. There is a price to be paid for the decontextualization of learning, however, and it is to this that we now turn.

Beyond Pupils' Control

Advocates of 'liberal education', an education detached from particular applications and devoted to the pursuit of the various forms of knowledge because they are intrinsically worthwhile, defend it as a means of developing citizens who can 'shape purposes for themselves and seek to satisfy those purposes' (Bailey, 1986). This is an entirely acceptable goal, but we have to ask whether the kind of subject-based schooling which represents 'liberal education' in most schools in fact provides for the development of this kind of thinking.

There is reason to believe that traditional schooling encourages in some pupils a passive acceptance of the status quo (Freidenberg, 1965; Hargreaves, 1982; Hammersley, 1977). It is not easy to determine whether this is the inevitable result of curricula which are divorced from real-world concerns or whether it is rather the result of determining pupils' achievement levels through examinations which mainly test the ability to recapitulate received opinions. Hammersley (1977) summarizes his conclusions:

> Pupils are ... encouraged to take classroom knowledge at face value rather than think critically. They are being socialised into a world in which knowledge is something external and beyond their control rather than being shown that knowledge is always produced by particular men [*sic*] in particular circumstances for particular purposes.... It denies pupils access to the means of producing knowledge, the means by which to challenge teacher-authority.

Such messages about their roles in school contain implications that may influence some students' view of their future roles in the world.

There have been various explanations of this lack of critical edge. For some commentators such as Atkinson and Delamont (1976) the tendency for school knowledge to be treated as absolute and authoritative is connected with the means by which teachers maintain their immediate control of pupils in the classroom. The teacher presents a 'working model' of the world to pupils and this 'provides the teacher with a resource in controlling the situation'. This must indeed be part of the mechanism that supports the normal curriculum, yet it must be added that Atkinson and Delamont do not discuss the possibility that the models presented may provide an uninformative or biased account of the world.

Teachers may at times find it useful to withhold knowledge. McNeil (1981), for example, observed three teachers teaching contemporary American history to senior high school students and noted that they not only avoided controversial contemporary issues but actively frustrated students' attempts to introduce current issues into lessons. The teachers did not have particularly conservative political views: it seemed that the form of knowledge and pedagogy that they practised was more closely related to the functions of education in a stratified industrial society than to those teachers' perceptions of how the world is. It would be interesting to know how often this is the case in different subjects and in different countries. To associate these characteristics of classroom epistemology solely with the teacher's need to manage children would be misleading since to idealize and unify knowledge – to show the world as simpler, more homogenous and more open to simplistic interpretations than it is – is a political act (Postman and Weingartner, 1966). Courses in business studies, for example, often present a highly idealized picture of the values and methods used by firms (Barnes, Barnes and Clarke, 1984). The exclusion of the students' existing knowledge and concerns both prescribes a passive role for them and frustrates their potential interest in the matters studied. There seems every reason for education to coopt the enthusiasm and commitment of the young rather than to frustrate it; those students who survive such treatment are likely to be those whose family support and sense of extrinsic goals are strongest.

One way in which social structure affects curriculum and teaching is that low-status subjects not infrequently change their content and procedures in order to gain status (Layton, 1973; Goodson, 1984). A subject will seek to gain status by substituting theoretical knowledge for activities demanding manual or other skills. Physical education took in elements of physiology and thus de-emphasized its focus upon physical skills and fitness in favour of book learning. Cookery and needlework became 'domestic science' and took in new social concerns, values and bodies of knowledge. The move is towards the theoretical and away from the practical, but often the result is not a move from repetitive skill learning to rational inquiry, since the theory may well be taught as inflexibly as the skills.

Educational institutions transmit preferred pictures of the world: it seems of crucial importance that, whenever these pictures include some representation of the learner himself or herself (and they almost always do), they should be active in responsible pursuit of goals, rather than a passive recipient of others' purposes. The traditional role of the learner in an academic curriculum is as the receiver of knowledge contructed elsewhere for purposes that he or she has not yet had an opportunity to grasp. We need to inquire whether a 'practical' curriculum would be any better.

A Practical Curriculum?

Saunders (1979; 1982) has presented a case for 'the learning of "action skills" (observation and participation) which are located or supported by reference to general theory or the "disciplines"', thus gaining the advantages of making the curriculum more active at the same time as providing access to more detached modes of thought. 'By including practical action in the curriculum it is possible to situate decontextualized meanings in issues arising in the physical and local environment,' he adds (1982). His formulation, though valuable, does not raise the question of a 'critical' element in such a curriculum.

The concepts 'practical' and 'relevant to the real world' are far from unambiguous. Gough (1985) has followed Schwab (1970) in modifying the distinctions made by Aristotle between 'theory', 'practice' and 'technique' in order to make important distinctions between kinds of curricula. (a) *Theoretic* operations are concerned with generalized propositional knowledge; (b) *technical* operations are procedures devoted to the production of specifiable products and events; (c) *practical* operations are concerned with actions which include choice based on socio-moral criteria. (See also Carr and Kammis (1986).)

All three kinds of operation are important, but Gough wishes to emphasize the central role that practical thinking and action should play in schooling. To illustrate *practical* activities he quotes Schwab's (1970) account of the cyclical thought processes characteristic of problem solving in real life:

We may be conscious that a practical problem exists, but we do not know what the problem is. We cannot be sure even of ... what it is we want or need.... The problem slowly emerges ... as we search for data, and conversely the search for data is only gradually given direction by the slow formation of the problem [quoted in Gough, 1985].

Schwab goes on to suggest that the search gradually moves into a second phase in which the search for solutions gradually replaces the attempt to define the problem, though even then there can be no certainty what information will be needed. He supplies the example of a person who seeks unsuccessfully to solve money problems by looking for ways of increasing income or by reallocating resources but ends by having to modify his desires: what began as a technical problem became a socio-moral problem. Hence Schwab's assertion that 'We cannot be sure even of what we want or need.' This account of what constitutes practical thinking can usefully be associated with Neisser's (1976) characterization of everyday reasoning as directed by feeling and values.

Gough's purpose is to argue that much of what is called 'practical' in school curricula is in fact 'technical' in his sense, that is, concerned with mastering standard procedures to specified ends. Practicals in school science, for example, are usually either rehearsals of skilful action or illustrations of theoretical propositions. Practical thinking in Gough's sense involves judgements about ends as well as means. 'Practical problems are essentially human problems,' he says. He does not deny the value of technical or theoretical activities, but wishes us to consider what dispositions underlie a learner's participation in each of them. My own formulation of the issue would be this: theoretic and technical learning casts the learner as receiver of purposes, frames and techniques constructed by others elsewhere; practical learning requires the learner to take a responsible part in the making.

There are not many teachers and other educationists who would dissent from the assertion that schooling should be concerned with 'the development of certain attitudes of mind, pre-eminent among which is the ability to look critically at one's world and to reach one's own conclusions about it, and indeed to achieve a measure of control over it' (Kelly, 1986). Real schooling is often very unlike this, however. Delamont (1983) relates a telling anecdote about a biology teacher who had set up the standard school 'experiment' of covering part of the leaves of a growing plant with metal foil in order to illustrate the action of light by measuring the presence of starch in the covered and uncovered parts of the leaves. On this occasion one of the students protested that the experiment would prove nothing, since any difference could be produced by the foil or some other unknown agent. The teacher was just about to respond when another pupil broke in to say that what the teacher said must be true or they would not be wasting time on it. Delamont uses this incident to distinguish between 'hot science', which involves genuine reasoning, observation and experiment, and 'cold science', which rests upon the uncritical reception of authoritative statements. The anecdote well illustrates both the characteristics of theoretical knowledge which is being transmitted irrespective of its relationship to the learners' pictures of the physical universe and also the way in which the apparently 'practical' may be coopted into the service of the theoretic curriculum. It is this that throws doubts upon those defences of traditional education which represent it as 'liberal' in the sense of developing students' abilities to form justifiable and informed judgements.

Genuinely practical education in Gough's sense would involve the learners in judgement, deliberation and choice; it would be 'hot', not 'cold'. Much school science is 'cold', but so is much school history, geography, maths and English. Can this be justified? Because schooling provides the arena in which young people are required to engage in displays which will initially determine their life chances, cold knowledge is firmly ensconced in education, for cold knowledge is easier to learn, to teach and (most significantly) to test. The British Government's Technical and Vocational Education Initiative can be looked at in the light of these considerations. Many of its formal aims might be taken to point towards 'practical' as well as 'technical' curricula, but it is far from clear that what schools put into practice will reflect these principles. Certification may prove to be the rock on which the government's policies for practical education will founder (Leach, 1986). Parents' and students' urgent demands for negotiable qualifications are likely once again to push schools back upon cold knowledge and upon 'technical' rather than 'practical' activities (Dore, 1976).

Technological thinking in the curriculum penetrates beyond the more obviously technical subjects. Langer and Applebee (1984), for example, point out that in some approaches to the teaching of writing the student is required to begin by formulating a 'thesis' which in effect requires him or her to know where s/he is going before the exploratory processes of composition have taken place, thus ignoring the discovery element in writing. As they put it 'Language events are driven by their purposes, not simply by their forms.' Other forms of academic learning are commonly open to similar criticisms.

It is the learner's desire to understand or to act that makes for 'hot' knowledge. In her critique of Paul Hirst's views on the structure of the curriculum, Marie Schilling (1986) says: 'In his overemphasis on the cognitive structure of human enterprises . . . he overlooks the purposes that gave them point.' Education is an ethical and political enterprise, not an epistemological one; right action depends on context and therefore cannot be universal. She takes the view that the curriculum should include practical reasoning which involves deliberation and choice and which cultivates 'playfulness, flexibility, openness to the alien, respect for what is different, empathetic understanding, trust, reasonableness, truthfulness, capacity for self-criticism.'

Our whole perception of reality is purposive: we construct our common realities on the basis of purposes which we partly negotiate with our fellows and partly construct ourselves, and these purposes can equally be seen as values. Even our curiosity and reflection is in the last analysis part of our reaching for a preferred picture of the world and of ourselves in it. 'Objects and events are not passively recorded . . . but acted upon and perceived in terms of actions performed' (Olson and Bruner, 1974). Our whole universe is action-oriented, and our school curricula should acknowledge this, for it is essential to educate young people in the processes of responsible choice. An education that is *solely* technical is no education at all. That is why we should be adopting a version of *the practical* which (like that recommended by Gough) acknowledges that students are purposive beings and that preparing them for life includes preparing them for critical choice. The theoretical and technical learning is useless without it, except perhaps as a method of social control.

Although most of those educationists who recommend a move towards 'practical' elements in the curriculum support their views with arguments based upon the dispositions that they believe should be fostered in future citizens, there is another line of thought. Learning that lacks the characteristics that Gough calls 'practical' may prove ineffective. I found it useful some years ago to make a distinction between 'school knowledge' and 'action knowledge'. I was wishing to point to differences in the way we know rather than in what we know. 'Action knowledge' is so integrated into our pictures of the world that it influences our behaviour: 'school knowledge' is held superficially and makes no contact with action. It is possible to distinguish 'deep' from 'surface' learning strategies amongst those displayed by learners (Bond, Keogh and Walker, 1985; Baird and White, 1982). Learners using 'deep' strategies attempt to relate new knowledge to their existing views of the world, making diverse links with personal experience and actively dealing with discontinuities and contradictions. Intention plays a central role in 'deep' learning strategies: the new knowledge is brought into relation with the purposive world of the learners, whereas 'surface' strategies occur where learners fail to perceive or create any relevance between the new and the old (Bond, Keogh and Walker, 1985). Practical learning will encourage and support deep learning because of its overt demands upon the learner's purposes. Surface learning does not affect those models of the world on which we base our actions and thus is ineffective and quickly forgotten.

Critical Teaching and Learning

The concept of a curriculum which is 'critical' as well as practical deserves further consideration. 'Critical' does not imply iconoclasm but a consistent practice of treating all accounts as requiring a justificatory context. It is not my intention to suggest that there is a critical 'faculty' that can be trained: the ability to take a critical responsibility for one's actions (or lack of action) derives from knowledge of the world. A critical curriculum is one in which knowledge is learned in certain ways. At the very least critical teaching implies the presenting of alternative accounts and alternative ways of carrying out a task, and with this the practice of exploring with students how the choice of one or other account or technique can be justified. The whole point of this is to make the processes of decision making and choice available to learners.

The call for a critical curriculum is not to be dismissed as facile liberalism. The real world in which schoolchildren are already living is not made of well-shaped issues with clear-cut answers. For the most part we have to choose to act on guesses about what is the case, guided by a background awareness of the world that is built up in a variety of contexts, most of them not academic. Our actions in real life do not conform to the technological ideal: we do not define goals first and then turn to investigating means; rational analysis of that kind usually takes place afterwards (Schön, 1983). Scientists turn back to construct logical justifications of what begin as intuitive hypothetical models that looked as if they might encompass the data. Yet school knowledge is usually represented as if it existed in some ideal realm of 'objective' knowledge, separated from any human knower and in particular from the policies and purposes of individuals. Of course, most teachers seek to avoid a crude transmission of their political or religious beliefs, yet whatever they teach is inevitably a pre-emptive choice – of these issues rather than those, of this evidence rather than that, of this discourse mode rather than another. How could it be otherwise?

Much schooling is based on the pretence that this is not the case, that there is an absolute truth to be transmitted. The students, however, pay a high price for this pretence;

> While a body of knowledge is given life and direction by the conjectures and dilemmas that brought it into being and sustained its growth, pupils who are being taught often do not have a corresponding sense of conjecture and dilemma [Bruner, 1966, quoted by Rowlands, 1984].

I would wish to go further and say that our understanding of the real world is in its very nature action-oriented: our hypotheses and guesses about how the world works are driven by our commitments, intentions and values. Active knowledge is purposive. It is organized as pre-emptive models of reality, as scripts than can in part be realized in the interactive roles we seek to play.

What is lost by the fact that much schooling treats the knowledge being taught as if it were neutral and as if it constituted the only possible account of the matter in question? Take, for example, a geography curriculum which in presenting an account of poverty in the Third World disguises the way in which such poverty is related to the economic policies of more wealthy nations. Geography should discuss not only how the world is but also consider views about how it should be in future (Hicks, 1984). Kilbourn (1985) discusses what he calls 'epistemological flatness' in science lessons; by this he means the practice of making assertions about the physical world without giving students access to any justifications. Aware of the difficulties of doing this, he asserts that teachers should be 'helping students to establish knowledge claims in some reasonably authentic fashion *for them*.' I see no reason why the same should not be argued for all areas of the curriculum; schooling has too long taken refuge in an unexamined positivism. If we wish to educate young people to take their place as adults, there can be no justification whatsoever in presenting them with other people's accounts of the world without giving them some access both to how those accounts were arrived at and to some of the possible alternative accounts and how they too might be justified. A 'critical' curriculum provides the only way of both avoiding indoctrination and recognizing that all knowledge is provisional. All teachers should seek to make the grounds of their beliefs available to students, and if this implies that they themselves will have to think more analytically about what those grounds are, all the better. Such criticism would not necessarily be sceptical; indeed, it might lead to young people having a firmer grasp of the reasons and values which support their beliefs and aspirations.

Positivistic assumptions that there exists a value-free knowledge to be taught in school are deeply embedded in our education systems. In the UK our public examinations are built upon such assumptions. So are teachers' normal practices in marking their pupils' work: Hull (1984) has pointed out how marking seldom puts students in the position of understanding the criteria used by the marker, thus reinforcing the students' tendency to direct their efforts towards superficially acceptable products instead of towards more effective learning strategies.

How accessible to learners are the criteria used by their teachers and those others who influence the content and nature of the curriculum? Learners should have access to the principles that justify learning this rather than that. There should be discussion of the nature of learning in each subject: the absence of this from the curriculum in Britain is not just a matter of the students' supposed immaturity; even in university degree courses there is frequently no discussion of the nature of the intended learning in that subject. Finally, students need to know the criteria on which teachers decide whether a piece of work has been satisfactorily completed, or on which they award marks comparing one piece with another or one student with another. Edwards and Mercer (1987) quote British primary school teachers who (surprisingly) say that they deliberately avoid such discussion in the interests of students' autonomy, yet the ability to choose is built upon awareness of others' perspectives beside one's own.

But awareness alone is not enough, since the learner is still implicitly deprived of the right to argue back. What is required is to give students access to the processes by which pictures of the world are constructed and eventually justified, and thus to alternative pictures which might reasonably be adopted. Students would become conscious of what many already understand tacitly: that knowledge is a human construct, perpetually open to revision. This would constitute a critical curriculum.

Arguments Against an Embedded Curriculum

If the curriculum were to move closer to the world outside school, several disadvantages might be expected. Learning might be focused on getting a task completed, rather than on understanding the context, conditions and purposes implicit in the task. The students would then learn how to carry out activities but not when and why, with the result that they would be qualified only to carry out others' purposes. (This presents in other terms the case for access to criteria made in the previous section.) The second disadvantage of a curriculum embedded in everyday life has often been pointed out in connection with the recommendations of the 'de-schooling' movement. If learning is to be carried on in the marketplace, then it is far more open to being captured and reshaped by an interested party; the interests of an employer or an official with whom a student spends time are not necessarily those of the student.

It has repeatedly been argued (Richards, 1978; Williams, 1977) that, if learners are not given access to the special 'ways of meaning' provided by the disciplines, then they will be trapped in the everyday discourse of the social milieu from which they come. If this is so, then a curriculum too firmly situated in the arenas of everyday life may well be in danger of disqualifying people from full participation in adult life. The idea of trapping learners in everyday discourse needs to be seriously considered. Does it imply that everyday discourse is unambiguously inferior to academic discourse? For some purposes it undoubtedly is. I notice in my own work with teachers that those who switch too readily into anecdotes about their pupils often find it difficult to justify and criticize their practices in the light of more general principles. How far should reflexive modes of thought be accorded an intrinsic value? Might there not be competent teachers without the habit of reflection? Many highly developed competences including language are not readily open to introspection. Moreover, everyday discourse is characterized not only by a lower level of introspective awareness but also by a quite different set of purposes and functions. For example, there has been much discussion recently of 'children's science', the ways of thinking about events in the physical world which children use to guide their actions and understanding (Driver, Guesne and Tiberghien, 1985; Hills, 1983). Our beliefs about how the world is are in essence the reflection of our purposes; our working categories are functional.

Does the fear that learners may be trapped in everyday discourse rest upon the assumption that part of the function of schooling is to empower the individual for future participation in a competitive society? In a country whose government is deliberately fostering competitiveness as a politico-social policy, is it the duty of a teacher to contribute to the socialization of pupils into such values? At one time or another most people, from whatever social background they come, need access to the interpretive frameworks provided by some of the disciplines, but we need it when we need it, not when someone else decides. At some times in my life I would have found linguistics boringly irrelevant and would have studied it under protest, but later I read enthusiastically in the field because it offered ways of thinking about issues which had by then become of importance to me. One of the difficulties about the argument based on right of access to the disciplines is that so many young people who are introduced to compulsory knowledge fail to gain access to anything from the enforced submission. This is not to shrug off our responsibility as adults to make some choices – or at least to join in negotiation – with young people who are not yet in a position to know what their future needs will be.

Is there any danger in schools that the frameworks provided by the subjects taught operate as blinkers, blinding the learners to other possible ways of seeing the world? I suspect that the danger is more often that students who do not make sense of what they are taught in school reject it entirely and fall back upon views of the world and ways of coping that they have found to 'work' elsewhere. Perhaps more dangerous is the effect upon students who are eager to be accepted into the club but who are enabled to join in the discourse in only the most superficial way. They are indeed at the mercy of the new frame of reference. They can only be protected from their enthusiasm if they are helped to get access not only to the results of the frame, but to the criteria, principles, methods and justifications that under-lie it.

How close are we willing to go to the real world? Connell *et al.* (1982) suggest that the curriculum should be organized around:

problems such as economic survival and collective action, handling the disruption of households by unemployment, responding to the impact of new technology, managing problems of personal identity and association, understanding how schools work and why.

These certainly sound like real-world problems; one difficulty for any teacher who encourages pupils to turn the curriculum into action in the world is that this action is necessarily political, in the sense of challenging access to resources and status, even when it is not involved with party politics. As McNeil (1981) suggested, most teachers do not see this as their task, yet an education which was genuinely directed to the real world would have to concern itself with issues like these, though it would also have to deal with much else.

What Should the Curriculum Be Like?

The decontextualized nature of schooling is at once its strength and its weakness. Schooling offers young people models of reality and at best allows them to try them out in an 'as if' mode which protects them from having to pay too dear for their mistakes and also from exploitation. On the other hand, school activities are often far removed from the learner's living purposes, which makes it difficult for some of them to be taken seriously. (My own writing, for example, arises from my current commitment to projects and persons: not so most writing done in school.) The models of reality offered to pupils are often invalid, a poor match for judgement and action in the world. Is it possible to bring schooling nearer to the real world while at the same time making alternative models of reality more available to young people rather than less?

The concept of closeness to the real world is, of course, open to a wide range of interpretations. Education for action should show awareness of the various ways in which we participate in the life about us. This would include not only the role of employee, but such other roles as member of a family, member of a club, trade union or church, and citizen with responsibilites and rights which include political power. The real world also encompasses interpersonal sensitivity, the unique interests, experiences and purposes of each boy or girl, and concern for people whom they will never meet. All of these should influence the curriculum, both in its content and in the roles which young people learn to play as pupils in school.

But the learner's view of the real world matters too. Much care should be taken to engage those aspects of life which the learners regard as urgent and relevant: this must involve some kind of negotiation between what adults regard as potentially useful and the learners' current concerns and interests. This is important because it is likely to influence whether the pupil learns in depth or superficially, whether what is learned becomes part of his or her action knowledge.

Schooling must not become merely 'technical' but should help young people to engage ethical and social issues both at a personal and political level. The idea of substituting 'process' for 'content' is nonsensical: understanding is impossible without knowledge. Academic curricula have been at fault not in celebrating knowledge but in teaching it as if it were monolithic and unquestionable.

The curriculum should be 'critical': a central purpose should be to give students access to the criteria being used by teachers in regarding some accounts as more truthful than others or some methods as more effective. The purpose would be to give students access to the grounds of knowledge, and thus put them in a position to act as participants and even to propose alternative criteria of their own making. Eventually the aim is to help them to make responsible choices in action, and this must imply giving them explicit access to the justifications, intellectual, social and ethical, for alternative accounts of how the world is and for the use of one technique rather than another. That is, the curriculum should be 'practical' in Gough's sense.

Teaching should enable the learners to make relationships between their existing pictures of the world and those which their teachers believe to be more 'valid', 'truthful', 'mature' or 'powerful'. Thus it would be acknowledged that, in the last analysis, however a teacher teaches, it is the student who must work upon his or her understanding. Talking and writing are of particular importance in this: by making his or her understanding of a matter explicit, a student moves closer to being able to control and if necessary change this understanding. It is appropriate in this volume to spend a moment in celebrating the contribution of James Britton to our theoretical understanding of this. He has always insisted that children are most likely to learn from writing or talking which is about something that matters to them as an audience who wants to hear and reply: teachers should encourage talking and writing 'for real' and not 'dummy runs'. It is this that will encourage and strengthen young people's ability to think and judge for themselves.

Adults need to be able to reflect and analyse as well as to act. Thus it is necessary to reconcile the embeddedness that can bring schooling closer to action in the real world with the detachment which schools also provide. It is this detachment that at best allows the learner the elbowroom in which to understand the world in a critical manner by providing occasions for him or her to reflect, choose and judge. It has already been suggested that it would be possible to design a 'practical' curriculum which would arise from closer involvement in the world of action, and which would also include access to more decontextual ways of thinking, approaching these in a critical manner. The failure of education has not been a failure of relevance to the economy, but a failure of relevance to the students' perception of what is worth doing. Detachment threatens that sense of relevance, so that any curriculum has to tread a narrow path between confining children to the reality they already experience and alienating them with what appear to be irrelevancies. There is cause for fear that either of the official policies with which this paper began would lead to an uncritical curriculum, one by promoting an unthinking pursuit of 'technique', skills and methods treated merely as means, and the other by a return to a curriculum which avoids controversy by transmitting pictures of the world which are so simplistic as to be finally untruthful.

Learning Listening
Gordon Pradl

As teachers we naturally have much advice to give, much information to dispense. If only our students would listen to us, the educational puzzle would be solved once and for all. Yet, ironically, students think they are listening all the time; in fact, they believe that schools are precisely concocted to make them listen as part of an endless, captive audience. But we know differently, for the continuing challenge of teaching/learning involves creating the right conditions of mutually intended attention, which inevitably leads us to the imperatives of relationship – of dominance and control, of sharing and trust, of collaboration and cooperation.

To give someone something, even knowledge, means we will have to come to terms with the other person's outlook on our very act of giving. For suspicion is constantly afoot. People who give exert a decided influence over those who receive; being on the receiving end, we hold disdain for those who would have power over us. And so as teachers we are constantly caught up in this dilemma that Soren Kierkegaard so precisely pinpointed:

all true effort to help begins with self-humiliation: the helper must first humble himself under him he would help, and therewith must understand that to help does not mean to be a sovereign but to be a servant, that to help does not mean to be ambitious but to be patient, that to help means to endure for the time being the imputation that one is in the wrong and does not understand what the other understands [1962, pp. 27–8].

The lesson Kierkegaard would have us learn, yet one we resist, even as we hear echoed its commonsense wisdom in our own experience, is simply that no one likes being placed in an inferior position to an advice-giver. Being sensitive to this possible resentment, the teacher serves as listener in order to draw out and explore the learner's evolving representations of the world. Teachers who would foster the student's emerging language competence grasp the importance of their selfless role.[1] Already secure in their obvious dominion over the learner, such teachers stand waiting to receive the performing inquiries of their students.

A concern for listening has been a crucial part of James Britton's lifelong preoccupation with language and learning.

Whenever Britton locates a point of emphasis in his thinking, invariably it involves some kind of active taking in of the world within an attending social matrix. Thus spectating, for him, is not an idle, languishing endeavour; rather, it is filled with high seriousness, the kind of seriousness many have attributed to play – that time when we try on the fit and possibility of a behaviour without suffering the blows of real consequences. Taking the role of *spectator* alternates cyclically with periods when we are *participants* in the ongoing affairs of the world, for as spectators we judge how validly these same affairs are being represented both by ourselves and others. Accordingly, when we spectate, we are testing the correspondences of texts – what is the goodness of fit for the words to the world and vice versa?

It is no surprise that the character of Britton's own professional conduct parallels his deep fascination with this *spectator* stance toward human discourse. The *spectator* stance is rooted in our profound human need to manipulate symbols and assess values. Through active spectating we forge a map of our accumulated experiences – a process involving sharing and negotiating, narrating and metaphorizing, legitimizing and invalidating. Consequently Britton has come to champion the role of *expressive* writing in education, whereby students come to determine the relationship that is emerging between themselves and the knowledge of others. Making knowledge personal requires language that is infused with one's own attitudes, connections, revelations. Expressive is not a melody of idiosyncracy, but a harmony of connection. It is listening to how one feels about what one knows or is coming to know. Without this conjoining relationship, this continuity between cognition and affect, at whatever level of maturity, a person's theories about the world remain out there under someone else's control and jurisdiction.

But, as Britton asks, why would anyone risk using language to generate an expressive genre, so filled with errors and misdirections as it is, unless there were others around who prized such writing, listeners who through their own acts of responsive listening reinforced the learner listening to herself. Thus, not surprisingly, when he and his research team (1975) were looking at the development of writing abilities of students during the early seventies, they found that little of the writing done by upper-level students was either expressive or addressed to a teacher as 'trusted adult'. Without an audience to encourage listening connections, there will be few forays into this forbidding territory, however central it might be to actual learning. As long as student measurement and subject evaluation hold priority, listening time can always be surrendered.

It may be easy to dismiss this brief for listening as being yet another apology for loose living and lax standards, especially in a climate where many are convinced that only objective and impersonal rigour and discipline lead to real mastery of a subject's content. But this opposition misrepresents the true dilemma of learning, namely that there is a *relationship* to contend with between the 'knower' and the 'known'. And, what is most important, we are now discovering, is that this relationship, between a sense of self and a sense of an impinging world made up of objects, operations and others, characterizes learning even in the youngest of infants. As Britton has commented:

we have begun to realize how language behaviour builds on earlier non-verbal behaviour: how cooperative routines set up between infant and adult, mostly in the form of play, increasingly generate *meaning* for the infant; and how early language comes in to highlight meanings already established in this way [1982b, p. 202].

The Earliest Listening Environment

In his study of the infant's emerging sense of self, Daniel Stern (1985) offers clear support for our intuitive grasp of the central role listening plays in a person's development. Drawing on a number of observations that have shown how infants 'have distinct biases or preferences with regard to the sensations they seek and the perceptions they form', and that from birth infants seem to show 'a central tendency to form and test hypotheses about what is occurring in the world', Stern demonstrates that early on the infant has a defined sense of self, one with clearly demarcated boundaries (pp. 41–2). In other words, differentiation between a me and a not-me, which psychoanalysis had posited as occuring much later in development, has now been shown to exist between two and six months. Further, the infant uses this sense of self to learn about the world during the endless series of encounters supported by the fostering stimulation of the parent or caretaker.

Included among the evidence which developmental psychologists have used to infer this sense of self are a number of 'experiments' with young infants which reveal their capacity to make fine discriminations among the objects of the presenting environment and actually to choose preferentially among a variety of stimuli. For instance, at four months infants were shown different animated cartoons side by side along with a sound track appropriate to only one (p. 85). Whichever image matched the sound track was the image attended to by the infant. In fact infants have been shown to notice a 400–millisecond discrepancy between an expected sound-sight relationship such as lip synchronization. Another experiment involved a pair of

Siamese twins who, being joined on the surface between the sternum and the umbilicus, were in a continual face-to-face relationship (p. 79). Observation revealed that they alternated in sucking each other's fingers. When the psychologist gently pulled the hand away from one twin's mouth, its attempt at recovery varied depending upon whose hand it was. If it was the twin's own hand, the hand itself strained to go back to the mouth, but if the hand belonged to the other twin, the head moved forward to recapture the fingers, precisely the kind of consistent body control one would expect if a coordinated and coherent sense of self existed.

Stern uses such evidence to sketch out the existence of four developmental stages ending with the infant's sense of a verbal self. What turns out to be crucial during each of these stages is the responsive listening role played by the adult caretaker. As the infant is solidifying its sense of self, it is learning a range of behaviours, such as agency, the appropriateness of which is determined by the kind of interpersonal relationships established during this period. Stern, for example, describes one mother, who was very dominating, listening to her own desires, not her daughter's:

She had to design, initiate, direct, and terminate all agendas. She determined which toy Molly should play with, how Molly was to play with it ('Shake it up and down – don't roll it on the floor'), when Molly was done playing with it, and what to do next ('Oh, here is dressy Bessy. Look!'). The mother overcontrolled the interaction to such an extent that it was often hard to trace the natural crescendo and decrescendo [sic] of Molly's own interest and excitement. It was so frequently derailed or interrupted that it could hardly be said to trace its own course ... [Molly] seems to have learned that excitement is not something that is equally regulated by two people – the self and the self-regulating other – but that it is mainly the self-regulating other who does all the regulating [p. 196–7].

Without the mutuality occasioned by responsive listening, Molly is developing a sense of self devoid of agency, and as such she will tend to avoid subsequent opportunities for inquiry and learning, feeling always a need to take her cues from others.

Stern's picture of the infant and its learning environment is characterized by an 'experience of being with an other'. The time the infant is with the caretaker constitutes 'active acts of integration', not 'passive failures of differentiation' (p. 101). As the infant attempts to fathom the regularity that appears to exist within this world of intersubjectivity, 'what is ultimately at stake is nothing less than discovering what part of the private world of inner experience is shareable and what part falls outside the pale of commonly recognized human experiences. At one end is psychic human membership, at the other psychic isolation' (p. 126).

The kind of responsive listening which is most supportive of the infant's developing sense of self, and which in turn will determine the person's frame of mind toward the future world of experience, Stern calls *attunement*. This is when the caretaker monitors the infant's states and actions of inquiry and provides feedback which in turn can be integrated and matched within the infant's perceptual field. For instance, 'the loudness of a mother's vocalization might match the force of an abrupt arm movement performed by the infant.' Through the means of *absolute intensity, intensity contour, temporal beat, rhythm, duration* and *shape*, the caretaker sends positive signals to the infant that its exploration of the world is both satisfactory and gratifying (p. 146). As Stern further elaborates:

An attunement is a recasting, a restatement of a subjective state. It treats the subjective state as the referent and the overt behavior as one of several possible manifestations or expressions of the referent. For example, a level and quality of exuberance can be expressed as a unique vocalization, as a unique gesture, or as a unique facial display. Each manifestation has some degree of substitutability as a recognizable signifier of the same inner state.... If one imagines a developmental progression from imitation through analogue and metaphor to symbols, this period of the formation of the sense of a subjective self provides the experience with analogue in the form of attunements, an essential step toward the use of symbols [p. 161].

Without this responsive listening represented at the pre-verbal stage by the caretaker's attunement, the infant is not properly prepared for the rush and crush of language looming on the horizon.

Not surprisingly, Stern is attracted to a 'dialogic' view of language, one which emphasizes that linguistic meanings in the world are jointly or socially owned, not merely personally controlled, even though this latter position has contributed in fundamental ways to the West's expectation of the individual.

The acquisition of language has traditionally been seen as a major step in the achievement of separation and individuation, next only to acquiring locomotion. The present view asserts that the opposite is equally true, that the acquisition of language is potent in the service of union and togetherness. In fact, every word learned is the by-product of uniting two mentalities in a common symbol system, a forging of shared meaning. With each word, children solidify their mental commonality with the parent and later with the other members of the language culture, when they discover that their personal experiential knowledge is part of a larger experience of knowledge, that they are unified with others in a common culture base [p. 172].

The infant's pre-verbal explorations have set the necessary conditions of perceptual and body knowledge that can now be linked with words. Words are initially given as a gift from outside by the caretaker, but there is a thought in the infant's head ready to receive it. Words, in this sense, serve as 'transitional phenomena', belonging neither completely to self nor completely to the other. Rather, they occupy 'a midway position between the infant's subjectivity and the mother's objectivity.... It is in this deeper sense that language is a union experience, permitting a new level of mental relatedness through shared meaning' (p. 172). But this union experience is dependent upon the mother deliberately supressing her own needs to perform for an audience. As Catherine Snow remarks, 'Mothers who talk a lot are apt to quickly leave behind topics that are of interest to the child. Children learn how to talk faster when mothers pick up on the topics the children introduce and request input from the children instead of always telling them what to do'.[2]

Finally, as Stern notes, the evolving presence of the word in this last stage of the infant's development of a sense of self provides a new way of storing and manipulating the motivated and episodic scripts that mark the world of social relatedness:

The advent of language ultimately brings about the ability to narrate one's own life story with all the potential that holds for changing how one views oneself. The making of a narrative is not the same as any other kind of thinking or talking. It appears to involve a different mode of thought from problem solving or pure description. It involves thinking in terms of persons who act as agents with intentions and goals that unfold in some causal sequence with a beginning, middle and end. (Narrative-making may prove to be a universal human phenomenon reflecting the design of the human mind) [p. 174].

Stern's synthesis is especially salient for our thinking about listening because it shows us the importance of pre-verbal ways of representing the world. These pre-verbal 'intentions' to make meaning out of the patterns of the world are quite complex and not simply the infant's reactions to the imperatives of its bodily functions. At this pre-verbal stage in the infant's development we notice a primary integration of affect and cognition. This should give us pause when later we tip the scales in favour of purely cognitive representations of experience owing in large part to the dominating presence of our verbal constructs.

Listening as Taking in the Other's World

To understand the dynamics of listening it is necessary to have some model of the individual's mental representation system and how that system might be subject to influence or change. Such a model, as Britton pointed out in *Language and Learning*, is found in the work of the psychologist George Kelly (1955). The fundamental postulate of Kelly's theory of personal constructs asserts: 'A person's processes are psychologically channelized by the ways in which he anticipates events'. Organized as it is around the idea that as individuals we carry constructs or mental models around in our heads which allow us to predict social events, Kelly's thinking views the notion of role and relationship as central to understanding human motives and actions.

These mental constructs that govern both perception and conception generally work smoothly, invisible to our conscious awareness or attention. Only through some breakdown in the system – what we sometimes label 'mistakes' or 'errors' when we get a response that we had not 'expected' – do we come to understand how powerfully determinant are the theories we carry around in our heads. Max Wertheimer tells the story of an anthropologist who was working on the grammar of a native language. On one particular occasion his informant was unable to translate a certain sentence. 'Puzzled, he tried to find out what words or grammatical inflections might be causing the trouble. It was only after some time that the native burst out, "How can I translate this sentence of yours: *The white man shot six bears today?* This is nonsense. It is impossible that the white man could shoot six bears in one day!"' (1959, p. 274). Failing to share the anthropologist's point of view whereby words need not match actual conditions in the world, the informant's linguistic behaviour was stopped dead in its tracks.

Yet, despite the control our theories of the world exert over our behaviour, these theories are subject to modification when they are exposed to the continual give and take of social relations. This dialectic of resistance and change constitutes the arena in which listening occurs. In this regard Kelly's 'sociality corollary' suggests that listening is not a mere activity we sometimes choose to do, but is indispensable to life itself: 'To the extent that one person construes the construction processes of another, he may play a role in a social process involving the other person.' This does not imply an exact eye-to-eye relationship; rather, if the venture is to be beneficial, there must be some mutual acceptance of the other's point of view. As Kelly explains, 'the person who is to play a constructive role in a social process with another person need not so much construe things as the other person does as he must effectively construe the other person's outlook' (1955, vol. 1, p. 95). With this in mind, we see that any taxonomy of listening will need to correlate both the needs and intentions of the speaker who is sending the message with the needs and intentions of the listener who is deciphering the message. Because these dimensions defy neat alignment, the listening puzzle remains complex indeed. A speaker, for instance, may *need* to be supported in terms of self-worth, even when his/her more immediate *intentions* appear to be directed at bringing about a change of opinion in the listener. If the listener fails to see beyond the intentions to this need, his/her message in reply may end by disrupting the communication. How many times have we seen a speaker deeply upset after an 'innocent' reply by some listener and the listener left wondering, 'But, what did I say?'

Having to balance conversational intentions with personal needs and, in turn, having to attempt to check that there is general agreement as to what background referent system is governing the conversation guarantee that taking in the other's world is a risky venture, one requiring conscious effort. In this regard it is useful to distinguish between listening which serves the other and listening which serves the self, though often these will be intertwined.

The kind of *responsive* or *reflective* listening I have been referring to serves the other by actively mirroring or playing back the speaker's utterances. With such a response the speaker can corroborate its intended effect on the listener or the effect of the written text on a reader. Such listening begins in attunement, as we saw at the pre-verbal stages of human development, and is a continuing source in the world for legitimizing or sanctioning the words and deeds of the speaker. We will, of course, also have had the experience of being helped by a listener even when he/she says nothing in return – no mirroring, no evaluations. Simply hearing our own words in the presence of another can be enough to trigger off connections, even solutions, that had previously eluded us.

Further extensions of this caring for the expression of the other, are seen in the *supportive* listening developed by Carl Rogers (1967). His form of creative, selfless listening involves a therapeutic technique which, in valuing and accepting openness, operates on the belief that the client should be responsible for his/her own determinations. Rogers's commitment to listening is realized in the language game played out in conversational sessions with his client. His conversational strategies try to withold evaluation, probing instead what the client is actually saying and feeling – 'Could you tell me more about this? How does that relate to what you said earlier? What made you think of that? Yes, that's interesting. Sure, I think so. Why not pursue more of the details?' The rules of this conversational technique of neutral encouragement and exploration were so explicit they even inspired an early artificial intelligence computer program called Eliza. Written by Joseph Weizenbaum of MIT in 1965, this interactive program showed a remarkable ability to induce people to believe that they were actually conversing with another person. Although a question may arise as to how far to take such non-directedness, from a supportive listening perspective it is really not non-directed at all; it is a matter of the client or speaker being served in such a way as to begin to create his/her own agendas.

Another kind of listening directed towards the other might be termed *protective*. When two people are arguing or when one person has angered or insulted another, conditions are ripe for the overt revelation of sensitive and potentially destructive material. A disparaging epithet suddenly bursts forth. Its power to wound deeply is great because we have been attending so long to the other person's themes and idiosyncracies that we know where he/she is vulnerable. In fact we spend a great deal of time covering, or ignoring through protective listening, these underbelly soft spots. The danger in this moment of anger – say in a lovers' quarrel when we abruptly lose sight of the other person's perspective – is that we stop listening protectively and go too far in giving voice to a name one cannot forgive or forget. Such escalation, especially in public, can end even a long-standing friendship with extreme prejudice. In serving the other we should always remember the role that discretion plays in our listening.

Listening which serves the self grows out of those many situations in which the messages we have to take in are conveyed within a strict 'transmission' context. Because such a context ignores the fact that meanings are socially constructed, we need to develop strategies for receiving the message so as to shape it for our own purposes. Such listening we might label *performing* or *rehearsing*. We incorporate the content of the message into our own words, making connections with our experience and previous knowledge. By giving the message back to the world of the speaker, we make it our own; or if the speaker is unavailable, we seek out others to try on our new script. Listening, in this sense, is never passive regurgitation – learners can assert control even within the 'transmission' model of education.

Finally, there is *reconstructive* listening, which, following the path of accommodation, makes our individual construct systems productive. Reconstructive listening is the mattock which breaks through the crust of our outdated beliefs. Unless we confront our own theories about human motives and actions with the construals of others and listen for the results, we have no way of monitoring and thus developing these theories in the first place. Attending to the results of our 'experiments' is akin to operating an early-warning radar system – we listen to the strength of the signals bouncing off approaching objects and adjust our behaviour accordingly.

If there are to be any participants in the life they are constructing, speakers are under certain obligations to help us play the role of listening *other*. Thus, in learning to participate in the social discourse of our speech communities, we come to master the particular constitutive rules that make conversational exchanges possible. Paul Grice (1975), for example, has attempted to capture the logic of conversation in what he calls the 'cooperative principle'. Basically, this includes four maxims: *quantity* (make your contribution as informative as necessary, but not more so); *quality* (don't say what you believe to be false or what you have no evidence for); *relation* (be relevant and coherent); and *manner* (follow the appropriate code of politeness – in other words, avoid obscurity, ambiguity, prolixity and disorder – be perspicuous, and, as Searle [1979, p. 50] adds, 'speak idiomatically unless there is some special reason not to'). Whether participating in a mutually initiated dialogue or being entrapped by some speaker such as happens when we receive one of those solicitation phone calls which increasingly plague the sanctity of our homes, these conversational underpinnings govern our basic expectations when we talk with others.

Though we constantly violate these rules, what is important to note is how these basic assumptions that we have about the other's contribution to a conversation even govern how we understand the intent behind a speaker's violation. What have been labelled 'indirect speech acts' are a case in point. Stating 'It's cold in here', for instance, more often than not is a veiled request that the listener shut the window or turn up the heat. Similarly, much humour and irony depends on the listener picking up a reversal of expressed meaning or intention.

In the area of monologue, specifically when someone is telling a story, implicit rules also obtain. Listeners constantly pressure the speaker to tell a tale that fits within some shared context. As William Labov remarks:

Pointless stories are met with the withering rejoinder, 'So what?' Every good narrator is continually warding off this question; when his narrative is over, it should be unthinkable for a bystander to say, 'So what?' Instead, the appropriate remark would be, 'He did?' or similar means of registering the reportable character of the events of the narrative [1972, p. 366].

This glue of shared context naturally binds speaker and listener together, for any speaker is in deep trouble when the audience is silently wondering, 'Why is he telling me this?' When this occurs there has been some error in correspondence between the emerging text and the set of listener expectations waiting to receive it. And such mismatches frequently arise because the speaker himself has not been listening adequately to the surrounding and shaping moments of the discourse.

Conversation, as opposed to one-way communication, assumes a mutual enterprise. The schemas being referred to by the words are being constructed even as the words are being uttered. Neither party assumes definitional priority in a true conversation and thus we see continual evidence of checking and rephrasing. In written texts we also see numerous explicit markers which connect writer to reader in this shared project of meaning making, though in modern writing these tend to be much less direct. I was struck by how much these markers, so reminiscent of speech forms, have receded when recently I read Rebecca Burlend's *A True Picture of Emigration*, an autobiographical story, written in 1848, about an English woman's homesteading in the United States. Continually Burlend establishes an immediate relationship with her audience by expressions such as:

And now, kind reader, if thou has any intentions of being an emigrant....

Having referred to the prairies, it may perhaps be necessary to be a little more explicit....

Let the reader imagine himself by the side of a rich meadow, or fine grass plain several miles in diameter....

Does the reader ask for an explanation? Let him consider for a while our condition.... [pp. 79, 83, 84, 112].

By addressing her reader so plainly, the author clearly locates her perspective and thus helps the reader entertain a more fully bodied picture of her communication intentions. Reciprocally, if the reader or listener is to complete the conservational link, she must not trick herself into assuming that words and worlds always mean the same thing. Shared referent systems are only built up slowly over time. For a person to listen with permeable constructs is an earned condition, a constantly practised way of life.

Listening to Ourselves

In *The Excursion*, Wordsworth describes:

> A curious child, who dwelt upon a tract
> Of inland ground, applying to his ear
> The convolutions of a smooth-lipped shell;
> To which, in silence hushed, his very soul
> Listened intensely; and his countenance soon
> Brightened with joy; for from within were heard
> Murmurings, whereby the monitor expressed
> Mysterious union with its native sea.
> [Book IV, l. 1132]

Having to say something, we wait impatiently, our ear pressed to the shell of our own thoughts. What correspondences will we discover between the demands of the present moment of communication and our yet-to-be-uttered words? We have all experienced the fear that the shell will be empty; but, if we attend, beyond the paralysis of self-consciousness, to the issue at hand, the loud roar of the sea follows.

Magically, it seems, much of our verbal power resides in potential body states. Our public utterances in other words rely on some inner reservoir of immediate intentions. They are not simply the result of isolated thoughts or speech scripts that have been carefully rehearsed in advance of the moment of delivery. Sometimes our ability to access specific verbal scripts even requires the circumstances of place; recall is blocked unless the context fits. I remember, for instance, having a secret fear of forgetting the combination of my locker at school. And whenever this fear came over me, I would try to rehearse the sequence of numbers, but inevitably my mind would go blank. Yet standing in front of my locker, actually engaged in spinning the cylinder with my fingers, the combination never deserted me.

Prior to its entry into the verbal world, the infant experiences a natural correspondence between its own bodily actions and the attuned responses of the caretaker. Out of this earlier integrated wholeness, we might surmise, grows the infant's eventual confidence in being able to represent the world with words, but this capacity for representation is inevitably tied to specific occasions. The listened-to infant learns that its agency will be equal to almost any present novelty. Because the infant associates these exploratory routines as leading to interpersonal satisfactions, a foundation is established for relating the affective with the cognitive aspects of language. In this way knowledge is person connected, at least when the infant's primary need for attention has not been thwarted. It is on this basis that we speak of being in touch with our intuitions. We know about the world through words which have been linked with bodily states, and this is what we feel when in uttering an expression we have the sensation of getting it right.

This phenomenon of inner listening, of feeling the necessary correspondences between our words and our intentions, has been explored by Britton in 'Shaping at the Point of Utterance' (1982). He emphasizes how the process is socially driven – that listening to ourselves and coming up with expressions that we feel are right for the occasion depend in part on the influence of audience. The guiding and caring presence of others, real or imagined, can help to draw out the words from us. Focusing specifically on the writer composing, Britton summarizes this relationship:

shaping at the point of utterance involves, first, drawing upon interpreted experience ... and, secondly, ... by some means getting behind this to a more direct apperception of the felt quality of 'experiencing' in some instance or instances; by which means the act of writing becomes itself a contemplative act revealing further coherence and fresh pattern. Its power to do so may depend in part upon the writer's counterpart of the social pressure that listeners exert on a speaker, though in this case, clearly, the writer himself is, in the course of the writing, the channel through which that pressure is applied [1982b, p. 143].

The implied conversation between ourselves acting both as speaker and listener is governed by the quality and quantity of our linguistic reserves which are built up through the frequenting of texts, both spoken and written. The language that we engage with is internalized 'through reading and *being read to*', and gradually a stock is built up that we can draw on at the moment of need. As Britton concludes: 'the developed writing process [is] one of hearing an inner voice dictating forms of the written language appropriate to the task at hand' (p. 144).

In 'Call it an experiment' (1987) Britton explores further these language resources which for the literate person have been accumulating over years of reading and rereading, especially those texts, literary or otherwise, that carry with them a distinctive style and rhythm. Probing his memory for the origins of literary fragments that had suddenly occurred to him – a poem by Stevens, a play by Auden – Britton touches upon the performance aspect of language:

identifying the source of a verbal fragment is, I am sure, a process of searching for a matching *sound* in my memory store. It seems likely that any item in that store will be more vividly represented when I have myself at some stage articulated sounds – creating a kinaesthetic as well as an audile image. The internalizations are not, I believe, usually the result of 'learning by heart' but are more often a result of increasing familiarity with text over a period of time – and perhaps in particular the outcome of repeated readings aloud [1987, p. 85].

In listening to his own language resources, Britton underscores the central role played by reading, which 'can have a cumulative effect upon memory so that we internalize general schemata for constructing a text, cadences that constitute both ways of sounding and ways of meaning'. Not to cultivate this resource for listening is greatly to diminish our integrative powers of self-expression.

The Teacher as Listener

To exhibit the kind of selflessness I am speaking of here is not to be sheared of identity or authority: as teachers we are not meek lambs drowning in the outpourings of our students. In fact, active listening suggests a strongly composed sense of self, for it involves knowing about intrusion and how one's ego (especially in the peculiar arena of teaching/learning) constantly risks swamping the egos of others. The teacher as listener provides the transitional space for the learner to move between one mental respresentation of the world and another.

Yet sometimes in our responses to student writing we fail to accommodate to the emerging words of the student struggling toward the expression of relatedness. Rather than join in some kind of natural dialogue, we seem obsessed with correctness and form, whether of product or of process. Consider, for instance, the following paper written by a twenty-one-year-old woman who only recently had come to the United States from Taiwan:

An unexpectant unfairness happened to Leo – a handicap. He lived in a very poor, longly, old little room. He only have his oldstyle tipewriter could play with, but there is a little business – selling pencils could convey him into a self satisfaction. As many people in the world, who love themselves and have a very dearing feeling to their parents. Leo's mother dead had bring to him an independed life. How a handicap like Leo could handle such a damn time? In his eyes, the world is charm and he 'guaranteed it'. In contrast, there are many people at our surroundings. They have given a healthy body. a wise blane and an advantage working change. Unfurnally, most of people do not appreciate it. They luck themselves to keep safeness, but lonly and could'nt be known. It had reflected to the high suicide rate. People should touch people, and make their life fill of energy. Don't curse at morning when we just wake up. To stay cool, and try to make a sweet day.

After reading this paper with a group of teachers who were considering the problems we face when teaching writing to students whose writing abilities are below expectations, I simply asked what questions would they like to address the author: 'Where would you begin your conversation with someone who said these things, had these thoughts?' The responses generally concentrated on form errors (spelling or 'What does "a very dearing feeling" refer to?') or focused on potential process problems ('How did you go about doing this?' or 'What do you want to say?'). Only a few teachers struck at the heart of meaning: 'Do you have any handicaps?' or 'Why do people not appreciate their "healthy body"?' The point I was trying to make involved realizing that there was a real speaking person behind this paper, a person who deserved listening to. And in listening we would be indicating our concern for establishing genuine conversation, as real people have outside of school. For in reading this paper my first curiosity centered on Leo: I was dying to know something about his handicap.

Of course, in our conversations with students, especially younger children, what we hear will not always be immediately understood. Oftentimes we would do well to puzzle more and judge less. Britton's story of Fat Ted and Knobby illustrates the listener's need to take a long view on the rush to interpretation:

Fat Ted was no real Teddy Bear but a wartime substitute, overstuffed and unfluffy. By then he was also worn threadbare in patches from much affection, though this had done little to soften his sullen expression. Fat Ted and Knobby (a loose-limbed and under-stuffed toy dog) were in conversation with their four-year-old possessor when I overheard her saying to Knobby, 'You see, Fad Ted was very, very naughty, so – (pause) – he grew up.' Of all concerned, it seemed that I was the only one who was puzzled; the puzzle stayed with me and it was some time before I solved it to my own satisfaction [1978, p. 33].

How does the listener make sense of a puzzling remark, Britton wonders. While suspending judgement, the listener strives for context and connection. Imagine for a moment a world which yokes 'naughty' with 'growing up', and you begin to grasp some picture of the child's imagined view of human behaviour wherein only the young are naughty, never the adults (regardless of whatever other bad traits they might be felt to have!). So to grow up is literally to leave 'naughtiness' behind. Still, as caring listeners it may be a while before we can incorporate the referents of the other into our own world view.

What we seek to develop for ourselves as teacher-listeners is a kind of facilitating social script, one that embodies the values of reflective listening. Such facilitation supports and encourages as it draws the learner forth. This means we are striving towards that interpersonal role relationship described as *mature dependency*. Infants, because they are unable to survive without their mothers, determine the immature end of the dependency continuum. At its opposite is not independence, but rather the kind of relationship that is possible between two friends, or two learners, or two workers, or a wife and a husband. Each involves a kind of reciprocal dependency that in fact defines maturity (a social concept) as opposed to self-sufficiency (an individual concept). And the right kinds of listening allow for the reciprocity that makes mature dependency possible: the capacity to play a social role in relation to someone else while allowing others to play a role in relation to you. In this way listening is not merely a route to learning, it is learning itself.

Our responsibility as teacher-listeners never stops – there will always be one more story waiting to be told by a student. And deciphering its point, not merely pinning on a quick label, requires a great deal of energy and a great deal of restraint. For after a while one's alertness fails, having endlessly to contend with growing selves vying for attention. So we need also to recognize the sheer drain, the personal costs extracted from the listener, and thus find ways of creating settings where in turn teachers will experience others who reflectively listen to them, to their stories, to their real concerns. Still there is no escaping the central role the teacher as listener plays in the education of the young. As Britton concludes:

We must be careful not to sacrifice to our roles as error spotters and improvers and correctors that of the teacher as listener and reader. I could sum it all up very simply. What is important is that children in school should write about what matters to them to someone who matters to them [1982b, p. 110].

If no one is listening to children their power and confidence with language inevitably withers.

Notes

1. One etymology of 'listening' even suggests its roots are to be found in a Sanskrit word meaning 'obedience'.
2. Quoted in 'Talking to the baby: some expert advice', *New York Times*, 5 May 1987, p. C11.

Part Two   Literacy and the Growth of Consciousness

The essays in this section are research documents about children learning, but the way the writers look at what is happening and the way they talk about it is distinctive. They do not argue much, though they make their assumptions clear; rather they patiently take the reader through the conversations which are the stuff of the essays, pausing as they go to comment on what is happening. In the later essays the writers use details from the life of classrooms as starting points or illustrations for theoretical arguments whereas, for these writers in Part Two, the interchange with the child is the actual matter in hand. One might say that while the focus in Part Two is on the developing self, in the rest of the book it is on the impinging world.

Myra Barrs introduces the section with her discussion of the central role of symbolic behaviour in the development of literacy. Gesture, makebelieve play, drawings and paintings represent children's ideas of reality. Vygotsky has suggested that all these forms may play a part in children's entry into the more abstract symbolism of print. Myra Barrs documents and discusses some of these transitions in her examples of children's drawings, and first attempts at writing and shows the interrelationship of both modes of representation.

The other three essays in the section are narratives about narratives – records of the children's drawn and written representations of happenings in their lives and of their speculative unwinding of the lives of others, and all these floating on a sea of talk. Furthermore, in these essays we can see 'learning with' in action. The teachers are 'scaffolders' in Courtney Cazden's sense of the metaphor – active but gradually retreating partners in a joint enterprise.

Henrietta Dombey describes two story sessions, one at home and one in a nursery class. In the first we see two 'readers' following in talk a story presented in pictures with minimal text. The session's sole aim is the enterprise of the story and its attendant speculations and we catch the pleasure of both readers in what is going on. Henrietta Dombey then goes on to explore the extent to which the particular quality of the session at home can be carried over into teaching in a classroom.

Margaret Meek is interested in the way children gradually learn the conventions of books. Beginning with the same picture story book used by Henrietta Dombey, she draws attention to some different things. She asks what are the things that a text teaches and shows a reluctant young reader beginning to learn the contexts and conventions of the picture story book – author, audience, print that is not part of the story, the story contained in the turning of the pages, and so on. In the end the child had found a world he liked and also knew how to get into. She refers to many books and their illustrators, and the ways in which these books teach children the rules of the game which reading stories is.

The essay by Amanda Branscombe and Janet Taylor is another version of the social interaction described by Courtney Cazden, but this time it is social interaction among peers. The authors describe shared journal writing in a kindergarten class. Each child writes a journal that is a chronicle of real events in his or her life and together they decide on the event they are to write about – the same event. The authors then show how the children's talk is used to construct knowledge about the writing system, to learn to make representations of events in drawings and letters, and to form a supportive community. The children's intentions are made explicit in the talk and the teacher ensures their decision a smooth passage.

James Britton says that we rationalize and logicalize our memories into narrative form. Here we can see this being undertaken first in talk – 'Which story shall we write about today?' – and then in pictorial and letter form. In the first essay in Part Three Claire Woods takes up this theme – English classes as places for evolving autobiography, but this time with a broader perspective. She sees all the experience of school (and home) as a potential continuing text. She suggests that the notion of a 'connecting conversation' as a part of English teachers' view of school learning might serve to take them into fields often thought to belong to other subjects but which she sees as part of each student's evolving autobiography.

Drawing a Story: Transitions between Drawing and Writing
Myra Barrs

Recent attempts to understand the beginnings of writing have often become preoccupied with the emergence of identifiable features of the written code – with the transition from early scribbles to letter-like forms and eventually to orthodox writing – and, with a few honourable exceptions, have lost the focus on meaning. For instance, Glenda Bissex in her long and absorbing study of her son's early writing development (1980), though she suggests some fascinating lines of inquiry (his preoccupation with lists, notices, sign-making and newspapers; his early assumption of a mature persona) never pursues them with the same energy as she brings to the tracking of his personal spellings, and her book becomes eventually a study of his ortho-graphic development. If reading is not decoding, then neither is writing *en*coding, and it is important not to concentrate too narrowly on the externals of writing development.

Learning to write is 'learning how to mean' on paper. Part of this is learning the writing conventions of one's culture and, in the case of English, becoming sensitive to the peculiar nature of the spelling system. Part of it is becoming aware of the bigger shapes, of genre and of the patterns of written language. But the essence of the activity was described by Vygotsky as 'the representation of meaning by symbolic signs' (1978). Unless we hold on to the definition of writing as a meaning-making and symbolizing activity, we may fail to recognize important aspects of development, such as the role played by drawing in children's growth as symbolizing beings.

Several commentators have referred to the links between drawing and writing in children's early writing. Ferreiro and Teberosky (1982) asked their child subjects to differentiate between drawing and writing both in their own acts and in adult acts. (Their interventions, as they acknowledge, directed the children's attention to writing as the more significant activity.) They found that most of their five/six-year-old subjects 'knew the differ-ence' between drawing and writing. Similarly, Harste, Woodward and Burke (1984) observe that 'we have found that all children by the age of three differentiate between writing and drawing'. They show by their examples that children's 'scribbles' designated by the children as writing are observably different from those that are designated as drawing, and they also recognize that art is part of writing for young children, who move backwards and forwards between the two modes. All these researchers, however, are mainly concerned to establish that the children they study can distinguish between the *appearance* of drawing and the *appearance* of writing; they focus on the emergence of writing-like forms that approximate to adult forms, and on children's knowledge of the externals of the writing system. The researchers pay less attention to the 'drawings' or the 'writing' as significant symbolizing activities, to the meanings that are being expressed through them, or to the question of which mode the children use by choice. Ferreiro and Teberosky do note that their subjects often drew in response to requests for them to write. The researchers comment: 'The fact that children provide an iconic representation of the object when asked to write seems significant since we do not suggest that they do so.'

Vygotsky, in a characteristically rich and dense chapter (1978), suggests that 'make-believe play, drawing and writing can be viewed as different moments in an essentially unified process of development of written language'. He admits that this notion, given the state of psychological knowledge at the time, 'might appear to be overstated'. But as we observe young children's play, their intense involvement in symbolizing activity, the way in which their early drawings are interwoven with dramatic play and their early writings with their drawing, only a view as broad as Vygotsky's of symbolic development seems adequate as a basis for an examination of the development of writing in a full sense.

In what follows I look at some of the links between drawing and writing, initially by examining the role of the pictographic in children's written language development, and then by considering the more obscure and interesting question of how children may continue to use drawing as an important element in their writing and as a means for symbolizing meaning, even when their understanding of the system of written language is well established. In addition I consider the developmental relationship between different kinds of symbolizing activity.

The pictographic element in children's writing development has not been given much attention in recent studies of early writing. It seems clear that many children do employ a 'pictographic hypothesis' about writing at some point, and that more may be perhaps learned about children's understandings by examining these genuine hypothetical systems than by focusing exclusively on the appearance of writing-like marks or letter-like forms. This point is convincingly made by Luria in the article (1983) that Vygotsky draws on extensively in his chapter on 'The Prehistory of Written Language' referred to above. Luria set out to look at young children's concepts of writing and their ability to use notation as a tool before they had learned to write. The youngest children (four/five-year-olds), he found, were generally unable to respond to his requests. 'They grasped the outward form of writing and saw how adults accomplished it; they were even able to imitate adults; but they themselves were completely unable to learn the specific psychological attributes any act must have if it to be used as a tool in the service of some end.' One five-year-old child 'wrote' a number of scrawls on the paper. When the experimenter asked him what they were, he said quite confidently, 'That's how you write'. Luria comments: 'The child is interested only in "writing like grown-ups"; for him the act of writing is not a means of remembering, or representing some meaning, but an act that is sufficient in its own right.' This important distinction, between early writing which is simply the reproduction of the outer form of grown-up writing and writing which is actually used by the child to represent meaning, is crucial for any study of development and is the point which is sometimes lost in too close a focus on the appearance of the recognizable forms of alphabetic written language.

Luria describes the way in which some children, and particularly one five-year-old child, Brina, discovered in the course of experimental sessions how to use marks on paper as mnemonic signs, sometimes by the use of rudimentary pictographs. Luria gives a detailed record of the third experimental session with this child. The experiment took the form of a dictation; five or six sentences were dictated to the child, who was asked to record them in any way he/she liked 'in order to remember them'. In Brina's first and second sessions she merely made a line for each sentence and arranged the lines in columns. When asked to recall the sentences, she made no attempt to refer to the marks she had made.

In the third session the experimenter dictated the sentences that had been used in the second session again, with a few changes. But this time Brina adopted a different technique, as is shown in her verbal responses. In the following extract from Luria's paper the dictated sentences are given on the left and Brina's responses on the right:

1. Here is a man, and he has two legs.   Then I'll draw two lines . . .
2. In the sky there are many stars.   Then I'll draw many lines.
3. The crane has one leg.   (Makes a mark) . . . The crane is on one leg . . . There you are . . . (Points) The crane is on one leg.
4. Brina has twenty teeth.   (Draws several lines)
5. The big hen and four little chicks.   (Makes one big line and two small ones; thinks a little, and adds another two)

This 'shift to a meaningful depictive sign', as Luria terms it, signals Brina's discovery of the uses of writing, her ability to perceive her marks as 'differentiated expressive tools' and to use them in the process of mediated recall.

Luria suggests that, if children continued to develop their personal writing systems and did not learn alphabetic writing, then pictography 'would achieve a flourishing development'. Both he and Vygotsky were also interested in the transition from purely pictographic writing to a more ideographic style of writing which sometimes occurred when experimental subjects were asked to record more abstract ideas. This progression, from simple marks which act as a jog to memory, to pictographs, to more abstract signs, clearly parallels, ontogenetically, the phylogeny of writing systems.

It would be valuable to have more naturalistic observations of children's use of pictographic signs. James Britton has recalled (1983) how his grand-daughter, Laurie, seemed to hold, initially, a basically topographic hypothesis about writing (the position of marks on the paper recalling their meanings). When, as a 'waitress', she took down orders from Britton in the role of customer, she 'read back' his order according to the arrangement of her marks. From this she moved to a pictographic hypothesis when she 'drew' a letter to a neighbour which depicted five little circles, in a note which meant 'Please buy me some eggs'. Similarly, Shirley Payton, in her study of her own daughter Cecilia (1984), records Cecilia making a shopping list which included 'matches' as an item (Figure 1). The nature of the writing here is obviously pictographic.

An intriguing example comes from a Toronto classroom, where a seven-year-old Canadian-Vietnamese boy, who was already used to writing in English, discovered to his consternation that not only could he not always read back all of his invented spellings, but his teacher could not either. This revelation so disconcerted him that for a time he adopted a sort of back-up system of pictograms which he placed above any word of whose invented spelling he was unsure. This gave the effect of little diacritic pictographic markings and enabled him to read back his texts with confidence, without having to rely completely on his as yet imperfect orthography.

These examples suggest that the younger children were employing a transitional pictographic hypothesis, as they actively explored the nature of the writing system, before they fully understood its alphabetic nature – learned that, in Vygotsky's words, 'one can draw not only objects but also speech'. It is interesting to note in passing that children who are moving into writing sometimes produce drawings that are highly symmetrical,

Figure 1   A shopping list

C.:   I'm going to make a shopping list.
M.:   Write 'matches'.
C.:   All right. (Draws the shapes indicated by 1.)
        Is that 'matches'?
M.:   Not quite.
C.:   (Draws shape indicated by 2.) I'm putting the matches in.
M.:   Try 'Ribena'.
C.:   (Continues writing.)

regular and stylized, as if they were beginning to attend to the symmetry and regularity of print and attempting to make their drawings more writing-like.

Children may well assume initially that writing is a form of drawing, since drawing is a symbolizing mode that is established so much earlier for them. Iconically based ways of symbolizing and thinking about the world continue to be powerful alongside the written linguistic mode when that mode is eventually brought under control, and for certain purposes they may continue to be preferred. Even when children understand the nature of the writing system and have begun to be able to write independently, they may still feel able to 'say more' through their drawing than through their writing.

Drawing and writing, then, are frequently linked modes of expression. It is impossible to say how far this is partly a consequence of cultural and environmental factors. Certainly in children's experience of print in the world, the print is more likely than we generally recognize to be linked with pictures. Adults read texts in which illustrations and diagrams play a larger or smaller part, and children's books, magazines and comics are profusely illustrated. Photo-litho printing, television and computers mean that most of us are used to 'reading' picture and text together. Ferreiro and Teberosky (1982), in their investigations of reading, looked at children's responses to illustrated texts and found that they initially located the meaning in the combination of text *and* picture.

The other major environmental influence on children's drawing-and-writing is, of course, the influence of the classroom and of adult expectations. Anne Haas Dyson points out how teachers may 'set the order of production – first drawing, then writing' (1986), and thus affect the child's view of the task and of the picture-text relationship. The kind of paper provided or the media made available may affect the nature of the outcome. Most children in infant schools produce pictures with labels or story captions, or illustrated stories, and it is hard to say how much of their practice is spontaneous and how much a consequence of the routines in force in their classrooms. In one telling example from a classroom Dyson suggests how some of these routines may be viewed:

Brian: Why do we always have to write words? [Translation: Why can't we just write the pictures?]
Teacher: Well, I like to see what you're going to write.
Sara: Why can't you just ask us? [1983]

It may not be possible completely to separate out, but it nevertheless does seem likely that for many children drawing and writing are viewed as linked or complimentary in some way, and that drawing or picturing may continue to be a major means of symbolizing meaning even when they are quite able to write independently.

In a top infant class in Willesden, London, Sandra, a seven-year-old girl, was drawing a scarecrow, preparatory to writing about it. She had, with the rest of her class, listened to a poem about a scarecrow and pretended to *be* a scarecrow earlier, in the book corner, with their teacher. Now the teacher had written the title 'The Scarecrow' on the blackboard and invited the class to draw-and-write. As Sandra drew she told me about her scarecrow. It was full of straw and she drew the straw inside with gusto, making heavy pencil scribbles. At a certain point in making her drawing she remarked that this was a *lady* scarecrow. This struck me as an interesting departure from a conventional view of the task and I urged her to include the information in the label to her picture so as to draw the teacher's attention to the difference. Sandra was not at all keen to write this down. 'She'll know it's a lady 'cos it's a skirt', she remarked dismissively. I realized that she had conveyed her meaning in her drawing, which seemed to her to be as explicit as any written text. Once something has been clearly stated in this iconic way, a linguistic restatement may appear redundant to a child.

One seven-year-old girl, also a third-year infant, gave an interesting account of her 'home' writing compared with her 'school' stories. She was clear that there was a very considerable difference between the two, and that this difference was partly a question of the relationship between picture and text.

M.B.: When you are at home do you write stories as well?
A.: Yes, lots of stories ...
M.N.: Are they like these stories or are they different?
A.: They're different, much different. 'Cos I have to rush these 'cos to get in, onto the next book we have to do, like today I'll probably have to rush my number to go on to my spellings.
M.B.: I see. What a shame you have to rush. So what are the ones at home like, why are they different?
A.: Because I don't rush. And I make it a little bit more longer 'cos I got huge pieces of paper about I should say that big, half of this table.
M.B.: Oh, I see.
A.: It's about up to there really.
M.B.: Yes. Oh, and you like having a nice big space to work on?
A.: Yes. Because if I did it when the twins were around they'd screw my paper up and draw with my other pencils that I have to do it.
M.B.: Yes.
A.: 'Cos I do it in all sorts of coloured felt-tips.
M.B.: That's the pictures?
A.: And the writing, I go pink, blue, or like, pink, dark blue, light blue, something like that.
M.B.: Do you do that? Does it make the story better?
A.: Makes it more colourful really.

She spoke of 'drawing a story' and described what she meant by this.

A.: 'Cos I like drawing stories and making things up and things, sort of things like that.
M.B.: The drawing is part of the story is it ...
A.: Yes.
M.B.: For you?
A.: I just write a little bit near each picture and just carry on with a picture, a little bit of the story by the side of it, a picture, sort of thing like that.

Clearly text and pictures were much more closely integrated in her 'home' stories than in her 'school' stories, and this seems to be true of many children's 'home' stories. Dyson has remarked how frequently children's spontaneous texts are composed of multiple media, and how these interwoven strands are pulled apart in school or in writing tasks undertaken for researchers (1986).

These few examples suggest that, for the young writers described, writing may not yet have become a fully detached symbolizing activity. It is still in some important way bound up with picturing, and the child's meanings are located in a combination of picture and text, with no clear boundary between them.

The way in which these aspects of a child's 'text' are seemingly bonded together has awakened echoes for me of a passage in one of James Britton's essays, where he explains the Piaget–Bruner framework of child development – the enactive/iconic/linguistic stages. What Britton's explanation most helpfully clarifies are the *transitions* in this model, and the way in which development can be viewed as, first, the addition of a new mode to the established modes and, then, the gradual freeing of the new 'system of representing the world' from the previous ones. He focuses particularly on the transition from language which is linked to movement and perception, what he calls 'speech-cum-action', to language which can transcend the immediate situation. The passage comes from Britton's introduction to the Penguin edition of Luria and Yudovich's *Speech and the Development of Mental Processes in the Child* (1971), and though it is long, it will be helpful to quote it in full:

Piaget and Bruner have shown that young children represent the world to themselves first in terms of perception-cum-movement – and I put it that way to indicate that the two are inseparable; and later also in terms of visual imagery, or in perception freed from movement, and that the simultaneity of visual representation compared with the serial nature of perception-cum-movement results in a better organized system of representing, a more effective filing system for experience.

These two models of representation are well established before the third, linguistic mode, comes into operation. When, at about two years of age, a child begins to speak, so achieving the third system, his talk is used as a means of assisting the modes of representation previously acquired; that is to say the modes of movement and of perception. In fact, his language is at first tied to the 'here and now', limited (with a few notable exceptions) to speech about what may be seen and handled in the immediate situation. It is speech-cum-action, or as Luria calls it, 'synpraxic speech'. Its function as such is to facilitate activity in the here and now, activity in terms of movement and perception. Parts of the monologue of the four-year-old we quoted above will serve to illustrate this earlier stage. ('Well, if you could look after these two elephants ... I'll go and see about this ... this panda. Well, all right. He squeezed out, and he got in. Shut the gate again ...', etc.) As we read it with imaginative insight, I believe we can sense the fact that her speech operates as a way of assisting her moves in the game.

But at one particular point in that monologue, we find language operating differently. She talks of things she *wants*, things that are not there in front of her – first 'the cage', and then 'the zoo man': and having spoken of him, off she goes to get him.

This indicates what really amounts to a fourth kind of representation. Just as movement-cum-perception provided the basis from which the second stage was reached, that of perception freed from movement, so language tied to the here-and-now forms the basis from which there develops linguistic representation freed from these bonds, freed from its dependence upon movement and perception. At this fourth stage words come to be used not *with* objects but *in place of them* [Britton, 1971].

The kind of progressive freeing of spoken language from action and perception described here seems to me to offer a fair parallel for the way in which written language, which has its roots in dramatic play and in picturing, is initially bound up with these other modes of symbolizing, only gradually and sometimes over a very long period becoming a free-standing symbolizing activity. Borrowing Britton's terminology, we might speak, in connection with the children's 'texts', that we have been considering, of 'writing-cum-drawing' which will provide a basis from which writing that is independent of other symbolic systems will develop. Some such account of the links and transitions involved is needed for any exploration of the relationship between the three modes.

The juxtaposition of Britton's account of the Piaget–Bruner model with Vygotsky's tentative account of the development of written language offers, moreover, a potentially powerful framework for observing children's development as symbolizing beings. For it is clear that just as children explore the world initially with their bodies, then by looking ('perception freed from movement'), finally adding language to these ways of investigating and controlling experience, so at the level of these symbolizing activities there is also a developmental progression from one mode to another to be discerned, though the interactions between modes are as important in this developmental picture as in the ones that Britton summarizes. It also appears that these different ways of symbolizing the world (dramatic play, picturing and writing) correspond closely to the earlier developmental stages (enactive, iconic and (spoken) linguistic). They involve the use of the same aspects of the self and may even develop in a corresponding order – though here I am obviously speculating. With a guiding framework of this kind, however, it becomes possible to speak more confidently of symbolic development, to have a standpoint for observing whether there is such a progression from one symbolizing mode to another, and also a basis for analysing the links and transition between them.

Evidence of developmental progression from one kind of symbolizing activity to another is not easy to find, but Howard Gardner, who has explored in many works the relationship between these symbolic domains, has suggested that drawing which has a symbolic intent develops later than dramatic play. In his study of artistic development, *Artful Scribbles*, he argues that the beginnings of meaningful symbolic graphic activity can be seen in most children around the age of three; before this he sees children as rehearsing a growing vocabulary of shapes and schemes which reflect their growing control of the movement of their arms and wrists and of their pencils, but which are not deliberate attempts to symbolize objects or events in the world. He contrasts this with the earlier emergence of symbolic dramatic play. 'At a time when … symbolic play sequences denote dressing, going to bed, or playing house, the forms which are drawn remain just forms.' It seems plausible that dramatic play, where the 'medium' is children's own bodies and voices, should be more available and more readily developed than the other forms under discussion, which involve the use of tools and, in the case of writing, the understanding of a system of second-order symbolism. But there may well be different accounts of the time relationship between the emergence of different symbolic systems. In order to be more confident about such relationships and to view development across the symbolic systems we would need to bring together the work of writers who have studied development in the different domains, and to find out more about individual children's developmental paths, taking their dramatic play and picturing into account alongside their written language development.

Another transitional symbolizing activity comparable to writing-cum-drawing, is the drawing-cum-dramatizing which many younger children engage in. Once children's picturing is established it is observable that, in some children at any rate, it is accompanied by commentary, often dramatic commentary, and that the creation of a picture therefore corresponds to an enacted drama. A striking account of this kind of dramatized picture making is Sylvia Feinburg's article on her son's battle pictures (1976). Many parents recognize this account of a common but rarely recorded activity, and I have described another instance of picturing accompanied by excited dramatic commentary in my article 'Maps of Play' in press.

In her article 'Transitions and tensions: interrelationships between the drawing, talking and dictating of young children' (1986) Dyson gives several examples of children living out their drawings and accompanying them with a stream of commentary, often dramatic in character.

Five year old Rachel is engrossed in the drama unfolding before her, as she draws and tells a story about a distraught mother on Christmas Day:

And she (the mom) couldn't find the door . . . the way to find that Christmas tree. She was trying to get to the other side to get her little baby. . . . And she was trying to get her 'cuz she might get hurt. She's just a little bitty girl. And they saw a – No. I don't know how to write (draw) that.

Dyson is interested in the way in which the talk that accompanies drawing helps to direct the activity, and she therefore attends not only to the dramatic or storytelling language, but also to the children's organizing talk, their interactions with other children and their personal comments. However, her article offers several examples of children whose talk is strongly focused on the figures and events in the pictures, and which is close to the language of dramatic play. One boy's pictures were, typically, action pictures which depicted events, often violent in character (Figure 2).

Although Jesse was capable of drawing basic forms for people, vehicles and houses, he seldom did so. In his efforts to play out an action, he did not labour over each figure. . . . His drawings thus reflected his energetic style – they were typically a tangle of curved lines, dots and splotches of color. Yet . . . Jesse's talk during drawing clearly conveyed his meaning.

Dyson comments on the vividness of the language surrounding the drawings that children like Jesse did and contrasts the abundant language

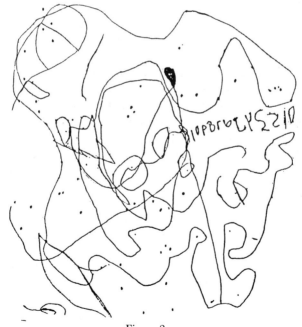

Figure 2

of their talk with the unemotional brevity of the texts that they dictated to their teachers after the event. Jesse's text, for instance, read:

> This is a time bomb.
> The time bomb is on a light.
> And it blowed up a light.

Dyson's exploration of the field of symbolic development and her appreciation of the 'fluidity and diversity' of young children's behaviour in drawing and writing is one example of the way in which researchers and educationists have begun to tease out the implications of Vygotsky's chapter on the 'Prehistory of Written Language'. Robert Gundlach in 'Children as writers: the beginning of learning to write' (1982) is also interested in the way in which 'the child . . . extends the function of several symbol systems – of speaking, drawing and play – into the new activity of writing'. He takes particular note of the way in which children 'extend the function of play into written language' by experimenting with role in their writing and he offers a number of examples.

In the following passage . . . the rhetorical question (and answer), the making of categories and distinctions, even the chatty, tour-guiding style, all may be seen as elements of the child's enactment of the role of the writer of expository prose for children. In trying on the writer's voice, the child is also trying on the writer's uses for written language.

'A human body is a anemll. An anemll is not a hummen like you. You are a special hummen anemll. You are diffrant! Do you Know? Well I dont think you do. Well I can exsplane the hummen body. Oh I haveant tolled you about the anemll! Well Ill tell you about the gray squirrel. When the mother squirrel finds new pussy willow buds to eat she knows that spring is coming!'

One unifying factor which runs through all these activities is, as Dyson's work emphasizes, spoken language. Dramatic play, drawing and writing too are often accompanied in young children by a stream of talk. The important role of spoken language in relation to all symbolic activity is stressed by Vygotsky, who sees it as the basis of all symbolic systems. 'We feel that Hertzer is most justified in asserting that primary symbolic representation should be ascribed to speech, and that it is on the basis of speech that all the other sign systems are created' (1978).

The other element which is common to all the symbolic activities under discussion is story. The imaginary worlds which children create through their play come into being and are shaped and developed by narrative. Frank Smith (1982) names the urge to create worlds as the main reason why children learn to read and write: 'I suspect that children happen to learn about written language, if appropriate demonstrations are available, because writing is a particularly efficacious means of accomplishing that which the child's brain is perpetually striving to do in any case – namely, to create worlds.'

But children are already experienced world makers and narrators through their oral storytelling and their dramatic play and picturing by the time they come to write.

It seems that over time these different symbolic activities become detached from one another and free-standing, though it also seems likely that they never lose some sense of interior connection. In later imaginings and creative activities it may be that children and adults continue to draw unconsciously on allied forms of symbolism. During writing or painting, for instance, it may well be that some form of interior enactment takes place, experienced more consciously at some times than others. But in general it is to be expected that symbolic expression in all these areas will become more differentiated, independent and self-referential.

However, for some children writing and drawing seem to go on being linked for much longer than they do for others. These children continue to make a great deal of use of picturing, by choice, to express their meanings and may find it hard to make the transition from writing-cum-drawing to writing, possibly because drawing is technically easier for them, but possibly too because drawing seems to them superior as a means of expression. As Dyson points out, despite the interrelationships that have been the subject of this article, each symbolic system is a unique system and 'meanings encoded within the space/time dimensions of a visual world may not be easily translated into those of a world of words' (1986a).

Drawing is certainly a better medium for representing certain meanings, and it may be helpful to consider what it is that some children can do through drawing that cannot be done through writing – what it is that they are obliged to give up or do without when they write rather than draw.

First, certain kinds of description and analysis are obviously better done through drawing and diagramming than through words. Drawing can show how things work much more efficiently than writing can – engineers, architects and designers use drawings to convey their thinking, and Alex Issigonis has remarked that the engineer who cannot draw cannot communicate with his colleagues. In Figure 3 Steven's drawing of Optimus Prime is dynamic as well as descriptive. It both analyses the construction of Optimus Prime and also shows the actual moment of his transformation from the leading Transformer, the leader of the Autobots, into a lorry. Children who are accustomed to making use of drawing in this way to record their observations and their knowledge may legitimately feel that

Figure 3

they can convey more through such diagrammatic drawings than they could through writing. The child who recorded his observations of tadpoles in the picture shown in Figure 4 obviously put more information and energy into the drawing than into the writing underneath.

But surely written language is a better medium for telling a story? Many children would disagree. They are experienced viewers of television narrative and readers of comics, and are used to the way in which a narrative can be carried virtually entirely through pictures. From the point of view of children who have developed their drawing to a point where they can use it for quite complicated narrative purposes, language may seem a less satisfactory medium for storying. Many children's pictures are dynamic rather than static icons and show movement, 'before' and 'after' states and violent action. Such drawings adopt or invent conventions to show trajectories, lines of force, heat, light, explosions and sometimes other events such as a gaze lighting on an object or, as in this example, telecommunications signals:

A term later, the day after a trip to Heathrow airport, Maurice . . . drew a picture, in pencil, of the airport. He had drawn the control tower, transparent. Showing two men, both with headphones, and microphones under their chins. From the head of one man he had a dotted line to the aeroplanes 'banked up' in three circles in the sky,

Figure 4

one on top of the other. To the same man, he showed, through dotted line, receiving signals from the large radar he had drawn. The second man he showed by the same manner was concerned with the planes lining up on the runway, waiting to take off. He had drawn the DC10 that he had been on, transparent, showing himself going down in the lifts to the kitchen, and sitting alone in a seat, drinking orange. The large hangar, with the engineers working on a plane. The coach was waiting in the right-hand corner.

'Maurice, you've remembered so much.'

He smiled broadly, stopped, leaned across his picture and put dots from the air controller's head across to the ground controller's head.

'E's got to know what he knows or be a crash', he said when he had finished the dots [Gilbert, 1984].

As is clear from this description, narrative drawings have the advantage of being able to show events that are happening simultaneously in different places, which prose, being linear, cannot do. They can also show, within the same frame, an event at different stages of its development (a technique often used in early painting). For children who have found these kinds of ways of conveying their meanings through drawing there may be few apparent advantages in writing as a medium for narrative.

Whereas in a detailed narrative drawing it is possible to show the setting for an action in minute particular, in prose it is hard to provide such a

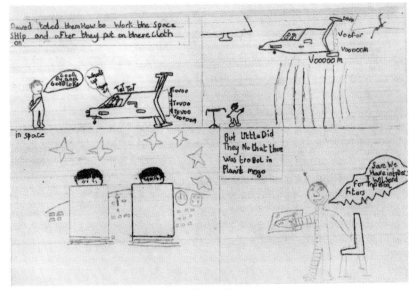

Figure 5

detailed context. Visual information is easier to take in quickly than verbal information and children who are adept at reading visual information and at conveying a complex situation in a drawing may be frustrated by the problems of trying to communicate a comparable amount of information in written language. This was the impression I received when I interviewed Ian, a ten-year-old boy from Kensal Rise, London, about his own work. Ian's graphic style was extremely sophisticated and he had drawn and written several full-length cartoon stories; his written stories, however, were much less assured and complete. Figure 5 is an example of his cartoon storying, a page from a narrative in which two boys take a trip in an inventor's new spaceship and are attacked by alien fighters in space.

Clearly, Ian has a very good command of this medium. He can tell a story economically in a series of images, using words occasionally in speech bubbles or captions. Where language is used it is not at all informal, despite the pop nature of the medium; it is comic-book 'high-style'. 'But little did they know that there was trouble in Planet Mogo' reads the caption to the last frame, while the Mogo alien observing the progress of the boys' spaceship on his video screen announces to his commander 'Sir, we have intruders, I will send for imperial fighters'.

Ian continually varies viewpoint and scale throughout the story, revealing a very extensive visual vocabulary. The silent frame captioned simply 'In space', with its pilots' eye view of the instrument panel and the stars beyond is particularly striking. Images like this give the impression of a visually sophisticated narrator who has absorbed many comic-book conventions and is enjoying using them in his own stories.

In an interview Ian explained how much he practised his drawing, and said how much he enjoyed telling a story in this way through a combination of words and pictures. I asked him whether he would mind writing stories which had no pictures in them:

Interviewer: How do you feel about writing just ordinary stories now, I mean if you just had to write ordinary stories like this on paper?
Ian: Well, it's all right. Wouldn't be too bad.
Interviewer: Wouldn't.
Ian: No.
Interviewer: But you prefer to use the illustrations?
Ian: Yeah.
Interviewer: Tell me why.
Ian: 'Cause they know, they know, when we do that they know what's going on, mostly they can, they can, when they read it they know what's going on but they can't see what's happening. Like for instance say that, em, they's in a spaceship right, and one of them said, 'Look out', they wouldn't know who it was, like, same if it was picture they can see the face and the other one sit there and then you can do a thing that says 'Look out!'
Interviewer: So they can see the whole situation.
Ian: Mmmm.

Ian was struggling to express something that he thought was of importance here and his hesitations are a result of this. He seems to me to be drawing attention to the relationship between action and context that I mentioned earlier. Readers of written stories 'know what's going on' but they cannot 'see what's happening' as well as if the scene were drawn. In a picture the whole physical context can be shown, including the characters present, their appearance, their position in the scene. The reader/viewer can see the whole situation and can see also who is speaking the dialogue; the speech-bubble convention means that there is no confusion about who is saying what.

It seems as if children like Ian have to learn to leave out a great deal of the kind of detail they are used to including in their narrative drawings if they want to make a written narrative that works. The information they have been used to conveying in drawing may be too detailed to relate in words without slowing down the story. They may have to settle for greater selectivity and suggestion in their narration, telling the story through partial information rather than making the reader aware of the whole scene.

Writing is often a question of leaving out rather than putting in detail; writers learn how to make readers do the necessary imaginative work by leaving the 'gaps in the text'. Exactly what role words can have in telling a story may be unclear to children who are very strongly oriented towards visual narrative. One teacher has given me an account of a six-year-old boy whose pictured narratives were immensely detailed and exciting, but whose written stories consisted of nothing but untagged dialogue and transcribed sound effects, as if he were writing soundtrack.

Most of the young writers/picturers I have referred to in the last few pages have been male, and there does seem to be a gender dimension to the question of the relationship between writing and drawing. My own observations and those of teachers I have consulted suggest that boys rather than girls are inclined to go on using picturing as a means of storytelling, and that this difference may relate to differences between girls' and boys' pictures. Girls' pictures frequently have a more static, iconic character than boys' pictures, which seem more likely to express action and convey a sequence of events. Boys' pictures also frequently reflect a preoccupation with television narratives and especially with superhero stories such as 'He-Man' and 'Transformers'. The strong influence of such television fantasies on children's dramatic play has been described by Vyvyen Paley (1985) and is just as marked in their narrative pictures, which obviously draw on the style of television graphics and related superhero comics.

Dyson also observed marked gender differences between girls and boys in their drawing. She noted clear differences in the themes they chose in the classroom she studied. Boys depicted explosions, battles, 'displays of power and motion', superheroes and monsters. Girls drew happy little girls and cheerful small animals, butterflies, birds and flowers.

... unlike Jesse, who produced quick sketches, Regina spent a great deal of time detailing her pictures, particularly the girls. As she talked and drew their hair and clothes, one might think she was dressing her dolls rather than drawing her girls.

She remarks of the same child that her pictures represented a static present time, rather than any past or future events:

Her interest was primarily in the actor or character being depicted, not in the actions over time. As each new figure was added to her drawings, it became the central topic of her talk and was not necessarily connected to other figures. She engaged in no dramatizing actions or language; her talk, therefore, did not convey such motorsensory qualities as volume, force, speed and emotional tone which were so dominant in Jesse's case [1986b].

What kinds of transitions will these children have to make as they move from drawing via writing-cum-drawing into writing? Will their handling of written narratives reveal any differences comparable to those found in their pictured stories, differences not only of theme but also of style and method?

Studying the development of children's writing-cum-drawing makes clear that drawing is not only part of the 'prehistory' of written language, but also part of its history. Even when written language is technically within a child's control, drawing may continue to be an important medium for the expression of meanings, and quite a long transition period may be needed (in some cases several years) before the links between the two activities are dissolved. This transition may come about differently for different individuals, and there may also be differences of gender and culture to explore both in children's drawings and in the relationship of their drawing to their writing.

All these explorations, however, need to form part of a much larger study of children's development as symbolizers – as the creators of imaginary worlds which are sometimes enacted, sometimes pictured and sometimes written into being. Such an approach may seem unmanageably broad, but is the only one adequate to encompass the full range of activities which prefigure, support and contribute to children's growth as writers. Moreover it is an approach which properly locates the beginnings of writing not in any desire to reproduce the outward form of adult behaviour, or in what Frank Smith calls 'a largely mythical compulsion to communicate', but in the impulse to create.

James Britton (1982a) has recognized that we have not yet acknowledged the essential contribution of other forms of symbolic behaviour, gesture, make-believe play, pictorial representation' to the process of learning to read and write. He continues:

It remains for me to point out that make-believe play ... storytelling, listening to stories, pictorial representation and the talk that complements it, story reading and story writing – these are all activities in the role of the spectator.

These are the activities which enable children to represent, review and re-enact life, the better to understand and control it. It seems all the more necessary to stress their importance, and the central role of symbolic behaviour in the development of literacy, at a time when the government's core curriculum is likely to marginalize further the place of the arts in education. The source of the passion and energy in young children's play, which in favourable circumstances can flow directly into their early narrative writing, is nothing less than this urge to order and comprehend experience by turning it into art.

Stories at Home and at School
Henrietta Dombey

Twenty-five years ago, crammed into a 'temporary' lecture hall at the London Institute of Education with dozens of other English postgraduate students, I began to feel my excitement about education crystallize into the beginnings of understanding. School had long seemed capable of being much more powerful and interesting than what I had experienced as a pupil. So, fired by ideas encountered at university, I had plunged untrained into a secondary modern in the East End of London, where the children's failure to hail me as their saviour had given me a brutal surprise. Somewhat chastened, I hoped the Institute would help me find ways of making constructive contact. Of course, it is impossible to outline all that I learned about education from the lectures, seminars and chats in the pub with Jimmy and his colleagues, let alone all I have gained from his writing. But there was one particular lesson that Jimmy taught that year which made me feel I was coming home.

With characteristic subtlety, width of reference and theoretical depth, and yet with a lightness of touch, a lack of pretentiousness and a clear indication of affectionate involvement, Jimmy would intersperse his lectures with tape recordings and sharply drawn sketches of his own children learning to master their mother tongue. At a time when in the West at least the study of child language was only just beginning, this was not what we expected. We were all aspiring secondary teachers and had certainly not arrived at the Institute ready to listen to the speech of a two-year-old. But as we learned to admire the power and complexity of the achievement, we also learned that to limit the theory and practice of mother-tongue teaching to the confines of the classroom is to become institutionalized. We were shown that the most fundamental learning taking place in the more open and emotional circumstances of home, where security and enjoyment are the prime concerns. We learned that, to develop our pedagogical practices in school, we should look very carefully at the best that goes on at home.

When shortly after my PGCE year I found myself teaching inner-city seven-year-olds with little experience, interest or competence in reading, I knew that to draw on my own memories of sharing books at home with my mother would put me on sounder territory than studying the handbook of a reading scheme or the behaviourist textbooks then in vogue. By and large the children and I flourished as we shared texts as varied as Dr Seuss's *Green Eggs and Ham* and Ruskin's *The King of the Golden River*. But, of course, problems remained, the greatest of which was that this way of teaching reading was looked on by my colleagues as distinctly odd and rather suspect. I could say little to reassure them.

In the years since then as teacher, parent, teacher trainer and researcher, I have been concerned to find out more about what goes on at home in successful preschool learning about books, stories and reading, to discover which parts of this learning are translatable to the classroom and to document what this process of translation involves. But others have had different concerns.

These days shops are full of preschool courses to prepare your child for formal education which set school up as the model for home learning. The parent is expected to develop a more formal relationship with his/her child. Yet the vast battery of studies of child language carried out in the intervening twenty-five years has shown us that home is where the most powerful language learning takes place, and that this learning results from activities undertaken not for formally defined educational reasons, but because they are interesting or enjoyable in their own right. Compared to this intense, extended and dynamic home learning, school learning in the early years can have a fragmented, mechanical and often rather tedious quality. If we are to improve this we need to be clear about what makes such home learning powerful and the reasons as well as the procedures for translating something of such learning into the school classroom. As a contribution towards this I want to describe two story sessions, one at home, the other in a nursery class, which show something of what the early stages of literary experience can look like, and how a strong sense of story sharing at home can enrich teaching in the classroom.

The first storytelling is unremarkable. Anna and her mother are engaged in the nightly ritual, common to so many families, of the bedtime story. The scene is domestic and comforting. But if we look closely we can see some very powerful learning taking place on a number of different levels, learning that can help to explain why, as Wells (1981) shows us, children from homes such as Anna's have relatively few problems with the formal initiation into literacy which they encounter in school.

Three-year-old Anna and her mother are reading *Rosie's Walk* by Pat Hutchins. As her mother reads, Anna is hearing linguistic forms rather different from those of conversation. Even in this brief and simple text there are words, phrase structures and clause patterns that young children are unlikely to hear in conversation. Anna is unworried. She treats as interesting acquaintances words such as 'beehive' and 'haycock'. When her mother reads the opening line: 'Rosie the hen went for a walk', Anna shows no puzzlement at that literary information-bearer the post-modified noun phrase, perhaps because she is already familiar with much more complex manifestations, from Sendak's *Where the Wild Things Are*, for example, where Max discovers 'the magic trick of staring into all their yellow eyes without blinking once'. Nor is she disconcerted by the density of the clause structure: seven adverbial phrases in the first clause seem to pose no particular problem. Anna is certainly learning new linguistic forms, but this is largely a tacit process. Her conscious attention is directed not at the spoken words or at their printed counterparts on the pages in front of her, but at the narrative constructed through those words and at the world out of which that narrative comes. For the reading is interspersed with conversation in which mother and child are concerned partly to establish connections between the narrated events and Anna's own first-hand experience and partly to construe the pictures. Their overriding concern, however, is to realize the narrative, to actualize the potential narrative structures and to build a complex textured and coherent whole.

In *Rosie's Walk*, where the words take us round Rosie's pretty and unmechanized farm and safely back home for dinner, the printed text is uneventful, but the richer story, sharp with the constant threat to the innocuous hen of being pounced on and eaten by the unmentioned fox, is to be found in the pictures. As they look at the pictures, the comments of both mother and child focus on what Barthes would see as the kernel events of the fox following Rosie and his desire to eat her (Barthes, 1975b). They ignore the satellite events of the frog on the lily pad and the goat by the hay. Outside the story context these pictures could be read in many other ways, but mother and child are reading them for a particular purpose – to establish the story and to actualize what Barthes terms the hermeneutic code of this verbal and visual narrative (Barthes, 1975a).

In doing so they are not using the stance of the narrative text. The sure voice of Genette's *classical subsequent* narration has been replaced by the tentative voice of the spectator who feels an excited uncertainty about the events she is witnessing. Their comments represent the actions and characters as operating in the present not the past: what is in the picture is happening now, whereas what is in the verbal narrative has already happened. The ever-present sense of uncertainty about what might happen next is in marked contrast to the immutable certainty of the narrative. Mother and child seem to be concerned not simply to establish an invariant story, but also to construct a fictive world where many things might happen. Anna's mother says with apparent conviction, 'I think he's going to get her this time', despite the fact that she has read her the story many times before and both know that the fox will be perpetually frustrated in his attempts to catch Rosie.

Within this story world there are many things to talk about and, as other readings of the story indicate, at each reading they construct a different 'reading'. Yet where they talk of what might happen, their speculations are rooted in the logic of the story. There is no suggestion that the fox might get bored or be caught in a trap. For the convention of the story (and for most others Anna has encountered through books) is that the characters behave autonomously and consistently, the significant events that take place are the outcome of this behaviour, and the setting is one in which the social and mechanical complexities of the modern world are, by and large, kept at bay.

Anna and her mother do not question the deviations of this story logic from the logic of literal everyday reality. They accept the genre of folk tale and move around happily in a world where hens have clear ambulatory intentions and mealtimes curiously like our own.

Underneath the surface of this narrative and inside the explicit phrasings of text and conversation lie potent meanings and implicit themes of danger and the return to safety, justice and morality. Anna and her mother enjoy exploring these themes as together they construct narratives whose very removal from literal reality – to worlds where hens harvest corn, mice help cats, small boys venture out across oceans on their own – provides a third area in which parent and child can explore important concerns in safety, where they can set aside the inevitable conflicts of the day and share a mental world without either intruding on the other's privacy. It is hardly surprising that so many parents and children feel such a potent pleasure in the experience. And such early encounters with narrative can be powerfully important in shaping children's understanding of both literature and life.

But these understandings do not come ready-made with the oral delivery of the text. Paradoxically the loose and shifting structures of conversation permit mother and child to actualize the tighter and more complex structures of narrative and to explore their implications. Like most three-year-olds, Anna has extensive experience of conversation. She is an expert at this form of discourse and knows well how to take the leading role. As do most rapid language learners, she initiates some two thirds of the exchanges with her mother and will press further if her mother's responses are not satisfactory. Like most caretakers of fast-learning children, Anna's mother plays a supportive and self-effacing role: Anna is the conversational virtuoso while her mother remains the unobtrusive accompanist. The conversation that surrounds this story reading follows this pattern, and thus the discourse structures Anna is familiar with serve to elaborate and articulate the less familiar structures of the narrative. What is new is not merely juxtaposed with what is familiar: it is through the familiar that the new is given its coherence and significance and enters Anna's possession.

Anna is being initiated into the process of reading as a process of active meaning construction in which the reader makes personal sense of whole texts. Her mother makes no attempt to disentangle the various levels of linguistic and literary understanding of which such meaning making is composed. At one and the same time she is increasing Anna's familiarity with the peculiarities of the situation of story reading (rather different from sorting the washing or playing with the Lego), enlarging Anna's sense of the kinds of propositional meanings of which stories are composed, extending her repertoire of the distinctive lexical and syntactic forms that realize meanings in narrative texts, and constructing rich and resonant narratives which shape Anna's way of seeing the world. There is no pre-learning of the vocabulary, no preliminary session with post-modified noun phrases, nor any exclusive attention to the sequence of events *per se*.

Instead, all this learning of new forms and meanings is organized and ordered by a central literary purpose: to produce, celebrate and give personal meaning to a whole narrative that brings its own semantic reward. Anna's mother acts on the expectation that this will be enjoyable to Anna and that a determination to savour the story will drive Anna to make sense of new forms as she constructs new meanings and provide her with the conditions that make it possible for her to do so. Her mother does not see her job as ensuring either that Anna has 'understood' each new word or structure or that she can give a literally faithful account of the events of story. Indeed, there is an implicit assumption that to do any of these things would be a distraction from the central activity.

The denotation (and connotation) of the lexis, the meaning relations realized in the syntax and the event structure of the story matter only in terms of their contribution to the narrative Anna is constructing in her head. And there is no one correct internal narrative. What matters is that Anna should construct something pleasing to herself and that this pleasure should be shared between mother and child. That Anna sees a richer understanding as more rewarding is evidenced by such questions and observations as 'How they, how the fox just don't get out?' and 'D'you know the fox can't get Rosie in in in her cage'. The explanations her mother offers are in response to Anna's questions: they are not items on a didactic agenda whose completion will indicate a correct reading of the text.

Rereading of this and other texts deepens Anna's understanding of the narrative wholes and of their parts, of the functions and of their forms, and makes each narrative more firmly her own. As she comes to know a number of texts very well indeed and to apprehend (albeit intuitively) the relationship between the forms and meanings of which they are composed, she will be able to make satisfying sense of more complex texts and demand fewer rereadings. But all this learning will take place simultaneously on a number of different linguistic and literary levels while her attention is focused on the larger semantic structures. Through her use of intonation and her responses to Anna's queries, her mother's mediation will assist Anna to conquer this new territory. As Anna becomes more experienced, this mediation will be less necessary. Already Anna is using her knowledge of other stories to help her gloss new ones: familiar forms in new combinations help her construct new meanings, familiar meanings help her make sense of new forms.

The conversation with her mother provides Anna with an external model for the internal conversation with the author that is necessary to any but the most superficial reading of a narrative text. Thus unwittingly following Vygotsky's much quoted observation, her mother helps Anna to do in partnership what she cannot yet do for herself (Vygotsky, 1962). And with each new narrative Anna's own internal dialogue will play a larger part in giving her a sense of the whole. But in this process of developing a richer experience of narrative she will proceed along a broad front, as she must if the activity is to be intrinsically rewarding. For an adult to abstract one element from the narrative and 'teach' it to Anna would be to rob her of the pleasure of making the narrative her own. Although she is not in any conventional sense yet reading independently, the process Anna is engaged in has the key features of Rumelhart's (1976) account of skilled adult reading: it is simultaneous, multi-level, interactive processing.

When Anna goes to school she will take with her an extensive, complex and personal experience of stories that will allow her to make her own sense of more unadorned tellings. But many children start school with little or no experience of this sort. Indeed Wells's (1981) Bristol study showed the experience of hearing stories read to be the most significant differentiator between the linguistic experience of children from different social classes. Heath's (1982) work in Carolina presents such differences as part of a much wider set of cultural differences concerning the role of the written word in the family's affairs. It is not to disvalue the oral culture which they bring to school to say that the homes of many children starting formal education have not given them the foundation they need if they are to take possession of the literate culture of the society in which they live. Nor is there any evidence to indicate that children from homes without a culture of book sharing have any compensatory experience of oral narrative. So it is in school that many children must start to build their literary experience.

But school is not usually the most supportive environment for this enterprise. A study by Lomax (1979) shows that it is precisely the children from non-bookish homes who choose not to listen to stories in school. Other studies show story reading in the early years of school to be typically more orderly and much less enjoyable than at home (Wood, McMahon and Cranston, 1980; Tizard and Hughes, 1984). The multiple distractions of the nursery and reception classrooms, the increased formality that comes with coping with large numbers of children and the attendant organizational demands all conspire to make school a very different place from home and suggest that a school-based initiation into the reading of literature must inevitably be a very different matter from the urgent intimacy of home story reading. Perhaps the most significant pressures towards making school so different from home are the teacher's nagging sense of what the syllabus expects and the firmly held belief that school is the place for serious business.

But some teachers do manage to create something broadly similar to the story reading that goes on in Anna's home. Mrs G. is sharing a story with children whose homes have given them little experience of this sort. Her actions and her interpretations are guided by her complex understanding of literary experience and of what learning to read is about. But she is also guided, and is very much aware of this, by her memories of the intense pleasures of sharing stories with her own children. What results is a dramatically enjoyable event, rich in tacit learning of a sort very similar to Anna's experience at home.

In some respects the situation is indeed more orderly than at home, as the children are expected to stay with the storytelling and not intrude other activities or concerns into the situation. Attempts to do so are quietly ignored or rebuffed: there is no room for the tolerance Anna's mother displays towards Anna's wandering attention. But within the tight boundary of this situation there is considerable informality as one of the children sits of Mrs G.'s knee, another turns the pages and Mrs G. gives them all an experience in which they are allowed to do more than just sit quietly. Today Darren, a recent and distractable arrival, has chosen the story which is again *Rosie's Walk*.

Mrs G. does not stay as close to the words on the page as Anna's mother. Her reading markedly expands on the printed text, making explicit the pictorial narrative of the hungry fox as she articulates all his frustrated attempts to seize Rosie and Rosie's blithe ignorance of her danger. The satellite elements such as the frogs on the lily pad are given a kernel status in her narration as they croak a warning to Rosie. The children have heard this story before and on occasion join in Mrs G's repeated formula 'Rosie just keeps on walking'. Twice the children respond to her intonational invitation to them to complete this sentence. In response to a similar invitation Simon completes a sentence with the word 'nose'. At the end he contributes a semantic extension to the narration with the highly appropriate words 'And then she came home'. Teacher and pupils together have created a narration rather different from the printed text, one that denies the listener the delightful sense of knowing more than the words say, but also one in which the children are materially involved and which orders the complexity of the pictures in terms of the kernel events.

In and out of this dialogic narration Mrs G. and the children weave an animated conversation. Just as in the storytelling at Anna's home, the lexis and syntax of the narration are expected to do their own work without conscious attention. Instead, as they talk they focus on the narrative which concerns events totally removed from the children's experience and yet maximally familiar. These children have had no direct contact with foxes, hens or haycocks, but attempting and evading capture are everyday experiences. So Mrs G. judges that the life-to-text and text-to-life moves, so often a feature of her story readings, have no place here. Instead she focuses on enlarging and elaborating the event structure or, as Barthes would call it, the proiaretic code (Barthes, 1975a). She enriches the sequence of kernel events, drawing in the pictorial elements of the watching mice and the frogs on the lily pad. And with the children she gloats over the juxtaposition of the fox's base intentions and the undignified situation in which they land him and triumphs in Rosie's repeated escapes from the danger of which she is so blithely unaware.

Like Anna's mother, Mrs G. does not single out any one element for didactic treatment. She certainly does not interrogate the children at the end: there are no oral comprehension exercises in this classroom. She is concerned more with the story's present and future than with its past. She invites the children to join with her in shaping that present as with questions such as: 'What does the fox want to do with her?', eliciting a chorused reply that carries echoes of the pantomime: 'Bite her, eat her. Eat her'.

But all this conversation has a disorderly appearance. Interruptions from the children abound in Mrs G.'s storytellings and increase markedly over the school year. In this March session there are twenty-five in only 132 exchanges. Mrs G. seems even to encourage these interruptions, often breaking off her storytelling to respond to them, as when Chris, alone in his confused perception of the story, shows some puzzlement:

Mrs G.:	The fox sits there thinking, 'Ooh, this is my chance to get Rosie'. She just keeps on walking.
Chris:	Did that, did that, did that chicken get up there?
Mrs G.:	Pardon, Chris?
Chris:	Up in there.
Desmond:	Up there.
Mrs G.:	What's up there?

This tolerance of interruption is part of a wider pattern that accords the children greater conversational rights than is usual in the classroom. In this storytelling Mrs G. responds to over half of the children's initiations. Lee speculates that the fox will splash in the water and fail to get Rosie. Simon bets the goat could eat the fox. Mrs G. listens closely and responds in ways that recognize the validity of their contributions.

Far from being socialized into a secondary, responding role found by so many investigators, these children are increasingly assertive, and most of their assertions are relevant to the business of constructing a narrative. Over the months they have come to learn that declarations about their cats, toy lorries and blue jumpers are not likely to be received with interest at storytime, and neither are generalized observations about the habits of frogs or snakes. Mrs G. is not encouraging verbal anarchy but active participation in the construction of narrative.

And yet she is often curiously unresponsive to questions. The children tend to use their questions to ask her for information they do not have, seeing her as the primary knower, as Chris does in the extract above. But Mrs G. does not wholeheartedly accept this role. Unlike the children around her she can read, and she knows far more about the world of the story than they do. But she does not insist on this superiority. Her own questions give her equal status with the children and imply a joint exploration of the text rather than the privileged examination of the children's knowledge that seems so typical of school classrooms (Sinclair and Coulthard, 1976; Stubbs, 1983).

When she asks, 'D'you think the mouse is trying to tell Rosie something?', she implies that their views are as valid as hers. The four-year-old's keen sense of conversational control is not substantially dented in this classroom. Indeed, the interpersonal patterning of these exchanges provides a greater degree of continuity with their home experience than young children are normally permitted in their early years at school and seems an important contributor to the ease and eagerness with which they enter the world of narrative.

Of course they do not initiate as high a percentage of the exchanges as Anna does at home, and of course there are some twenty of them to only one of her. But the movement is in this direction. This is not to say that Mrs G. has abdicated the teacher's role: she draws clear ideational boundaries around storytime. Within these she encourages the children to initiate observations and interpretations of what they are both seeing and listening to, and in her responses to their contributions she gently nudges them towards the kernel events. Thus she directs them into the text, sharing with them her own processes of making narrative sense and encouraging them to engage in a similar enterprise. Through the means of familiar interpersonal patterns, she steers the children towards a new ideational coherence.

Schools can never be exactly like home. Because she knows her daughter so well and because of the intimacy of the situation, Anna's mother needs little conscious effort to help Anna make personal sense of the narratives they read together. But Mrs G. knows that the forms and meanings of written narrative are strange to the twenty or so children in her charge and that she has a comparatively short time to make these familiar to her children, with their varying temperaments and experiences of which she knows so little. She has to be more deliberate. Early in the school year she starts with the conversational forms familiar to them, through which she gives them a taste of the meanings that can be created through narrative. As the year progresses and as the children gain an increasing familiarity and respect for these meanings, she moves from dialogue towards monologue and introduces forms which realize narrative meanings more richly.

But she sees the encouragement of overt participation to be vital. Whereas at home with her daughter Anna's mother can safely rely on the three-year-old's lively interest in the event which is after all largely under the child's own control, in school Mrs G. is far more consciously concerned to prompt her children towards the active involvement she sees to be necessary for literary satisfaction. This means helping them not only to construe the fictive characters and events in the light of their own experience, but also to predict what will happen next and to test their predictions against the evidence of the verbal and pictorial texts.

Like Anna's mother, Mrs G. makes it possible for her children to engage in simultaneous multi-level interactive learning with the focus on the construction of narrative. Like her, she acts both as model reader and as mediator between child and author. But although intuition plays a large part in guiding her actions, so too do conscious thought and deliberation. Anna's mother sees that she is sharing a pleasurable experience. Mrs G. sees that she is teaching children to read. Where she differs from very many teachers of young children is in taking her intuitions into the classroom instead of abandoning them at the school door, and in seeing that these intuitions can be knitted together with ideas culled from careful study, discussion and reflection.

Mrs G. recognizes the value of her experiences at home with her own children and, drawing on her classroom skill and her educational and literary knowledge, attempts to create an experience of a similar kind in school. That she is substantially successful in this enterprise is shown by the fact that towards the end of the school year all her pupils have developed a marked interest in books. At the end of a morning in June all except three of the children in the room are immersed in books, individually 'reading' their stories aloud, with Glenda singing Lobel's *Mouse Tales*. If this is not considered objective evidence, their own storytellings provide a convincing demonstration of growth in their mastery of narrative. Whereas at the beginning of the year they need considerable prompting and support to produce a halting succession of often fragmentary and largely inexplicit statements about the pictures in the books in front of them, at the end of the year even those who have not participated before in invited storytelling produce extensive and coherent narrations with highly explicit language, including elaborated adverbial and noun phrases and extensive use of cohesive devices. In October Richard, eager to tell Eric Carle's *Do You Want to Be My Friend?*, can manage only an announcement of the title followed by the words 'and that' repeated sixteen times. But in July he produces a telling of the three bears that is twenty-three utterances long, an orderly, patterned and highly explicit sequence leading to the turning point of Goldilocks's escape and possessing much of the texture of the folk tale. Lee, uninterested in telling stories at another's behest in the earlier part of the year, gives a 'reading' of Peter and the Wolf in June that includes creatures with such literary forms as 'a duck under water and a fish deep under water'. These are not trivial achievements. These children are gaining a command of the forms and meanings of written narrative that will permit them not only to make active sense of the stories they hear, but also to predict the words on the page in the books in front of them when they begin the business of learning to read for themselves. From the work of the Goodmans we now know enough about the early stages of reading to recognize the central importance of this prediction (Y. Goodman, 1968; K. Goodman, 1973).

But teaching of Mrs G.'s sort is rare in schools. And at the present time there is a very real danger that learning, which we can glimpse in action but which is not amenable to any simplistic measurement, will be marginalized in favour of what is more readily assessable and more obviously appropriate to the business of formal education. It is far easier to test the number of letters a four-year-old can recognize (or the number of words a seven-year-old can identify) than to discover what a child has learned about the language of books, about the meanings that can be created through this language and about how a text can be interrogated. And yet we know this kind of learning to be at once quite fundamental, extremely complicated and unevenly distributed. We need to help our teachers, whether experienced or novices, to provide all young children with experiences that will make it more possible for them to become active readers of literature. To do so we need to recognize that there are many important home truths still to be learned.

Children's Books Referred to

E. Carle, *Do You Want to be My Friend?* London: Hamish Hamilton, 1971.
P. Hutchins, *Rosie's Walk*. London: Penguin, 1970.
A. Lobel, *Mouse Tales*. London: World's Work, 1972.
J. Ruskin, *The King of the Golden River*. London: Constable, 1851.
M. Sendak, *Where the Wild Things Are*. London: Penguin, 1970.
Dr Seuss, *Green Eggs and Ham*. New York: Random House, 1960.

How Texts Teach What Readers Learn[1]
Margaret Meek

This article is a workshop rather than an essay or a lecture. To make the most of it you should refer to the texts – in most cases books for children or young readers – which I have used to illustrate the central points. You will find a list of these at the end, and I shall mention some other interesting books which have helped my thinking.

Everyone knows that the most significant things about reading are the most obvious. When Frank Smith first said that children learn to read by reading, we all agreed. We even felt that something had been revealed to us. In fact, good readers have always taken that for granted. Our commonsense notions of skill and expertise tell us that those who are good at something – making pastry or money, playing golf or bridge or the violin, or inventing computer programs – achieve mastery by practise, pleasure and persistence. Reading is no different from anything else we learn, except perhaps in that we have to learn to do it if we are to be recognized by others as someone who can learn.

By reminding us of what we know, Frank Smith reclaimed reading for learners, freed teachers from enslavement to pedagogic methodology, and let us rediscover reading as something with language as its core. It then followed that children's aptitude for learning language early and well guaranteed that reading and writing are obvious social things to do in any community where written language is part of our social function as human beings[1] (Heath, 1983).

There are many more obvious things which successful readers learn without ever being taught. So obvious are they, we seem to have missed them out of our accounts of reading and reading instruction. Most of what now follows is a list of the ordinary things that readers do without seeming to have learned them as lessons. If we look at these a little more closely, they may turn out to be less ordinary than we first believed. If it is also true that readers learn them without reading instruction, perhaps we shall discover more about the constituent parts of the reading process.

Begin with yourself. Try to put together your autobiography in reading. (If you do not want to do it now, save it for a ruminant moment, a walk or a way of escaping into your head in a boring meeting.) What can you remember of learning to read? Who was with you? Where did it happen? What did you do? Summon up your best recollections and you will probably remember two things above all others – the difficulties and successes you had on your way, and the important turning points in your understanding of what reading was all about. Ask yourself why you are interested in reading. Scan your present reading habits. (No guilt, please, about the pile of unread books beside your bed.) Then ask yourself what you think these recollections will tell you that you think you do not know about reading. The only necessary condition for this exercise is that you should tell yourself what you already know you know, as if you were thinking of it for the first time. What comes clearly and easily to mind?

I see myself in a Scottish village primary school industriously pleasing my teacher with my rendering of *Little Red Hen, Chicken Licken* and *The Three Billy Goats Gruff*. My grandparents, all of them, read to me and told me stories – the endless ramifications of Scottish history and legend which I believed had happened in their lifetime instead of centuries before, if at all. My childhood Sundays clanged with pulpit readings of the Authorized Version of the Bible, *Pilgrim's Progress, Paradise Lost*, heroic accounts of African missionaries. The weekdays, cold and dark in the wartime winter, were a muddle of whatever was around, Grimm, Scott, *The People's Friend*. Reading was a form of displaced action for an asthmatic; I could talk about things as if they had happened to me. That I was 'good' at reading never crossed my mind, but I liked the approval which linked pleasure and virtue. I could not understand, when many years later I first met someone who had never learned to read, why the process should be so difficult. The shock of recognition which brought all of this back was my first reading of Sartre's autobiographical account of his early adventures in his grandfather's library. Read it if you can; the book is called *Words* (Sartre, 1964).

What I next have to say will be difficult to believe. In all the books I have read about reading and teaching reading there is scarcely a mention about what is to be read. Books are, as the saying goes, taken as read in discussions about reading teaching. The reading experts, for all their understanding about 'the reading process', treat all text as the neutral substance on which the process works, as if the reader did the same things with a poem, a timetable and a warning notice. They *know* this is not the case, but somehow the differentiation between reading a threatening letter, a file or 'the mind's construction in the face' is not regarded as part of what the reader does.

Not only that, these experts often fail to remind themselves that reading does not happen in a vacuum. The social conditions and surroundings are important too. For we have been inclined to think of reading as a silent, solitary activity so long that we have neglected those things that are part of our reading together. People singing hymns in church are usually reading the words. Their social reading is different from that of the unemployed scanning notices in an employment centre. The reading process has always to be described in terms of texts and contexts as well as in terms of what we think readers actually *do*.

My disquiet about reading experts is that they decontextualize reading in order to describe it. They are casual about texts. Those whom I want to call 'expert readers' – critics, subject specialists, writers, English professors, publisher's editors and text consultants – make the same kind of mistake. They believe that there exists a group of well-read who have a common background of texts which they all know and to which reference can be made at all times with common understanding by those 'in the know'. But they have very little curiosity about how readers in their specialism *come to know* how to read the texts of their subject. I guess that any doctor, chemist, physicist or medievalist will tell you that he/she did nothing different from the reading most people do, except that his/her texts were special. That is obvious.

My main point is very simple. We learned to read, competently and sensitively, because we gave ourselves what Sartre called 'private lessons', by becoming involved in what we read. We also found we could share what we read with other people, our friends, our colleagues, our opponents even, when we argued with them. The reading lessons were not part of a course of reading, except of the course we gave ourselves in our interactions with texts. If we can at this point acknowledge the importance of these untaught lessons, I think we should look at them more closely, beginning with the beginners.

How the Book Works, How the Story Goes

Most children come to school with a crop of reader-like behaviours and an awareness of what they expect reading to be like. They can distinguish makes of motorcars, road signs, wrappers on favourite chocolate bars. If someone has read to them, they can turn pages, tell a story from pictures, recognize advertisements on television and know that print is common in their world. If they have not had much experience of books, there are still other 'literacy events' in their lives (see, for example, Goelman, Oberg and Smith, 1984).

Many early reading skills can be missed by teachers whose training has been strictly geared to 'schooling' literacy. Teachers are naturally concerned about what pupils have to learn and their responsibility for teaching these things, so they sometimes undervalue what the children have already discovered about writing and reading. If there is no place or chance for beginners to demonstrate what they can do, what they know will never be part of their teachers' awareness.

Any significant reading research I have done rests on my having treated anecdotes as evidence. Take the case of young Ben, who had been 'offered' to one of my students as a beginner in need of extra attention because of his slow progress with the phonics check list. The student and I picked him up in the school corridor and went into a quiet corner to look at the new book for which I happened to need just such a reader – a review copy of *Rosie's Walk* by Pat Hutchins. We read it together.

First we looked at the cover and talked about the hen, the fox, the bees, and the trees with apples and pears. Ben was the leader in this discussion. He recognized the hen coop, the windmill, the farm buildings, the sun and the cloud ('There might be rain'). All of these are represented in the formal terms of the artist's design for the page; there is no attempt at realism, the fruit hangs in rows and the landscape is stylized. Yet we seemed to talk naturally about Rosie 'living' in the hen coop, despite the fact that Ben's London is far from a farm. I doubt that he had ever seen a windmill and he had never encountered a fox. Yet he picked out the elements and seemed to anticipate something of what the story might be about.

Before we opened the book there was a kind of tacit agreement by Ben that Rosie the hen might be a suitable protagonist for a tale. As her creator draws her, she is; her antecedents stretch back beyond Chaucer's Pertelote, whom she resembles. Do you agree with me so far that these are reading lessons? If so, how do we come to know the character in a story whose fortunes we are to follow? Is it not in the repeated encounter on each page with the recognizable object or person? If so, then going on seems to be the best thing to do, page-turning to see 'what happens next'. Again, we have always known that, but forgotten how we learned. Where our sympathies are engaged there comes a cohesion of *textual* concern, even when the text is pictures. Rosie is a continuing presence; so is the fox, although his name is never once recorded in print; he is never mentioned.

When we open the page at the first two-page spread Rosie is in her coop at the left-hand side – where the reader's eyes naturally go if the books are not an entire novelty. Beyond her, on the right-hand page, is the farm, now with more buildings, and beyond it a cornfield, a distant goat, a tractor, a cart and beehives. There is no sign of the fox. The print on this page is 'Pat Hutchins, ROSIE'S WALK, The Bodley Head, London, Sydney,

Toronto'. Most accomplished readers turn this page, taking the conventions of publishing for granted. My clever student read the words out and we talked about where books are made. Ben said this was the third time he had seen the title; he recognized it. Explaining Pat Hutchins took a little longer but the first-edition hardback has her picture on the back flap. That someone wrote the story and drew the pictures was a new idea for Ben; he wondered if he could see her. We said he might, for she too lived in London. As this was not an instructional situation in his eyes he knew he could tell us to turn the page, which we did and found the same words again, this time in tiny print with the publisher's address and the date. When did you learn that you do not read these words as part of the story?

On the facing page we next read: 'For Wendy and Stephen'. Here Ben was quickly alerted. 'I know that says Wendy,' he said. 'Her peg is next to mine. And I know Stephen, that's his name.' So we embedded this successful recognition (called 'world to text' by the experts) in the idea that authors and artists make books for children they know, but other children can read them.

If you are already bored by these details you might want to stop here, but not before I suggest that understanding authorship, audience, illustration and iconic interpretation are part of the ontogenesis of 'literary competences' (Culler, 1977). To learn to read a book, as distinct from simply recognizing the words on the page, a young reader has to become both the teller (picking up the author's view and voice) and the told (the recipient of the story, the interpreter). This symbolic interaction is learned early. It is rarely, if ever, taught, except in so far as an adult stands in for the author by giving the text a 'voice' when reading to the child. Wendy and Stephen are replaced by other nameless children, in this case thousands of them, whose interpretations of the words and pictures may be as numerous, but are scarcely ever inquired into or understood for what they are. Ben knew Wendy and Stephen and he found their names in the book. That was what we knew, but we were sure there was more to know about the nature of his understanding. The next bit of the argument is easier if you have the text:

Rosie the hen went for a walk across the yard around the pond over the haycock past the mill through the fence under the beehives and got back in time for dinner.

There are thirty-two words in one sentence and twenty-seven pages of pictures. One word 'haycock' is different in the North American text where it is 'haystack'. No one now speaks of haycocks; they have almost disappeared from our fields. But the word is familiar in a special sense to those children who recite 'Little Boy Blue'. Rosie's actual walk is described in the pictures in the terms of the size of the trees, the nearness or distancing of the goat and the windmill. A rake, a pond, a haycock, a bag of flour hanging out of the mill, beehives and a group of carts become traps for Rosie's pursuer, the fox. The words to be read reflect a quiet stroll. They are balanced by an expression of knowing insouciance on Rosie's face. Does she know he is there? That is a secret, but the reader decides. Rosie never looks behind where all the action is. The fox, with his eyes constantly trained on Rosie, falls a victim to every hazard until he is stung by the bees into retreat.

Ben enjoyed the book so much that we read it four times more. By the end of the afternoon he could tell the story and nearly match the words, so we said he could read it by himself. I do not mind if you say he had 'just memorized it'. My recollection of and conviction about this encounter is that Ben had a genuine reading experience which made up for the disappointment, the exclusion, the failure with the phonics check list. He had been in the company of readers who welcomed him as one of them; he had met an artist-author whose text had helped him to learn significant reading lessons. At the end he *possessed* the text, so that even when I took the book away with me to write about it, I took his reading with me as part of my understanding, and left him with the story to tell to someone else. He had also learned how a story goes in a book; that is, the reader tells it to himself, and every time he went back to the beginning, there it was again. Yet every reading yielded something more.

Because our concern is with the interaction of young readers with texts, we may pass over too quickly the skill and understanding which underlie the making of picture books. We take the simplicity of the words for granted. *Rosie's Walk* seems simple; it is a classical story (beginning, middle, end) with clear antecedents in every little red hen back to Aesop. But each double-page spread with its three words of text is full of possibilities. At 'over the haycock' there are terrified mice, a static tethered goat, the fox leaping so near to Rosie. (The reader has to 'read' the scratch marks that indicate jumping.) On the next page the fox is buried in the hay: there is a different expression on the face of the goat, Rosie is walking on. This pattern comes four times. By the time the reader gets to 'through the fence' he or she knows to look ahead to spot the next obstacle. But on this occasion the author has changed the rules. The fox and the reader have ignored the empty cart which the jumping fox tips so that it knocks over the beehives; not exactly what we expected, but there as a possibility from the very first picture.

By this time you may have had enough of Rosie, but young readers make us patient. Let me summarize what rereadings of this famous walk tell me about what is there to encourage the emergence of children's 'literary competences' and to establish, for me at least, the necessary connections of literacy and literature. Begin with the testimony of one of my Canadian colleagues who had introduced Rosie and the fox to a reader of Ben's age. Pointing to the fox he said: 'Who is that?' 'McDonald Big Ears' was the prompt reply. Thus we can say that a page in a picture book is an icon to be contemplated, narrated, explicated by the viewer. It holds the story until there is a telling. So in the beginning the words are few; the story happenings are in the pictures which form the polysemic text. The reader has to learn which of the pictorial events carries the line of the story, while each rereading shows that other things can also be taken into account. Gradually the reader learns that the narration is made up of words and pictures, together. The essential lesson of *Rosie's Walk* depends on there being no mention of the fox, but the reader knows that there would be no story without him. Nowhere but in a reader's interaction with a text can this lesson be learned. It is a lesson we take with us from wherever we first learned it to our understanding of Jane Austen.

How do children distinguish the heroine from the villain? How does an author 'recruit' their imagination and 'sustain their emotional regard', or rather, how do they let her (Bruner, 1986)? What do they presuppose will happen, and what, exactly, is the satisfaction of the happy ending that Tolkien calls the 'eucatastrophe'? Is it an evaluation of the rightness of things that one comes to expect in a story when it is less evident in life itself? If so, where does this moral judgement come from, if not from games with rules? Is reading an elaborate game with rules? What relation has this game with rules to children's deep play and risk taking? Some of these questions can be answered by watching children's interactions with texts. My contention is that reading demands explanations beyond the information given about the surface features of language, important as that undoubtedly is.

One thing more. In all children's stories there are cultural features which locate them in a tradition. *Rosie's Walk* is a tale in the tradition of Western Europe. There is evidence that its counterparts exist in other cultures. We have passed beyond the monocultural nature of literature and literacy, so now we need to know how it is read where the text is in languages other than English.

If some of the foregoing has made sense, you should now want to read books written or made by those who take children seriously as readers. Artists and writers have a vested interest in the young because they have innocent eyes, language in the making, fewer presuppositions about the predictable and less experience of established conventions of narrative.

They can be counted on as allies by virtue of their curiosity and a huge desire to learn how the world works. In addition, children's picture books are international currency; the texts are more easily translated than most. The tradition of modernism is strong. Using Bruner's metaphor again, we can see that the artist or storyteller 'recruits' children's imaginations by presenting them with the familiar in a new guise or by making a 'logical' extension of the real. When Bear in Anthony Browne's story goes for a walk he takes his pencil and draws himself out of trouble. Innovations are common in children's books because they are seen as forms of diversion. In his story about Bear, Anthony Browne's stylized jungle has flowers and plants with faces and *ties*, which children usually notice before adults do. Skilful makers of children's books exploit this freedom on behalf of their readers who are entering new discourses. As we have just seen, they create patterns and vary them. The reader enjoys both the security of the familiar and the shock of novelty. Sometimes the critics are reproached by the artists for their failure to understand that they are dealing with the descendants of Blake, Hogarth, Caldecott and Tenniel.

Reading Secrets

John Burningham's picture books are reading adventures with deep reading secrets. *Mr Gumpy's Outing* appears at first to be that most ancient of story kinds, the cumulative tale, which owes its success to the simple trick of building a story one step and, in a book, one page-turning at a time.

Mr Gumpy owned a boat and his house was by a river.
'May we come with you?' said the children.
'Yes,' said Mr Gumpy, 'if you don't squabble.'

That is how traditional storytelling dialogue works. Now it takes over the narration.

'Can I come along, Mr Gumpy?' said the rabbit.
'Yes, but don't hop about.'

The cat, the dog, the pig, the sheep, the chickens, the calf in turn ask Mr Gumpy's permission to board his boat. They are given leave to join the others on condition that their behaviour is decorous. Each animal makes the same request and is given the same answer; that is, the meaning stays the same but the form of the language varies.

'Have you a place for me?' said the sheep.
'Yes, but don't keep bleating.'

'Can you make room for me?' said the calf.
'Yes, if you don't trample about.'

'May I join you, Mr Gumpy?' said the goat.
'Very well, but don't kick.'

The reading lessons, about how dialogue appears on a page, the formal ways of making requests, the way the sentences appear on a page, go hand in hand with what children have already begun to discover about language as 'a rich and adaptable instrument for the realisation of intentions' (Halliday, 1969). But there is more:

'May I come, please?' said the pig.
'Very well, but don't muck about.'

'Can we come too?' said the chickens.
'Yes, but don't flap,' said Mr Gumpy.

I would say that this is the most important lesson of all, learned early and relearned every day, as each one of us stretches our language to reconstruct, remake, extend and understand our experience of living in social contact with each other. When we want to make new meanings we need metaphor. Here the young reader discovers that the admonitions, 'don't flap' and 'don't muck about' are two-sided phrases with bilateral meanings. In the context of Mr Gumpy's boat, the words mean more than they say.

In a later book, *Granpa*, John Burningham exploits this dialogic game even more subtly. He leaves gaps in the text to be filled with the metaphors of his paintings of the seasons which suggest the passing of time, over a year in the narrative, over the lifetime of Granpa. The text is entirely the conversation of a little girl and her grandfather. They talk about flowers in the greenhouse, the possibility of catching whales when they go fishing, what happened when Granpa was young, what they might do when he recovers from feeling unwell. The resonances of the simplest of dialogue turn-taking are about where babies come from, what is the difference between girls and boys, how memory works, how stories are to be read, what is possible, what is death and loss.

In *Come Away from the Water, Shirley* Burningham uses two modes of narration simultaneously. On the first page we see an only child and her (elderly?) parents arriving on a pebbled British beach with deckchairs and a picnic basket. Thereafter, on the left-hand page, we see the parents, seated. The text is on this side only. It consists of phrases British children have heard since sea bathing became our annual endurance test, reflecting here the unadventurousness of adults:

Of course, it's far too cold for swimming, Shirley.
Mind you don't get any of that filthy tar on your nice new shoes.
You won't bring any of that smelly seaweed home, will you Shirley?

The facing pages are full of action. The reader sees Shirley and her imaginary dog rowing out to meet a boatload of pirates who make the adventurous pair walk the plank. They escape by diving into the sea, the dog with a treasure map in its mouth. They dig up the treasure and, crowned with gold, sail back just as Shirley's mother on the opposite page is saying, 'Good heavens. Just look at the time. We're going to be late if we don't hurry'.

You will already have grasped that the artist uses the conventions of realism to convey the life-to-text nature of the portrayal of the parents, with the Thermos flasks and father sleeping under his newspaper. And we know just how the words sound if we have ever been at the beach or on a picnic during draughty, changeable August. Across the page Shirley is free to be adventurous in the ways that books and stories have taught her. The surprise for the reader, and the reading lesson, lies in the discovery of the two kinds of storytelling side by side. To be a reader you have to learn the conventions of both. Burningham is suggesting that what seems real in stories is just as conventional as what seems fantastic. What matters is to know the rules of the game the author is playing. Shirley does not bring her gold back to her mother. She knows which things are appropriate in which contexts.

Lessons in Discourse

According to Shirley Brice Heath (1983), fantasy in texts for children is a social as well as a literary understanding. My feeling is that the nature of 'made-up' stories is not well enough understood by those who are confronted by the strength of imagination in childhood, when the inner and outer realities are closer together. *Come Away from the Water, Shirley* shows how texts teach how they are to be read, so that there is no problem about which of the two stories is true. They both are.

Children quickly learn the rules for 'how things work around here'. Having done so, in behaviour and language, they know that the rules can be broken, by parody, for example. There are alternative versions of nursery rhymes, Christmas carols, national hymns which never find their way into books, all of which show that, when they have learned the rules, children know how to subvert them. A joke is often the best reading test.

The authors who exploit their art and the illustrators who make pictures with secrets link what children know, partly know and are learning about the world to ways of presenting the world in books. These presentations are lifelike, that is, the reader senses their relation to psychological reality. But they are also scandalous, excessive, daring possibilities that the real world, the world of adults, might not endure, but which are real to children. Look for the picture books of Edward Ardizzone, John Burningham, Anthony Browne, Quentin Blake, Shirley Hughes, Janet and Allan Ahlberg and, of course, Maurice Sendak. Read them with your most adult awareness of life and literature and text, and you will see that the invitations they offer to young readers are far from infantile. Children who encounter such books learn many lessons that are hidden for ever from those who move directly from the reading scheme to the worksheet.

Compare the textual variety of children's picture books with that of reading schemes. You will see how the interactions made possible by skilled artists and writers far outweigh what can be learned from books made up by those who offer readers no excitement, no challenge, no real help. Let children talk to you about what they see in the pictures; they look more closely than their skipping and scanning elders. Do not explain everything: leave some of the artist-author's secrets for another time. What texts teach is a process of discovery for readers, not a programme of instruction for teachers.

Clubs, Networks and Spies

Frank Smith says readers belong to a club. I think they are members of networks, sometimes like spies. They do not all read the same books, but they know the people who like the books they like, and they also know the groups they might like to belong to. They look out for the books that other children like, and they reread old favourites. But it is not so easy to find yourself in a familiar network as it was when there were fewer texts in school. We all read the same ones in my day. Now the number of children's books published each year would take a seven-year-old until seventy to read.

When I read with inexperienced readers I find that their difficulties lie not in the words but in understanding something that lies behind the words, embedded in the sense. It is usually an oblique reference to something the writer takes for granted the reader will understand, so that the new text will mean more than it says. Imagine a smart detective standing over a corpse and remarking 'Curiouser and curiouser', where a phrase from *Alice in Wonderland* is set into another book as if to say 'This is a well-read detective' or in order to draw a parallel with *Alice*. It is a very ancient habit to make texts polysemic. With Chaucer and Shakespeare it was not plagiarism or showing off but a form of tribute or flattery. With modern novelists it might be anything from crossword puzzles to irony. Readers sometimes feel they are really rewriting the story as they read it. Barthes calls some of this 'writerly' text. To read writerly text you have to do at least half of the work.

It does not sound like something you expect beginning readers to be good at. Well, again they take lessons. Most people have in their heads verses from childhood, groups of words, sayings, rhymes that are part of the texture of the language, spoken or written. As a writer you could count on the children knowing, say, Humpty Dumpty or Old Mother Hubbard, Jack and Jill, Cinderella perhaps. That's what Janet and Allan Ahlberg do in *Each Peach Pear Plum*. The young reader does not have to know about Tom Thumb to be able to read the words 'I spy Tom Thumb'; the invitation from the artist is to find him in the picture. But if the beginner has heard of him before, in a rhyme or in another book, there are two kinds of finding: one of the boy hiding in the picture, the other of the fact that Tom Thumb is also known to the Ahlbergs in the way that we all say we know Jane Eyre or Billy Bunter.

Experts tell us that the lucky children are those who are read to. If they know stories or rhymes by heart, they bring the words *to* the page when they read for themselves. They discover that you can play with language in both speech and writing, and they also learn not to expect the same sense from 'Diddle diddle dumpling, my son John' as from stories about a first day in school.

The most important single lesson that children learn from texts is the nature and variety of written discourse, the different ways that language lets a writer tell, and the many and different ways a reader reads. Go back again to your own learning. How did you know when you were reading a joke? Didn't you practise asking them before you fully understood the puns of the 'Knock, knock' game? Wasn't it the conspiratorial feeling of the exchanges that pleased you? Irony – not saying quite what you mean – is likewise socially learned. We saw the beginning of it in *Rosie's Walk*.

As the Learning Goes on: The Transition Stage

Experienced literary critics, those who never read children's books now but whose memories are laden with the rhymes of childhood, tell us that there is enough childhood lore in all literature to be fed into stories at all stages of learning to read, right up to Joyce's *Ulysses*. Those who know how to recognize bits and pieces of other texts in what they read find it is like the discovery of old friends in new places. They feel they are sharing a secret with the writer (that conspiratorial feeling again). They become 'insiders' in the network.

Children enter the intertext of literature, oral and written, very early; as soon as they know some nursery rhymes, in fact, and later, when they have amassed the lore of the school playground, they are able to recognize in their reading what has been in their memories for some time.

The best example of what I am trying to explain is another book by the Ahlbergs. (They have a special kind of insight into the part the oral tradition plays in the lives of children.) It is called *The Jolly Postman, or Other People's Letters*. Readers of about seven or eight enjoy it because they know that letters are good things to get, and other people's letters have secrets you're not supposed to read. In the book the Jolly Postman, who rides a bicycle, takes letters to the homes of some characters from nursery rhymes. The connecting story is told in rhyme. But the intrigue lies in the fact that some pages of the book are envelopes containing the actual letters which the reader takes out and reads. So here is Goldilocks, writing to apologize to the Three Bears for breaking and entering. The Wicked Witch gets a flyer from Hobgoblin Supplies Ltd, who make special offers for Hallowe'en boots, deadly lampshades, newts, boy powder, and books of foul spells. A publisher sends to HRH Cinderella a little book of her recent adventures specially prepared on the occasion of her wedding. Here is my favourite, addressed to B. B. Wolf, Esq., c/o Grandma's Cottage, Horner's Corner:

Meeny, Miny, Mo & Co. Solicitors
Alley O Buildings, Toe Lane, Tel. 12345

Dear Mr Wolf,

We are writing to you on behalf of our client, Miss Riding Hood, concerning her grandma. Miss Hood tells us that you are presently occupying her grandma's cottage and wearing her grandma's clothes without this lady's permission.

Please understand that if this harassment does not cease, we will call in the Official Woodcutter, and – if necessary – all the King's horses and all the King's men.

On a separate matter, we must inform you that Messrs Three Little Pigs Ltd are now firmly resolved to sue for damages. Your offer of shares in an apple-picking business is declined, and all this huffing and puffing will get you nowhere.

Yours sincerely,

Harold Meeny

Inside the verse text of *The Jolly Postman*, in the envelopes, are texts whose conventions are drawn from the world of actual literacy events: personal letters, publishing, the law, travel brochures and advertising. The contents refer to the world of the fairy story. The Ahlbergs never make mistakes in reaching their readers, so they know that this intricate intertext will be read by those who are ready to read it.

On the surface intertext can seem to be a kind of literary joke; underneath it is a very serious business, part of the whole intricate network of words which mean more than they say. Readers of *The Jolly Postman* enter the world of 'If on a winter's night a traveller . . .'. They also find themselves in the network of political propaganda and other less honourably subversive texts.

This intertextuality cannot be a feature of the reading scheme, which offers words to be read only in order to reinforce lessons that are taught *about* reading rather than learned *by* reading. The result is a divergence in competence and understanding between young readers who have entered the reading network through the multiple meanings of polysemic texts and those who may have practised only on the reductive features of words written to be 'sounded out' or 'recognized'. Those who have had only the latter experience often feel that they are missing something when they read a text which they know means more than it says.

Examples from Middle Childhood and Longer Texts

We are talking about *narrations*, ways that the tellers of stories in books teach children how to read them. We have looked at some of the ways in which modern artists make storytelling in picture books as intriguing as the seductive narratives of television. We are bound, as a result, to acknowledge the power of images – that is, non-verbal representations of ideas (connected, of course, with imagination) – to be, in the early stages of reading, as important as words. Think of the appeal of Raymond Brigg's *The Snowman*. Evidence from research emphasizes the importance of images. It is schooling and the teaching of reading as a concern with words alone that put into our heads the notion that books with pictures are a preliterate form of storytelling, while all the time the very force of television shows us this is not the case.

What counts in children's climbing up through their school years is the ability confidently to tackle longer and longer stretches of continuous prose, in both reading and writing. But, like adults, children take time out. Outside the classroom, the library, the bookish, they find the popular culture of childhood in comics. Looking back at the debates which have ranged around these productions, I am surprised that we have ignored for so long the reading skills they taught our readers. The classic comic demands that two interpretations be made together, of pictures and text. Balloon dialogue (and the one with the wavy line for 'thinks'), inset sketches, drawing 'asides', together with the reader's impulse to keep the story going while taking all this in, should have alerted us sooner to the ways by which the young reader becomes both the teller and the told, what Bakhtin (1981) calls 'the dialogic imagination'.

And this is reading in its social context; readers of comics swop them, act out the farces which they enjoy, and know that the adults are in two minds about their worth. It is well nigh impossible to read a comic *to* a child. To read one *with* a child, an adult has to be accepted as a peer, and even this is thought of as a kind of intrusion.

In *Chips and Jessie* Shirley Hughes combines as many of the discourse forms as any nine-year-old will have encountered. In devising an intriguing form of storytelling she mixes the conventions of the comic with 'straight' bookish text, and thereby shows what pictures can do that text cannot. For example, overlapping events that occur at the same time can be depicted simultaneously but have to be related sequentially. Her skill in exploiting this mixed form can be seen in the episode of Chico, the hamster brought home from school, who escapes and is lost. There is a lull in the rush of events at the point where Chico has been replaced by another hamster and all seems well. The formal story text says:

That evening Chips and Jessie were sitting on the kitchen table at Chips' house. Mum had taken Gloria to visit a friend and Grandpa was working in his garden shed. It was getting dark. Jessie was keeping Chips company by telling him all about a very spooky film she had seen on TV. It was about a man who had been locked up in a terrible prison on an island from which no one could escape, even though he had done nothing wrong.

Above the heads of Chips and Jessie are the words of their dialogue:

Above that is a picture of their mental image of the prisoner and another of the dungeon. Then, on the next page, as Jessie describes the prisoner scratching on the wall, the reader *sees* the missing Chico in the rim of the picture as he makes his way down behind the kitchen wall towards the taps and the sink.

This particular kind of multiconsciousness, apparently so natural in childhood yet culturally and specifically learned, is passed over as children are taught to pay attention only to words in books. The ousting of images by text has not been an unmitigated gain in the teaching of literacy, as we are only now beginning to realize.

More Learning

Perhaps at this point we should remind ourselves that these are not the only lessons children learn: the stories themselves, what they are about, are also lessons of a kind, the kind that most adults are more concerned with when they talk about a book being 'suitable'.

When children read comfortably, when the rules of 'how the story goes' are quickly and familiarly settled between author and reader, reading feels easy. Readers know they can read, and authors can take their skill for granted. Teachers are so relieved that they encourage the young to go ahead as fast as they can. It is usually a good time for new readers to learn other lessons, but if they do not get the stories that help them, they are running on the spot instead of striding out.

Let us stay with the familiar kind of story for a little, the one where the hero or heroine is involved in unexpected events or suffers a temporary desolation but all comes right in the end. In books written in the last thirty years these tales of childhood have presented to young readers a version of being young which is optimistic and, on the whole, comfortable. There are certain tacit assumptions within them that this is what childhood is, or should be, like.

When the structure of the story is familiar, readers are free to look at other possible lessons to be learned from events they may never encounter and kinds of people who may never cross their path. Now the reader is to ask: what would I do if I found myself in that situation? Do I or do I not care for people like that? Is there a part of me that understands them?

Here begin two kinds of explorations, of the value system that prevails in the world and the one revealed in the text, and also of the way narratives handle these things, not only in the conventions of the realistic tale but also in the more metaphorical instances in folk tales and legends. Readers have to confront truth/falsehood, trust/betrayal, heroism/cowardice, unselfishness/self-concern and all the other ways in which our interactions with each other are construed and presented in life and in stories. Both life and text have to be interrogated about 'the way things might be'. *Sir Gawain and the Green Knight* brings up all of these puzzles at once, but they are also present in the work of Enid Blyton and Roald Dahl, which children read with great pleasure.

'Who is the reader to become, during the time of reading?' is a powerful question from Wayne Booth (1984). We know from children's addiction to the Famous Five and their fondness for *Danny* and *Boy* that they are trying out different kinds of companionship, perhaps of those whose lives seem to involve them in more risk-taking than their own. If they read all the works of these authors, and many children do, they come to the question: 'Do I want to read about these people any more?' when someone asks them what they like or puts in their way something different. It is at this moment that the kind of telling comes into focus, a chance to read not so much about different people but to read about people differently.

Readers who read a lot soon discover what is suitable or unsuitable in a story. In fiction, as in life, it is a judgement they learn to make from evidence they understand. Instead of condemning some children's stories as 'unsuitable', adults need to take time to help children talk about what they read so that they learn to express their judgements, however tentatively at first. Many a good reading lesson from an undistinguished book has been smothered by too emphatic classroom demands for the reader to pronounce immediately on characters or actions, when a time for thought might have been more helpful.

The signs of genuine reading development are hard to detect as they appear and bear little relation to what is measured by reading tests. For me the move from 'more of the same' to 'I might try something different' is a clear step. So is a growing tolerance of ambiguity, the notion that things are not quite what they seem, even in a fairly straightforward tale about, say, a family seaside holiday or the unexpected behaviour on the part of parents.

Two texts help me to distinguish moves in children's reading. The first is *The Iron Man* by Ted Hughes. It can be read with pleasure and understanding by children at all stages in school, from the reception class to the sixth form. This is not exaggerated praise but a serious claim, and what happens is not a smooth progression but a series of loopings back to find new awareness in oneself as a reader. Some of the youngest readers see as deeply into Hughes's stated intentions for the story (Hughes, 1976) as do the oldest. The crossing point from reading and understanding 'what happens' to the Iron Man to interpreting the mythic implications comes for most children when, in answer to the question 'If we had Mr Hughes here, what would you like to ask him about his book?', the child says, 'Where did he get the idea from?' The idea is the meeting place of reader and writer, the intersection of culture and cognition; the readers are now writing as they read.

By the time they are eight, or a little later, children are generally expected to choose books for themselves. Those who know that authors help them to make sense of the story are more patient with the beginnings of books than those who expect to recognize straightaway what they have to understand. The common phrase for this process is 'getting into the story'. Practised readers tolerate uncertainty; they know that sometimes the author is building up suspense and that the puzzle will be resolved if they just keep reading. I wish I knew more about how we learn to tolerate uncertainty in our reading and what we are really doing. W. H. Auden (1963) says that we go on reading books we only partly understand if they have been given to us by someone we like and we want to be thought well of by him or her. Many a good tutor has let fall the title of a book, implying that of course the student will want to read it. Remember the early untaught lessons of approval and virtue? I doubt if this kind of suasion is very prevalent nowadays, but surely we should continue to help young readers to 'get into' books until they are confident that they will not be daunted. We need not do more than reduce some of the uncertainty; the author will take over where we leave off.

My second special text – the best example I know of a story for readers near the end of their primary school – is one which does everything I have already mentioned. It is based on a subtle play of intertexts which a young reader will certainly 'get' and understand and thereby feel confident, perhaps even superior, in the 'knowingness' that it produces about reading itself. It is called 'William's Version' and is by Jan Mark. See if you have to tolerate the uncertainty of the beginning.

William and Granny were left to entertain each other for an hour while William's mother went to the clinic.

'Sing to me,' said William.

'Granny's too old to sing,' said Granny.

'I'll sing to you, then,' said William. William only knew one song. He had forgotten the words and the tune, but he sang it several times, anyway.

'Shall we do something else now?' said Granny.

'Tell me a story,' said William. 'Tell me about the wolf.'

'Red Riding Hood?'

'No, not *that* wolf, the other wolf.'

'Peter and the wolf?' said Granny.

'Mummy's going to have a baby,' said William.

'I know,' said Granny.

William looked suspicious.

'How do you know?'

'Well – she told me. And it shows, doesn't it?'

'The lady down the road had a baby. It looks like a pig,' said William. He counted on his fingers. 'Three babies looks like three pigs.'

'Ah,' said Granny. 'Once upon a time there were three little pigs. Their names were –'

'They didn't have names,' said William.

'Yes they did. The first pig was called –'

'Pigs don't have names.'

'Some do. These pigs had names.'

'No they didn't.' William slid off Granny's lap and went to open the corner cupboard by the fireplace. Old magazines cascaded out as old magazines do when they have been flung into a cupboard and the door slammed shut. He rooted among them until he found a little book covered with brown paper, climbed into the cupboard, opened the book, closed it and climbed out again. 'They didn't have names,' he said.

'I didn't know you could read,' said Granny, properly impressed.

'C–A–T, wheelbarrow,' said William.

'Is that the book Mummy reads to you out of?'

'It's my book,' said William.

'But it's the one Mummy reads?'

'If she says please,' said William.

'Well, that's Mummy's story then. My pigs have names.'

'They're the wrong pigs.' William was not open to negotiation. 'I don't want them in this story.'

'Can't we have different pigs this time?'

'No. They won't know what to do.'

'Once upon a time,' said Granny, 'there were three little pigs who lived with their mother.'

'Their mother was dead,' said William.

'Oh. I'm sure she wasn't,' said Granny.

'She was dead. You make bacon out of dead pigs. She got eaten for breakfast and they threw the rind out for the birds.'

'So the three little pigs had to find homes for themselves.'

'No.' William consulted his book. 'They had to build little houses.'

'I'm just coming to that.'

'You said they had to *find* homes. They didn't *find* them.'

'The first little pig walked along for a bit until he met a man with a load of hay.'

The story proceeds in this dialogic format, with William countering his Granny's telling of every event in the old tale with a version of his own. Granny struggles to continue the narrative. When William has diverted her at a crucial point, she says, 'Why don't you tell the story?' William then produces a green scarf called Doctor Snake. Granny tries again. William adds aleatoric interventions which he seems to find in the book he has taken from the cupboard. The final argument is about the fate of the wolf. Granny tells the traditional ending: 'and the wolf fell down the chimney and into the pan of water and was boiled and the little pig ate him for supper.' The result of this is a wild tantrum from William, who then offers his version:

'The little pig put the saucepan on the gas stove and the wolf got down the chimney and put the little pig in the saucepan and boiled him. He had him for tea, with chips,' said William.

'Oh,' said Granny. 'I've got it all wrong, haven't I? Can I see the book, then I shall know, next time.'

William took the book from under his pullover. Granny opened it and read, *First Aid for Beginners: a Practical Handbook.*

'I see,' said Granny. 'I don't think I can read this. I left my glasses at home. You tell Gran how it ends.'

William turned to the last page which showed a prostrate man with his leg in a splint; *compound fracture of the femur.*

'Then the wolf washed up and got on his tricycle and went to see his Granny and his Granny opened the door and said: "Hello, William".'

'I thought it was the wolf.'

'It was. It was the wolf. His name was William Wolf,' said William.

'What a nice story,' said Granny. 'You tell it much better than I do.'

'I can see up your nose,' said William. 'It's all whiskery.'

I have read this story many times in class and elsewhere. The effect is always one of great delight, but you and I know that there is deep play in this text. William's version is older than even the tale of the three little pigs. He is 'positioned within' the story his grandmother tells; the new baby is a great threat to his identity, to his self-love. Like the story, he suffers displacement. Young readers recognize this effect even before they have the means or the understanding to explain it. In its turn the text gives them a site, a location for the pursuit of their understanding. I don't want to press too hard the notion of the 'ego as a critical construction' but Lacan's (1977) ideas are germane to our coming to know how children are subjectively located in language and culture. Any consideration of texts for children has to encounter the intertext of the reader's unconscious at some stage. The reading lesson here is that texts reveal what we think we have successfully concealed even from ourselves.

Adult Lessons

As we become more experienced in reading so we can become less and not more skilled. In some ways we even make one kind of reading do for all. I mean this in two ways: first, we read only what we find comfortable, rushing through novels to finish the story and then going on to another one. Then, if we are reading teachers or teachers of literature we may adopt too easily patterns of work which do not encourage us to inspect what we do. Habitual readers can become less adventurous than their skills allow. It is like driving in second gear in a high-powered car.

We can understand this if we go back again to our own reading, the kind we do with ease and pleasure. We can manage most texts, the written papers which impinge on the run of our ordinary lives, because we know what they refer to and the kinds of responses that are expected from us when we fill in tax forms, write reports or take time with boring but important matters from the bank. But how often do we who teach children to read, or who read on their behalf, give ourselves reading lessons? When do we read a new novel twice, that is, if we are not going to teach it for an examination? Do we even do that when we are going to read it to a class, once to see 'what happens' and again to see if we can penetrate the secrets of 'how it's done' or 'what more is there here?'

Children read stories they like over and over again: that is when they pay attention to the words – after they have discovered what happens. Adults, generally, go on to the next book, so that *how* we read is not part of the consciousness we bring to texts. We usually do not need to ask because, for our comfort, it is often 'another of the same'. I find that I give myself reading lessons when I write reviews – a stringent discipline if it is done well. I admire good reviewers very much, so I do not let myself read anyone else's piece until mine is safely beyond my reach for revision. It is the writing that makes me aware of what I am doing when I read.

I am also very curious about how other people read, not least because there seems to be no end to the interpretive possibilities of some texts. Certainly, all readers bring different things to the text, but this makes me keener than ever to know what makes the difference. How did we discover that certain ways of saying things are meaningful in the first place? What does the order of words on the page do to the way I look at things? Jerome Bruner (1986) says that if we ask a reader what kind of a story he or she is reading we are not expecting the reply to tell us about the nature of the text but about what is happening to the reader. When I asked a six-year-old which part of *The Iron Man* she liked best, she said: 'My favourite is "delicacies".' Here is what she was remembering:

The Iron Man gazed, and his eyes turned red. He kneeled down in the yard, he stretched out on one elbow. He picked up a greasy black stove and chewed it like a toffee. There were delicious crumbs of chrome on it. He followed that with a double-decker bedstead and the brass knobs made his eyes crackle with joy. Never before had the Iron Man eaten such delicacies.

The word summed up the whole section of visual concreteness; she brought back the picture with a word. The others in the group taking part in the discussion nodded. They knew exactly what she meant, although the chances are that their images were quite different.

Teaching Lessons

Young people nowadays practise their interpretive processes mostly by watching television. They find difficulty in tolerating the slow speed of classical texts where the scene has to be set in passages of description before the action can get going. They are also less tolerant of passages of text recall, especially if there are other stories embedded in these. A visual flashback goes over the same kind of ground, literally in a flash. 'Getting into' a novel like *Huckleberry Finn* needs a fair amount of tolerance of uncertainty. How would you deal with the part where Huck is complaining that Tom Sawyer is always making up adventure games from stories he has read in books?

I didn't see no di'monds and I told Tom Sawyer so. He said there was A-rabs there too, and elephants and things. I said why couldn't we see them, then? He said if I warn't so ignorant, but had read a book called *Don Quixote*, I would know without asking.

Huck wants real adventure while Tom re-creates book adventures for real. Later Huck and Tom have 'real' adventures which become part of the virtual experience of every reader of the book. When a novel as 'layered' as this is turned into a film the 'meanings' have to be translated into the semiotics of the visual. What disappears is not the plot, the characters or the recollections of what happens, but the experience of reading. Television and books are allies. I do not believe that the one drives out the other. But we need to be clearer about the kinds of 'reading' offered by both. I find I need the young to teach me as much as I think I can teach them. One of the sharpest late reading lessons I have learned is to *let* the texts teach the reader, as I would do in the case of *Huckleberry Finn*. The problem for teachers in secondary schools is to give students enough experience of different kinds of text while exploring the secrets and lessons of only some of them.

If we want to see what lessons have been learned from the texts children read, we have to look for them in what they write. Of course, they draw on the whole of their culture if we let them. We have to be alert to what comes from books as well as from life. This topic must wait for another occasion.

By this time you will have reduced my repetitive arguments to the idea that 'real' books are good reading texts for learners because they introduce children to the discourse styles of various genres. That is true, but it is not the whole story. Experimental authors are constantly changing the genres. All over the world new writers appear, writing in their English, a different cultural stream from the deep old channel of the Thames. Their narrative styles are different; they draw on different intertexts. They have their way to make. Children too have different demands. I have rested my case on narrative fiction, but every area of knowledge teaches the apprentices how people write in that domain. That is the lesson of the history books, the geography folder, the science manual, the engineering drawing. These teach their own lessons, yet we know very little about how these lessons are learned. All scientific discovery is as dramatic as the events in a novel or a film, but in the written report to the learned society the excitement must be edited out. Topic discourse, says Harold Rosen (1984), 'covers its narrative tracks'. This is another text-taught lesson.

The case for narrative fiction is best made in a short statement by Jonathan Culler (1977), from whom I borrowed the idea of 'literacy competences'. He is discussing ways of reading 'the text as an exploration of writing, of the problems of articulating a world'. He says that the job of the critic and that of every reader is 'an attempt to capture its force. The force, the power of any text, even the most unabashedly mimetic, lies in those moments which exceed our ability to categorize, which collide with our interpretive codes but nevertheless seem right.' He goes on: 'Fiction can hold together within a single space a variety of language, levels of focus, points of view, which would be contradictory in other kinds of discourse organized towards a particular empirical end.'

Strange as it may seem, the reading of stories makes skilful, powerful readers who come to understand not only the meaning but also the force of texts. It is a strong defence against being victimized by the reductive power of so-called 'functional literacy'. It also makes writers.

Tailpiece

If you think that the arguments of this article are too impressionistic, too shallowly rooted in empirical evidence, may I direct you to the main source of my conviction. For more than five years my colleagues and I examined the reading of a group of adolescents who had been deemed to be unteachable. In fact they had learned too well too many unhelpful lessons. They had never been trusted with real texts. Their early encounters with reading had not included books as a source of pleasure, play, desire. At best they could say a few words after prompting. They had been given only conditional entry into their culture and they wanted nothing of the tyranny of literacy. We gave them real books and showed them how texts teach (Meek *et al.*, 1983).

It is hard for anyone whose life has been enriched by books to exclude the young from this source of pleasure and serious reflection. What we have to realize is that the young have powerful allies in a host of gifted artists and writers to help them to subvert the world of their elders.

Note

1. An earlier version of this article was published as a pamphlet by Abel Press, PO Box 6162, Station C, Victoria BC, Canada. The current version is published, again as a pamphlet, by Thimble Press, Lockwood, Station Road, South Woodchester, Stroud, Gloucestershire.

Children's Books Referred to

J. and A. Ahlberg, *Each Peach Pear Plum*. London: Kestrel, 1976.

J. and A. Ahlberg: *The Jolly Postman or Other People's Letters*. London: Heinemann, 1986.

A. Browne, *Bear Hunt*. London: Hamish Hamilton, 1978.

J. Burningham, *Come Away from the Water, Shirley*. London: Cape, 1977.

J. Burningham, *Granpa*. London: Cape, 1984.

J. Burningham, *Mr Gumpy's Outing*. London: Cape, 1970.

S. Hughes, *Chips and Jessie*. London: Bodley Head, 1985.

T. Hughes, *The Iron Man*. London: Faber, 1968.

P. Hutchins, *Rosie's Walk*. London: Bodley Head, 1969.

J. Mark, 'William's Version' in *Nothing to be Afraid Of*. London: Viking Kestrel, 1980.

'I wanna write jes like in dat book!': Talk and Its Role in the Shared Journal Experience
Amanda Branscombe and Janet Taylor

Justin's house burned
He couldn't help it.
Justin could have burned down too.
He's lucky.
They think somebody set it.
Then cops came and got 'em.
I came by Justin's house one day.
If it had been brick it wouldn't have burned.
My house is brick.
I'm sad for Justin cause his house burned.

This narrative was told by a six-year-old kindergarten child two months after he had written about this event in his shared journal (Taylor, 1984). It illustrates how he is using talk to contextualize the experience of his classmate and make it more a part of his own life (Britton, 1982b). He does this by reshaping the event for himself as well as others and by pulling it into his world through personalizing the meaning. He allows himself and the listeners the event's experience from the safety of what Britton refers to as the spectator role. In this role he is able to empathize with the tragedy, express relief that his friend was not harmed, provide commentary on the cause and prevention of such a tragedy, and assure himself that such a disaster could never happen to him ... 'My house is brick.'

This illustration highlights how one child, over the course of a year in which he participated in shared-journal writing, elaborated and refined his schemes about the composing process by using talk to develop perspective taking and to adapt to his social environment. The purpose of this chapter is to describe how the role of talk is used in shared-journal writing to construct knowledge about the system of writing, to learn to write, to decontextualize and contextualize discourse, and to form a supportive community so that these can occur.

Young children come to know the forms and functions of their oral language through continual interaction with significant members of their immediate social community. They use talk to test hypotheses they construct, and they refine their earlier schemes on the basis of the responses they get to that talk. Thus, children use constructive errors to progress through 'levels of wrongness' in talk as they apply rules related to the phonology, syntax, semantics and functions of their language. Through this process children gradually come to know and use the conventional 'adult-like' forms and functions of their language. This process is self-initiated and self-regulated and is motivated by their need to adapt to their social environment. The knowledge they construct and the level of understanding that they achieve by a certain age vary according to the personal character-istics of the child and the kind and quality of social interactions the particular environment allows.

Britton (1972) suggests that one of the ways talk functions in this process is in the shaping of the children's experience, so that they can better interpret that experience and learn from it. The incentive to do this is to share their experiences with significant members in their community. Britton asks:

Can this work with writing? Can the constant audience of the teacher and the even sharper shaping process that goes on when you write from experience – can this – continue to serve for the child as the talk with his parents has served him in infancy [p. 98]?

We think it can, particularly if we carry the notion of the constant audience one step further. If, within the context of the classroom, interactive talk is used as an incentive and a vehicle for drawing a story from experiences and reconstructing that story into modes of discourse (such as expressive writ-ing) and for developing perspective taking, then children can learn not only from their own experiences but also from those of their classmates. This is an essential step in writing and in building a sense of community.

However, none of our beliefs could be elaborated without the acceptance of the basic tenet that children actively construct knowledge about written forms of language long before they enter school (Dyson, 1984; Ferriero, 1984; Ferriero and Teberosky, 1982; Goodman, 1984; Mason, 1981). This constructive activity seems to be characterized by a search for regularity and order in the use of graphic symbols to represent meaning (Bissex, 1980; Chomsky, 1979; Clay, 1975; Read, 1971), for the means by which to make sense of familiar print found in the immediate environment (Goodman, 1984; Holdaway, 1979), and for the usefulness of print as a social instrument (Dyson, 1984; Harste, Woodard and Burke, 1984). The process children go through as they construct knowledge about written language parallels the process used in initial language learning. Here too they proceed through various levels of 'wrongness' and require some form of social interaction to confirm or reject the hypotheses they hold about the nature of written language. Here too the knowledge children have constructed and their level of understanding about written language varies according to their social environment and their own personal characteristics.

Unfortunately when children enter school at five years of age, they often find that the means they previously have used to construct knowledge about oral and written language are not acceptable in this new social environment. Rather, schools often promote values that conflict with this constructive process. For example, children are encouraged 'to think for themselves' and to do their own work. Copying other children's work is thought to be shameful and quiet behaviour is usually encouraged. These values certainly do not encourage children to interact and exchange viewpoints with each other or even to interact with the teacher except at her initiation or when given permission. Thus children encounter a very different model for learning about writing, a model that presupposes that all children have reached a certain level of understanding (Ferriero and Teberosky, 1982), yet favours only those children who have reached that level. For this reason many children cannot benefit from the kind of writing instruction found in today's kindergarten and first grade classrooms.

This problem exists because traditional kindergarten and first-grade curricula are not based on what we now know about how children learn. Rather, they employ strategies of an outmoded and inadequate theory (Kamii, 1985) and an organization of the writing content that reflects adult notions about which aspects of writing are the simplest and most easily learned (Ferriero and Teberosky, 1982). The emphasis is placed on the surface features of writing such as the movement from left to right and top to bottom, the forming of letters, and on initial consonant sound-symbol correspondences. Little attention is given to the process of composing and to the function of talk in learning to write.

Recent research on literacy has given rise to a number of innovations for writing in the early grades. Knowledge that children can and do write using invented spellings (Bissex, 1980; Chomsky, 1979; Giacobbe, 1971; Read, 1971) has led to the use of personal writing in a variety of forms such as individual poems and stories, language experience charts and personal or interactive journals. However, little attention has been given to how children learn to differentiate writing from drawing, how they come to know that writing carries a message, and how they come to know that graphemes correspond in some way to the phonemes of speech. Until children construct this kind of knowledge, until they become familiar with the finite set of symbols used in writing, and until they can form these symbols and know the rules that govern their use, they cannot engage in personal writing activities. Thus these newer practices seem to favour only those who have attained a certain level of understanding about the nature of written language. These newer approaches also put considerable emphasis on personal expressive writing and overlook the need for children to extend their own experiences through listening to and sharing in the experiences of others. Furthermore, even with the new approaches, most teachers attempt to present the conventional symbols to the child and to encourage children to trace and/or copy them.

Ferriero and Teberosky (1982) suggest:

We must let children write, even in a writing system different from the alphabetic one; we must let them write, not so they invent their own idiosyncratic system, but so they discover that their system is not the conventional one and in this way find valid reasons to substantiate their own hypotheses with our conventional ones [p. 227].

They also suggest that curricula be reconceptualized to allow for the 'constructive errors' that children make as they move through different hypotheses about how to write, and to account for the wide range of difference between children in their development of written language.

Because of our understandings of researchers' work like Ferriero and Teberosky, we believe that curricula need to be reconceptualized not only to allow for the above, but also to provide opportunities for children to use talk and writing as a means of adapting to their social environment. The practice we suggest is shared journal writing.

Shared Journal Writing: 'I did that before, too!'

Britton (1982b) notes that language regulates and coordinates children's behaviour with others and with information so that the children can shape systems of connections that transcend here-and-now experiences and move them and their messages to written forms of communication. Furthermore, he states that by giving children a place and time to talk about events we give them the means to shape those events in language so that the events become more accessible to the children's learning process. This kind of talk, Britton says, is the way we make sense of our experiences so that we store in memory the meaning we have come to attribute to those experiences.

Talk among peers is one way to get at the kinds of language use Britton finds necessary. This talk seems to occur best in classroom communities that allow peer–peer interaction and reciprocity in the Piagetian sense of cooperation.[1] During this talk in the classroom the teacher must diminish his/her role of authority, as Cazden (in press) notes, to the point at which he/she is an onlooker who observes rather than an active participant who orchestrates.

Shared-journal writing (see Appendix below), used in several school systems in the southern United States, is an attempt to maximize opportunities for exchanging viewpoints through talk in writing-related tasks. At the same time it is an attempt to provide opportunities for children to take on and come to know the perspective of others. This is accomplished in the following way.

Each child writes a journal that is a chronicle of real events in the lives of members of their particular classroom community. Each day the children negotiate and collectively decide on the one event that is to be recorded for that day and then each child writes his/her own version of that event. Within this process the opportunity for the exchange of viewpoints exists. Three or four possible topics are offered by class members for consideration. These topics may be events that relate to happenings in the classroom, such as a visit from a local doctor; they may be events significant to one individual, such as the losing of a tooth; or they may be family experiences, such as a grandmother having a heart attack. From the questions asked, as well as from the verbal and non-verbal responses received, children learn to differentiate those events that seem trivial and mundane, those that seem to have universal appeal and those that are individual and unique.

The protocols used in this chapter to illustrate how children use talk were gathered as part of a year-long study of 180 state school kindergarten children and their nine teachers who were involved in the shared-journal experience. The children and their teachers were randomly selected and represented the demographic characteristics of their small rural, mill community in the southeastern United States. The protocols reflect the discussions and writings of the ethnic, as well as social and economic, backgrounds of the community. Those protocols cited in this chapter represent a cross-section of the research population and include children from each of the nine classrooms rather than one group of children who represented the entire population.

The following protocols,[2] gathered in December 1986, demonstrate the schemes that some children have constructed about selecting topics for writing in their journals. The first protocol demonstrates the children's generalizing and exemplifying topics from their class discussions. It shows the 'Aha' response that bonds child to child as they recognize a mutual experience – losing a tooth!

R: What do you write about in your journals?
C: Everybody in our class.
C₂: Just good and bad.
C₃: Terrible.
C₄: Cutting off a finger ... like that.
R: Who cut their finger like that?
C₄: Larry, he almost cut if off like this [gestures] and pulling a tooth.
R: Who pulled a tooth?
C₄: Stan.
C₃: I did too. Right here.

The next two protocols show how children build on each other's responses in their efforts to ferret out what makes one topic better than another. They reveal that to suggest a topic for group consideration imposes a certain amount of risk taking, in that what the child offers may not be valued by the group.

The first transcription suggests that children construct hypotheses about what topics might be selected. Both view 'bad' events as likely possibilities, while one of them hopes that 'getting a new doll' is sufficiently unique.

C: Whoever gets the most votes wins. I sure hope they write about me cause I got a new doll.
R: What do you vote about?
C: About terrible stuff happen and good stuff happen. When I say terrible stuff I mean bad stuff.
C₂: You think it in your mind. You've got to figure out what bad.

The second transcription demonstrates how five children explain the reasoning they use when selecting a topic. Just as in the preceding protocol, these children view catastrophes where community members are powerless as the best topics, but they note that 'little things' can be written about on other days.

C₁: I like to write about everybody in my class.
C₂: Like Lisa cut her finger.
C₃: Ann got some new clothes.
C₄: My sister cut her finger with a hook.
R: How do y'all know when something is good to write about?
C₃: People might die or something.*
C₂: Cause it should be real important. We can write about little things like people going to places and all the next day.*
C₅: Like Tammy [a classmate] is not coming back.
C₂: Like on somebody's ... Justin's house got burned down.
C₁: ... I'm glad my sister's birthday is in July 13th.
C₄: If we had both of those, I'd write about Justin's house burned down. He couldn't help that.*

All three protocols seem to indicate that as the children discuss which topic is best for a journal entry, they struggle with their earlier experiences in relation to their present and future experiences. These play a role in their present ideas about power and its limits for the individual and the community, values held by the community, the role of human suffering and joy within the individual's life, and the connectedness of their experiences to the lives of the entire community. This consistent, ongoing construction of the community and its life occurs because of the need of a journal entry for the day – so that the community has a record of its existence on that day. With that historical record, they begin to develop an understanding of control and ownership over events in their lives which allows them to move to ownership of the more abstract aspects of their community life, such as time. Because the children talk with peers and the teacher about these matters before writing, they are not overwhelmed by their tasks. They can count on those members of their community to help them construct their view of what is significant or memorable by focusing their discussion so that they consider 'What is it that makes today most special?' or 'What is it that will most help us to remember today?'

As children engage in the selection process, they often disagree as to which topic makes the day memorable. They must argue and state the reasons for their decisions in order to convince others of the wisdom of that choice. Each child who has offered a topic has made a personal investment in the process and wants the sense of power and importance that comes from knowing that everyone in the class is writing about his/her selection; thus this strategy employs an aspect of social marking.[3]

The strategies that the children use to determine the specific topic for the day vary according to the kind of topics offered, the individual offering the topic and the degree of dissent that occurs. For example, on some days a classroom event can be so significant that the children all agree that it is the appropriate topic for the day. On other days the children may resolve initial differences of opinion through discussion and negotiation and eventually come to agree on the same topic. In this instance perspective taking provides opportunities for children to hear the points of view of others and perhaps to adjust their own thinking in accordance with what they hear. In order to reach agreement they have to take on the perspective of another classmate. This kind of discussion and negotiation causes children to recognize that those first events that they thought were unique to them also happen to others. There is also a reciprocal and sometimes asymmetrical aspect of perspective taking in that children come to know that if we can write about someone else's topic today, then we might write about ours tomorrow. Thus competition is diminished as the process continues, and the individuals in the community develop more sophisticated strategies for topic offering and topic selection. Most of the children began constructing their selection process with the strategy of either 'my topic is best and should be selected', 'my friend's topic is best and should be selected'; then, they move to a more collaborative strategy that considers what is important for the community. By year's end the children have constructed such a highly autonomous community that often they have negotiated and reached a consensus on the day's journal topic in informal discussion before school, rather than waiting for the teacher-assigned journal time during the school day.

The following protocol from early in the community's development (December, 1986) demonstrates how the children are beginning to reject the notion that they select topics of importance on the basis of friendship. It also shows that when through negotiation they cannot resolve which topic is best, they vote and write on the topic that receives the majority vote. Finally, it explains, from their perspective, how the voting process works. Before the interviewers had even seated the children, the first child opened the interview.

C: They haven't wrote about me yet!
R: [to another child] Have they written about you?
C₂: They wrote about me on my birthday.
R: They did! Well, that's a special day. How do you decide what to write about each day?
C: We have to choose each other.
R: You choose each other. How do you do that? Tell me more about that.
C₂: We ask questions.
R: You ask who?
C₂: You ask the people you be writin' about.
C: We get three people to give [offer the topic].
R: What helps you decide who you're going to vote for?
C: Yourself.
R: How do you decide about yourself?
C₂: Think the most to write about.
R: Do you just vote for your friends?
C: Vote for your friends.*
C₂: No you don't.

While voting solves the problem of which topic to write about, it creates a kind of conflict for those who did not choose to write on that topic. In these instances the vote, reflecting the opinion of the majority of the class, forces them to deal with another point of view. Thus journal-writing procedures provide a variety of means for coordination of points of view between children that serve as a source for later individual coordination in that the individual must consider the story, the discussion and the vote in his/her writing.

The next two protocols are from group interactions during the initial sharing part of the shared journal. They demonstrate how the children negotiate their topic, build on each other's talk and create strategies that build the information needed for the community's record through their individual writing. Although the interactions and outcomes (as far as what was picked for the journal topic) are different, the children follow similar patterns in constructing the meaning of the event. The first strategy seems to be that the children 'stake their claim' that the topic is significant enough to be selected as the most memorable event of the day in their life and the lives of their peers. To varying degrees they do this through the structure of their presentations (narration or exposition), the openings of those presentations (fluidity and clarity), their answers to peers' questions and elaborations of those answers when necessary. The second strategy seems to develop around their taking responsibility for the management of the community in terms of turn-taking, respect for the questioner's need to know (information as well as levels of specificity about that information) and nonjudgemental recognition of any peer's question or statement. In return the community shows respect for that 'claim staking' by offering empathetic statements and by sanctioning its members when they repeatedly ask the same question, use inappropriate language, or challenge the importance or significance of the event before the appropriate time. By approaching the group interactions in these ways the children build their community, make it cohesive and live within it.

The first protocol demonstrates how one child's personal narrative becomes reconstructed by the community through his telling and their questioning of the event. As the community adds their perspectives and emotions to the narrative, they gain ownership of it and later select it for the topic to be written about that day.

N: ... a hill. There was dirt under the leaves and I was going down it. I started from my pavement and then went down it. I saw that tree and I couldn't turn my bike. I was going too fast, and then I ran into it.

C_1: Did it hurt?

C_2: Why're you go outside and ride your bike?

N: Oh, cuz I wanted to. [Laughter]

C_3: Why'd you want to go down that hill?

N: I was just going to go down to my house on my bike.

C_4: How'd you fall?

N: I didn't fall. Mmmm – my bike fell over when it hit the tree.

C_5:   Did the tree fall? [Laughter]

N: It was too hard. I was harder. [More laughter]

C_6:   Yes – me too. Like when – like when that – *

C_1:   Noam, Noam, did the bike break?

N: What?

C_1:   Did the bike tore up?

C_7:   Just talk. Don't say bike, Chris.

C_8:   Hey Noam, what colour was your bike?

N: It was red.

C_3:   Oh, oh, a coloured one.*

C_4:   Did your bike tear up?

C_1:   That's what I just asked him.*

C_9:   Did it have training wheels on it?

C_4:   Sorry [to child who said, 'That's what I just asked him.']

C_8:   Was it a big – was it a big wheel?

N: No, it was about two – about that high. [Gestures –]

C_1:   Oh, that must be – did it have a lot of [makes motion] …*

N: [Directs his attention to adjacent child, dialogue inaudible]

C_8:   Was it a four wheel?

N;   No.

C_9:   A bike …

N: … with pedals.

C_1:   Noam.

C_8:   I did that before too!*

C_1:   Noam.

N: I almost ran up the tree. [Laughter]

C_1:   Noam, did the tyre get flat?

C_{10}:   I said that.

C_{11}:   I said that first.

C_{12}:   I said that.

C_8:   Did it just go out? Did it – did the tyre – did the tyre bust? – little – little pieces?

N: No, my back tyre went flat.

C_{11}:   Did you cry?

N: No, I just said, 'What? How did that happen?'

C_9:   Noam, uh Noam, Noam, I say, did any rubber burn? Like when ya hit the ground real fast rubber sets on the ground.*

C_{10}:   Do you mean it burns like burn my hand?*

C_9:   Uh uh, when ya burn rubber that means it goes [sound] and starts spinning off. Then you burn rubber.*

C_{13}:   Did you get – off your bike to fall – to stop on braking?

N: I don't have any brakes on my bike. [Several oohs and ahs]*

C_{14}:   Oh that must be – that did hurt – I know that.*

C_9:   I have brakes*

C_{14}:   Cuz I have – it hurt.*

This protocol demonstrates the children's use of repetition, elaboration and questioning as they identify significant objects, details of the setting and sequence of events, and make connections between those. At times they elaborate through definition (burn rubber) which helps peers understand their view. At other times they personalize ('Oh, that must be ... that did hurt ... I know that'). And at other times they clarify ('Why're you go outside and ride the bike?'). All of these are necessary for children as they take meaning from a discourse (in this case, an oral discourse).

The journal entries that follow this interaction (Figures 1a-c) demonstrate that the children used most of the information they gained from the interaction both in the detail they used to produce the picture and the words they chose to construct their written message. For example, all of the children outlined their bikes in red or orange, showed some kind of hill and tree, and included this kind of detailed information in their writing.

The second protocol presents an incident where children question the reality of the event offered and thus doubt the sincerity of the speaker. When the child attempts to offer her personal narrative, her peers shift it to a

(a)

Figure 1   Journal entries about Noam's narrative. (a) Noam rode around the street until he fall. (b) Noam fell on a tree. (c) I wrote about me running into a tree.

*l Noam faLon atee BIc
Thu rsddys march 5p 1987

(b)

Thursday
March
1987

i Ro
BAT
me
rohu
No TOAhie

(c)

discussion about planting seeds and collecting honey from flowers. This protocol demonstrates a high level of conflict between the children with regard to the importance of the topic offering, the fallacies in the child's presentation and the community's sanction of a topic offering which possibly violates their values about honesty. This conflict reaches such a pitch that the children call in the teacher for more information. They did not select this topic as the one to be written about in their journals.

A:	It, uh, my mama wanted some flowers and we went to the woods to get those flowers while I was feeling better.
C_1:	You were –
T:	Jane, wait.
C_2:	I don't think that's important.
C_3:	Well, we can write – we can vote on it.
A:	She jis wanted some flowers, Kenny.
C_4:	Why did she need some?
C_5:	I know.
A:	To go in her flowerbed.
C_6:	To plant em? If you had some flowers and put em in . . . and put em in dirt then they'll fall out. You gotta put some seeds . . . cause it wouldn't have any roots.
C_7:	And honey. Honey belongs to the bees.
C_8:	Bees might be in there.
C_7:	Not honey. That's where honey lives – in flowers.
C_6:	Hu uhuh. They –
C_8:	They only live in honey flowers. Bees . . . um . . . live in honey flowers – Not in – no
C_2:	Honey suckers – only bees get honey suckers – What – what's got honey in it. Don't they, Mrs Calvin?
T:	Only bees get honey suckers – honey suckers?
C_8:	No.
T:	What do you think about that, John?
C_9:	I think they get it out of everyone that had been got some out.
T:	You think they find honey everywhere they – in the flowers? Or do you think they make the honey?
All:	They make the honey.
T:	That's why we get honey bees, isn't it? They take the things from the flowers and they make the honey. Y'all have any more questions to ask Anne?
All:	No
T:	All right then, Ann, sit down. We'll vote on Ann and Joe.

These children use the same strategies as in the first protocol to take meaning from the oral discourse. Because their discussion moves into the transactional voice, they engage in more synthesis and analysis of the information than in the first protocol (a personal narrative). The conversation also focuses more on the 'wrongness' or 'rightness' of the community's construction of the available information.

Unlike more typical kinds of sharing time events (Cazden, in press), these discussions indicate that children regulate themselves and match their expectations of good writing topics with their peers, rather than with the teacher or teacher-modelled format. Furthermore, they have the place and time to experience how to select a good topic, present it to their peer community and construct answers for each others' questions. They also have a place to shape questions that gather more information, point out inconsistencies and order that information so that they and their peers can better understand the topic's potential as a journal entry. This phase of shared-journal writing is the self-initiated, self-regulatory activity that helps children come to know what events in their lives are of interest to others; it continually builds their sense of community and develops a robust oral discourse that leads them to their written discourse about those events.

Talk During Individual Writing Time: 'They haven't wrote about me yet!'

As children begin their chronicling of the day's topic in their journals, they engage in spontaneous commentary-like talk with their peers at the writing table. This talk manifests itself in two distinct forms, parallel and collaborative, which seem to serve a number of heuristic functions for children. One function is the children's problem solving about the mechanics of writing, such as how to make letters, design their pictures or spell words. The second function served by talk is the differentiation and clarification of the information the children gathered during the earlier oral discourse. The third focuses on the way children deal with interpersonal relationships and their use of community property and space.

It seems that, as children use spontaneous talk in problem-solving situations, they again must coordinate the others' perspectives and information with their own. This external coordination seems to advance individual coordination and the child's knowledge about the nature of written language.

The following protocols from four small groups show the children's use of talk to help them explain their processes in shaping their journal's discourse. As these children problem solve, they use what Britton (1982b) calls 'the cumulative process of shaping and evaluating which gets things done'.

The first protocol (January 1987) demonstrates the power a child feels when her topic offering has been selected for the day. It also shows her taking the role of audience, who is monitor and evaluator of the other children's writing, which is a unique reciprocal function for both the child as writer and as audience.

C: We're writing about me today, Stan. My sister's name is Val. V-A-L. Write on here.

C_2: How about me? I'm doin' my journal.

C_3: I'm finished.

C: [to a new child who enters the group] You know what we're writin' about?

C_4: Yea.

C: Who?

C_4: You.

C: Get pencil and paper. [Spells her name for child] Do you see my brother's name is Dan. Then mine . . . [to another child who's writing] That's pretty good Lois.

C_5: What?

C: That pretty good. Make some circles to be his feet.

C_5: I already made 'em.

C: Make the table blue.

The second protocol (January 1987) shows one child helping another child with the mechanics of constructing written symbols and spelling. This peer teacher helps her classmate by dealing with the community members' property, demonstrating how to make a letter, offering a metaphorical relationship as visual imagery, making her own writing strategies explicit for the other child, and finally offering a model.

C: How do you draw a R?

C_2: This is my journal, ain't it?

C: Is this your journal?

C_2: OK. See a R. You get a straight line and then you go across. And then you do another one. Right? But, now put S.

C: How you write S?

C_2: See how a snake crawls like a [gestures] and go round. Oh yea, you go like that. No! T-I-N-A.

C: T! How do you make a T?

C_2: I.

C: How do you write a I?

C_2: Circle. Straight line. I put a little dot on top. You put a i. You put a A.

C: Did I do it?

C_2: N . . . You know how to make a N, don't you?

C: No.

C_2: Look at your date and copy the date.

During this time there was no teacher intervention to force interaction, so any cooperation, collaboration and/or conflict that occurred was completely spontaneous.

The third protocol (April 1987) has been included to demonstrate how other children use one classmate's spelling process to help them with the construction of their own spelling processes. According to Cazden (in press), children often serve as change agents in others' learning processes. These children freely admit that they cannot spell yet but can 'mock' mimic or copy their classmate, which in turn helps them. Because their classmate offers several strategies, models her process and reads *their present spellings so that they too communicate meaning*,* the other children are able to use her as a source to continue to develop their own systems of conventional spelling.

R: Tell me something. How did you figure out how to sound out words?
C: Sound the letters like sssss [makes the s sound] is s.*
R: Well, how did you figure out how to spell your writing?
C₂: Beth [C]knowed her.
C₃: We just ... sound it out. Beth knowed how and we mock her.*
C₂   See, my sister knows ... don't know how.
C₃: She [C] don't know how to spell 'Dear Parents'. She don't know how.
C: See, like when I was trying to spell 'stop' ... I just learned it cause I know I looked on the stop, stop sign and stop sign ... I don't ever look at it no more, and I still know it. S-T-O-P. And I not even looking at it.*
R: Beth, the other children say they use you to help them spell. How did you learn to spell?
C: I know how to spell uh school.
R: How?
C: S-C-H-O-O-L.
R: Right. Well, did you learn words that helped you make ... I mean, did you learn certain words first ... or what?
C: I learned 'cat' and 'dog' and 'cow' and uh animals like that and 'horse' first and 'house' and then names and like that and then uh I'm coming into bigger words. I thought myself into bigger words.*
R: And do you sound them out when you do that or do you learn ...
C: I sound them out and keep writin' em until I get it right.*
C₂: Everybody loves Beth.*
R: Well! Is it OK to spell part of a word in your journal or do you have to spell the whole word?
C₄: ... It tell you that you didn't know how to spell it good.
C₂: It [first letter] sound like the first word.
C₃: I know how to spell 'Dear Parents'.
C: You can just put the first letter and tell Mrs Carter ... Sometimes Kathy puts an e. Like when she's using 'the' she'll put a V for the T (she makes t sound) T ... in place of it.*

   The fourth protocol (April 1987) is of an entire group interaction as they write their journal entry for the day. It demonstrates how these children contextualize the oral discourse and construct it as a written discourse. It also demonstrates how the children deal with their fellow community members' property.

C_1: Clarrisa, how do you spell your name?
C_2: C-l-a-r-i-s-s-a.
C_3: How do you spell Clarissa?
C_2: C-l-a-r-i-s-s-a.
C_4: S-s-e.
C_3: Let me show you! Not s-s-e! S-s-a!
C_4: S-s ...
C_5: I want to see your journals. Let me see your journal, Susan.
C_4: C-a. Is it C-a-s-s-a?
C_6: How do you spell your name, Clarissa?
C_3: There it is right there!
All: [In unison] OK ... Oh! [then offer random letters from her name.]
C_4: C-l-i-s-s-a.
C_2: L!
C_5: S-s-s.
C_6: C-l. c-l. c-l ...
C_5: A-s-s ...
C_1: C-a ...
C_4: How do you spell 'school'?
C_6: S-s-a-a-s-p ...
C_4: You tried 'space', didn't you?
C_6: No, that says 'school'.
C_4: Oh!
C_7: What's the name of those flowers? [These had been mentioned during Sharing Time.]
C_4: Daffodils.
C_7: Daffodils?
C_5: Not uh ...
C_3: Buttercups!
C_4: How should I know which ones they are?
C_7: Do you?
C_4: Why did you ask that question anyway?
C_3: Daffodils.
C_7: I'm gonna copy yours. I'm not gonna write 'Steele'.
C_4: You know what Clarissa's ... Clarissa stole my uh party ...[Laughter]*
C_7: Clarissa stole my party. [More laughter]
C_3: Clarissa stole my baby ... kidnapped my baby.
C_1: Clarissa stealed me.
C_5: How did she steal?
C_7: Cause her name ... Cause her name is Clarissa Steele.
C_1: Clarissa steal my pencil.
C_5: Clarissa didn't do nothing cause she's still painting.
C_7: Karen, I got a clock thing like you got.
C_5: One at a time.
C_4: S-t-a-s-t-l-e.
C_5: I know ... I know what they is cause she tole me. They called ... uh, daffodils.
C_7: No, they're not.
C_4: They're not. They're called ... Let me think of the name.

C_5: Quit pickin' em.
C_4: They're called piedmont. They're called piedmont.
C_6: Piedmont.
C_5: That one!
C_1: I didn't. I didn't broke it. Somebody else did.
C_5: Somebody broke a pencil. Somebody broke a pencil.
C_7: How do you spell 'of'?
C_2: You look at that ... right there ...
C_5: You look at that one.
C_3: There's a broke pencil.
C_4: Look at what I got, Karen.
C_7: Who had some of these pencils with numbers?
C_4: John.
C_7: Then this is your pencil ... [discussion about pencil continues]
C_7: How do you spell 'they've'?*
C_3: 'They've ... 'mave' ...
C_4: You spell it like 'mave'.
C_3: 'Crave' ...
C_4: You know how to spell 'mave'?
C_7: How do you spell 'mave' and 'crave'?
C_4: Then spell 'they've'.
C_5: You're not suppose to write more than that ... Clarissa.
C_4: Listen! Clarissa Steele stole my party.
C_7: Clarissa Steele stole my cake.
C_3: Clarissa Steele stole my swimming pool.
C_6: Clarissa Steele stole my uh girlfriend house.
C_4: Clarissa Steele stole my girlfriend.
C_1: ... my girlfriend. That's what John said.
C_7: Clarissa Steele took my girlfriend to Florida.
C_5: What's the name of the flower?
C_4: I'm gonna' use this.
C_3: Uh, uh ... daffodils.
C_5: It's not a daffodil.
C_6: Azalea.
C_7: Azalea ... a-do-do ... azalea ... a-do-do ...*
C_4: A-do-do ...
C_5: Azalea ... azalea ... azalea ...
All: [unison] Zzzzzzz
C_7: How do you spell 'pretty'?
C_2: Pppp [makes sound]
C_7: Pretty?
C_4: Remember ... Mrs Black ...
C_3: You know what p and s spells.
C_5: How do you spell 'azalea'?
All: [Several children begin to make zea sounds]
C_4: Listen to this ...
C_7: Pretty.
C_3: ... zea, zea, zea ... azalea ...

C_7: I can spell 'pretty'.

C_2: Pink.

C_7: P-e ... p ... peddy ... ped ...

C_4: He spell 'pretty'.

C_1: Pretty.

C_5: He spell yucky!

C_1: I want a B.

C_5: Shut up.

C_1: What we write about?

C_4: Karen, look at my leg.

C_3: Zea ... zea ...

C_6: Look at that.

C_4: Put some lipstick on her.

C_6: Yea! Put some lipstick on her.

C_7: And she did!

C_4: She did put some lipstick.

C_3: My boyfriend comes over to my house.

C_5: I'm putting some.

C_4: Colour eyes, colour eyes ...

C_5: What colour are your eyes?

C_4: What colour are your eyes?

C_2: Brownish-green.

C_5: Brownish and green.

C_4: Say brown ... make 'em brown.

C_1: Zea ... zea ...

C_7: Clarissa Steele brought a pink azalea.

During this discussion, the children used language play about names ('Steele' and 'azalea') and spellings ('mave', 'crave', 'they've') seemingly to help them in constructing ways to use their information for prompting memory and for enjoying sounds of language. Through the coordination of language functions and their choices of collaborative or parallel talk, these children were able to differentiate their information, order it, get new information when they saw parts that needed more specificity, and finally construct a product that had experienced evaluative comments throughout the process and could communicate a message that others understood.

Journal entries from the children who engaged in this spontaneous talk as they wrote are shown in Figures 2a–d. As one can see, they used the group's information and either chose 'flower' or 'azalea' to name the flower Clarissa brought to the class. One also used the spelling for pretty ('ped') and the rhyming association strategy for spelling 'they've' ('vay'). One final point worth noting is that they concentrated more on the written message for chronicling this event.

☆Tuesday April 14, 1987
Cliríssa Stíllbrt
ZLY.

(a)

☆Tyesday April 14, 1987.

I BT Sm Zy Z and vy vvs pte

And I Td Mrs Bc mh

(b)

Figure 2 Journal entries written by the children about the flowers that Clarissa brought to class. (a) Clarissa Steele brought azalea.
(b) I brought some azaleas and they was pretty and I told Mrs Blackman that she could have them. (c) Clarissa Steele brought azaleas and they was pretty.
(d) Clarissa brought a beautiful flower.

TUesday April 14 1987
   Clarissastill Broughe
A h and vay way
Ped.

(c)

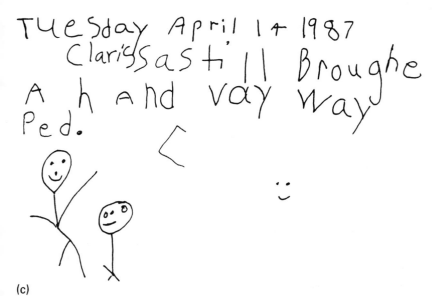

#tuesday April 14
87

Clarissa brought a beauti
                        Flower.

(d)

Some Final Thoughts on Shared Journal Writing: 'You gotta ... you gotta, you gotta make good stories'

The children's talk offered information to the researchers as we explored the role of social interaction in written discourse and in the formation of a community. It gave us clues in understanding how and what the children came to know. It also helped us understand how a child's internal constructions of knowledge developed autonomy for that child which allowed him/her to function as a valued member of his/her community. Finally, it led us to the opinion that the curriculum practice of shared-journal writing acts as a bridge from oral discourse to written discourse in narrative, expository and poetic forms. Because of the talk, the community and the shared writing, the children were able to make meaning from a context (be it learning environment, learning process, relationships, play productions, textbook, work book or story). We believe that the collective or mutual knowledge (Newman, 1986) aspect of the journal entry is the impetus for this meaning-making ability. It occurs in talk and then writing, which allows each child to know what all the other children are writing about and to evaluate how they are constructing both writing systems and written messages in comparison to his or hers.

Thus it was not surprising to us that by year's end these kindergarten children had begun to include journal-entry topics about published stories they had seen presented (puppet shows, plays) and had had read to them. Nor was it surprising that they were discussing and writing about these texts in the transactional voice that negotiates the text by evaluating it, pointing out ideas, events and characters, and then summarizing it. These children had had a place (shared-journal practice) to be both writer and audience, reader and respondent, so that they were able to pull this new literature into their worlds and own it just as they had with the child's reportage of Justin's house burning.

The last set of journal entries (May 1987) presents the children's first attempts at contextualizing literature from writing that came from an impersonal, unheard voice and an unknown face outside their community. In the first two entries the children seem to focus on identifying the kind of character the story uses (rabbits), the number of characters and the main character's name (Buttercup). For them, this identifying aspect is an essential connection for reconstructing the story for themselves and calls the story 'into existence' in the here and how (Britton, 1971). One child not only identified the kind of characters used, the number used, but named all of them and offered one event in the plot's action ('One went into the woods'). This child seems to coordinate identity (the rabbit) with a key event in his reconstruction of the story which moves his entry from here and now to a historical present – one that was constructed in another's imagination but can, through events described in words, be called back to the present (Britton, 1971) (see Figures 3a-c).

The last set of journal entries shows how children contextualize a piece of literature that had been presented as a puppet show. Just as with the preceding entries, the first child's commentary identifies the characters and their roles in the story. He does add an object (lamp) the story's main character uses, but his connections focus on identification rather than action, present rather than historical present. The second child identifies the kind of performance (puppet show) which frames her summary. Although she does not name the characters, she does offer a general summation of the key event in the story (boy marries princess). Her summary seems to indicate that she has reconstructed the story's plot for

(a)

Figure 3   The children's first attempts at contextualizing literature. (a) The little rabbit she named was Buttercup and she had 7 babies. (b) Buttercup rabbit had babies. The babies called a rabbit. (c) The little rabbit. His name was Buttercup. He had 7 babies and he named them Sunday, Monday, Tuesday, Wednesday, Thursday, Friday, Saturday. One went into the woods.

(b)

(c)

herself (see Figure 4) and has made meaning of it. The third child offers a detailed summary that includes the fact that she had seen this story which had characters. She notes key events and adds a commentary to the ending ('happily ever after'). Her journal entry suggests that she has complete ownership of the story and had reconstructed it for herself. Her comment to her teacher as she read this entry also shows that she has recognized conventional writing and hopes to produce it herself. When writing this entry about the puppet show, she pointed to a nearby book and said, 'I wanna write jes like in dat book!'

Critics of the shared-journal practice could attempt to reduce it to nothing more than a chronicling of children's gossip that does not allow children the freedom to pick their own topics. We maintain that such chronicling of daily events (which is really a child's community's history book) is close to the informal end of the spectator role's continuum, which

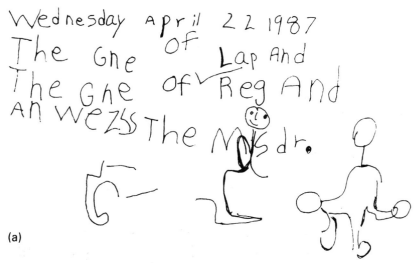

(a)

Figure 4   Contextualization of literature presented in a puppet show. (a) The genie of the lamp and the genie of the ring and Aladdin was the master. (b) We saw a puppet show and it had a boy and the boy was going to marry the princess. (c) We saw a puppet show. We saw a story about a puppet. And his lamp genie visited Aladdin. (He) had it (the lamp) to marry (the) princess and he went away mad. His uncle (came) but it was a wicked (man) and he got it. They lived happily ever after.

(b)

★ Wednesday April 22, 1987

mrq+y PS iS.
We 5d ʌ +y PT Sw and it Hd q BY
and tY BУ WS Gn to

(b)

★ Wедо-y April 22, 198

We went
W ewd 's
saw
And Za p, sT So
show
r a p
a
puppet

and
a n d
he got it.
h G n
They lived happily ever after.
d L hvar
his
h s z
uncle (came)
a c L
but it was wicked (man)
bT II wz a wKd
a
(He) had
d
(the lamp)
it to marry (the) princess
h a e T I M
and he went away mad.
F z z A n d re w he wava M d.
puppet. And
n r T. A n d
his ∟ lamp
genie visited
h z 6 a v v
Aladdin.
h u z I T 4 n t
We saw a
We Saw a
story about a
sTory a bou T a

(c)

has at its most formal end all the components and resources of literature (Britton, 1982b). D. W. Harding suggests:

What takes place informally in a chat about events is in essence similar to what is achieved by a work of fiction or drama. 'True or fictional, all of these forms of narrative invite us to be onlookers joining in the evaluation of some possibility of experience' [1962, p. 138].

The children who engaged in the shared-journal practice moved back and forth on the spectator role's continuum. They functioned as equal collaborators who were listeners, writers, readers, talkers, evaluators and builders. They focused on the meaningfulness of their lives and the lives of their fellow community members. From this they gained a sense of control and connectedness over their past, an ownership over their present worlds and hope for possibilities in their futures.

The following journal writing from one class seems a fitting place to end. The children chose it over another child's mother having a baby (a sure win on past voting occasions):

March 3, 1987
Yesterday Tommy's mom took him to the dentist to get his teeth cleaned. Mary's mama cleaned them for him.

This event might seem insignificant to us in our adult worlds, but to the children it was what reflected the values of their community and the memorable events of that day – that Tommy is a brain-damaged, lower-class black child, and Mary is a bright middle-class white child, and that Tommy offered this event seems to show the bridge of equality and connectedness in these children's lives. How they prize that connectedness is a memorable lesson and event for all.

Appendix: The Shared Journal

A shared journal is a chronicle of events in the lives of the children in a particular classroom. The process of shared journal writing includes the following steps.

1. Negotiation and collaborative selection of writing topic based on what children deem most significant to mark the day in memory.
2. Recording topic on appropriate page in journal using representational forms available to the child – usually drawing and/or some stage of writing.
3. 'Reading' their journal entries to each other and to the teacher.

4. Sharing selected entries of special interest to total class.
5. At month's end, sharing journal entries with parents.
6. After their return, using journals for a variety of problem-solving situations, such as determining the numbers of days from the time a tooth is lost until the appearance of a new tooth.

Notes

1. Cooperation is defined as 'any interaction between two or more individuals who are, or believe themselves to be equal ... any interaction in which there is no element of authority or prestige' (Piaget, 1976, p. 67, cited in Doise and Mugny, 1984, p. 21). According to Piaget, 'Cooperation between individuals in fact remains the first of a series of forms of behaviour which are important for the constitution and development of logic' (Piaget, 1960, p. 163, cited in Doise and Mugny, 1984, p. 21).
2. The protocols for this paper would not have been possible without the help of the children and their teachers. We extend a special thanks to those children and their teachers: J. Bice, D. Blackmon, M. Boos, S. Caver, M. McClelland, B. Sharman, E. Slaughter, J. Terrell and B. Thompson. We also want to express our deepest appreciation to the school system and the principal, R. Wagoner, for allowing us to work with the teachers and children.

Transcription key is R = researcher, C = child, T = teacher. Asterisks are used to help the reader locate key points within the dialogues. Transcriptions hold true to the child's use of syntax, but not to his/her phonology.
3. 'Social marking examines the causal intervention of social regulations as norms in cognitive development. This notion refers to links which exist between social relations in an interaction between individuals in a given situation and the cognitive relations inherent in certain properties of objects which mediate the social relationships' (Doise and Mugny, 1984, p. 30).

Part Three Coming to Terms with the World

A variety of factors have insisted that English teachers in the eighties re-create and re-establish the nature of their activity. English teachers are no different from other teachers in this, but they have perhaps a greater reason to feel the need to articulate anew some of the central dilemmas of secondary schooling in the eighties. They have, more than most, suffered from the squeezing of resources resulting from decline in public spending and falling birth rates. They have been one of the principal targets within the school system for a strident critique of the ways in which schooling relates to society, the economy, employment. More than most, too, they have been forced to come to terms with the changing nature of the school as a multicultural community.

One can see in the articles that follow some of these concerns and critiques becoming appropriated. Mike Torbe accepts the critique of language in relation to the real world on its own terms, and seeks to demonstrate that, properly conceived, language competence is as broad as English teachers have maintained, and that working with language in the world is a complex matter which is embedded in relationships. Implicit in this argument is the awareness that, for the development of young people, the actual contexts and purposes of linguistic activity need somehow to be reproduced in the educational process. To the extent that this has not happened in the past, the force of the critique can be acknowledged, but far from altering the main thrust of the teachers activity such approaches actually reinforce it. This echoes Peter Medway's perception that the English teacher's emphasis on the subjective and individual and the exclusion of the empirical may restrict and fragment the coming to terms with the world. It is, in his account, the participation of the young person in the adult world that is both extending and satisfying: language in 'motivated use'. Harold Rosen explores that most fundamental of human social and socializing activity, the telling of stories, and Claire Woods the role of autobiography as an aspect of language across the curriculum.

Tony Burgess takes up the question of 'difference' to consider whether the models of language development put forward by Britton and others need to be revised in modern circumstances and in the face of modern critiques. He thinks not, but is concerned that the models of language development, curriculum and process are in danger of becoming distorted, principally through a lack of 'history'. The paradigms do not change, though they may become expressed differently within the same humane context.

It is right that this section should close with teacher training, a process which needs to reflect so precisely the values and philosophies with which we seek to imbue education in the future. Arthur Applebee sees some discontinuities between what we know about learning and what we practice in teaching teachers to teach. In seeking to resolve these disjunctions, he argues for a model of 'reflective' teaching which is capable of transforming the vision of teacher as professional. His argument closes a circle on the first three sections of this book by returning to the scaffolding metaphor with which Courtney Cazden opened and to our conception of learning itself.

In Part Two the style of the teaching enterprise is striking: it is patient, sympathetic and closely observed. The teacher is certainly there and there is an accompanying style and voice, but the focus is intensely on the child. In the pieces that follow the teacher in some sense becomes an actor in a more positive way, still teaching, but also engaging with the world in a way that is parallel with the growing awareness of young people. The teacher acts and argues, asserts values and claims priorities.

Places for Evolving Autobiography: English Classes at Work in the Curriculum
Claire Woods

My story begins 2 years ago. It was one day in May 1982; my family and I were in our lounge. Everyone was very sad because it was the time for me to leave (escape from Vietnam). It was the fourth time I had tried. The last three attempts were not successful, but in my soul I was thinking 'I will make it this time'. We all cried. I kissed my mum, my grandpa, my grandmother, my brothers and sisters for the last time. Then I went out with my uncle to the bus station. We were going to catch the bus to Nha Tnang (the city near the beach). I did not let any of my friends know about it.

After 2 days living in Nha Tnang in my uncle's house, a strange man came to us and took us with him. We were taken to his home, and that night, we and five other people had to wade across a stream and get on a small boat. It took us to a deserted island. We were there for six days to wait for other people to come. Every night, more and more people came and on the sixth night, we decided to leave. The boat we used to escape was only about 12 metres long and 3 metres wide.

It was a cold, dark night and it was raining. We were all wet and cold but we were happy that we were leaving. We caught rainwater in a big tank because the amount of water we had was very little. That rainwater would help us a lot.... .

That night, when we were ready to sleep, we heard one of the men's voices shout, 'Ship! Everyone wake up – ship is coming for us.' We all woke up and looked where he pointed. I could see a lot of light very far away from us, but it was coming closer and closer. We were all happy. Mr Giang, our group's leader said, 'Write down in diary – 9.25 p.m., 25/5/82 – we saw first ship.' He was so excited. We all hoped that they would be very surprised to see us in this little boat and they would rescue us. We used a big piece of cloth and burnt it to make a signal. 'Bad manners,' someone said. 'That's all right, everyone calm down,' Mr Giang said. 'There must be a reason why they didn't rescue us. We are not out of the Vietnamese sea frontier. We will see a lot of ships tomorrow' [extract from an account by Long, fifteen years old][1].

'Boy! Your life isn't as boring as I thought it was,' I said to my father as I was writing down the last few words of his explanation.

'I've never really asked you much about your life but I sure am glad I asked you today because at least now I have an insight on an incident in your past.'

The year is 1965 in Ville Literno, Naples, Italy. My father, Giusseppe P – is eighteen. He is getting ready to board the ship that is going to take him to Adelaide, Australia.

It is the first of May and a lovely spring day at that. His parents walk with him down to the Naple's dock where they will see him off. Joe, my dad, studies the scenery for one last look as he walks down to the dock [extract from an account by Pierina, fifteen years old][2].

I cannot resist the autobiographical. When I read or hear people telling their stories, I am constantly fascinated and drawn into their worlds and experiences. I am propelled into ways of speaking or listening that I have not tried before. I become an invited watcher through a crack in the door opened for me.

Not so long ago a friend who is a committed spare-time writer of short stories invited me to the door of her family history when she asked me to read her fictionalized account of her great grandmother's life. The account is based on the many tales, anecdotes, snippets of family information, scandal, secrets and quiet whisperings she has heard from many relatives throughout her own life. It is accompanied by the old family photo album in which great grandmother, severely prim in black, seems still to admonish the family from her sepia portrait. I read my friend's words and through the door I went, to visit another family, in another time and another place.

Pierina and Long invited their teachers and classmates into their lives and families with their narratives which begin this chapter. They are of different times, places and ways of living and being. They are members of classes we teach.

This year eleven students (sixteen to seventeen year olds) with whom I currently share some time recently began an exploration of other people's lives by reading short stories, diary extracts, letters, oral histories and autobiographical accounts. After this flood of versions of others' lives, they eased with varying degrees of bravado and sensitivity into writing a focused account of one remembered incident in their own lives or a fictionalized version of an event in someone else's life, for example, that of their grandfather or grandmother. The autobiographical or biographical piece was to be stretched towards the fictional and shaped with a focus on the incident, an object, a person or an emotion. The intention was to draw the students into the quite difficult assignment of shaping a fiction in a particular way. In fact it was to make a mountain out of a molehill, as Graham Little (1987) has described the making of autobiography. 'Autobiography's first move,' he writes, 'is to make a mountain out of a molehill. Especially the life of the nonentity whose laundry list has to be inflated into a Magna Carta.' He continues:

Everyone should write one; indeed, should write lots, like painters repeatedly approaching the same subject. It's a comforting form of fiction. To shape one's own history, to arrange a bespoke background, to have a life at last, is a kind of snuggling down and dressing up at the same time.

We attempted to recognize the fiction inherent in autobiography and then to capitalize on it and extend it through talking and writing; indeed, to weave language with serious intent.

Our lives and those of our students are spun in words. There is no tie on time or place for such spinning. Professional writers and raconteurs know this only too well. Their chosen craft is word spinning, snatching the main threads and offcuts of their own and others' lives and shaping them for us to read or hear. The rest of us do not choose to craft as formally perhaps, but we do construct our lives with narratives. The child racing home to tell someone the dramatic moment of the school day; each of us turning to a friend to recount *our* version of an event; individuals offering their individual interpretations of and feelings about the headline news – 'I feel so sad for …', 'it reminds me of …', 'you can't believe it, can you?', 'remember when …', the cues to narratives and anecdotes of personal lives. They are also the narratives of lives shared in time and place. In these narratives is a meeting ground of the personal and the social, the individual and the shared, the private and the public.

They are narratives from individuals in their worlds and their cultures. A personal narrative is a cultural narrative, spun as it is within the understandings, traditions, ways of knowing, ways of speaking into which each of us is born and in which we each live and grow. We are constantly evolving our own autobiographies and thus constructing consciously and unconsciously our individual versions of ourselves and the pathways we tread through the worlds, spiritual and temporal, public and private, real and fantastical, we inhabit.

Thus evolving autobiographies are both about one's self alone and about one's self in community. Into each evolving autobiography are threaded the events of daily lives and of school days, snatches of other people's conversations, teachers' ideas and prejudices, the books read, the films seen and the ideas and experiences of countless others. These jostle for a place in the patterns we seek to create for ourselves of our own way of being or our own 'world representation'. As I write these two words I stop. I finger the bookshelves and draw out what is now a rather tatty book. It has that browned and dried paper smell of an old paperback. I read: 'Our world representation is a storehouse of the data of our experience …' Britton continues:

What I have loosely referred to as 'world representation' has been more elaborately christened 'a verbally organized world schema'. *Verbally organized*: what is organized is far more than words. Woven into its fabric are representations of many kinds: images directly presented by the senses, images that are interiorized experiences of sight, sound, movement, touch, smell and taste: pre-verbal patterns reflecting feeling responses and elementary value judgements: post-verbal patterns, our ideas and reasoned beliefs about the world: images derived from myth, religion and the arts [1970].

The words are familiar to us, as are the ideas which follow: that with words, with talk, we come to grips with experience, and that we create thereby personal contexts for events and happenings individually or jointly experienced. The notion of thus shaping our worlds with words, in talk or on paper, and the implications of this for what we do with children and students in schools for me had never been more powerfully expressed.

Creating the ways for such shaping to occur has been the conscious centre of all my teaching since my first encounter with Britton's ideas. It leads me to particular ways of working with my students. It has led me to working with teachers in writing workshops where their writing and performing are the focus for often difficult reassessments of their own teaching. In a real sense it has lead me and my teaching colleagues to develop the English curriculum guidelines and documents for South Australian schools which we have titles *The Connecting Conversation* (South Australian Education Department, 1987).

We recognize the seminal and shaping thinking of many others whose ideas have helped us to construct our texts for living, teaching and learning. Yet I venture that the constantly shaping voice for many of us as teachers continues to be that of James Britton:

We build in large measure a common world, a world in which we live together: yet each of us builds in his own way. My representation differs from yours not only because the world has treated us differently but also because my way of representing what happens to both of us will differ from yours. We are neither of us cameras. Admittedly, we construct a representation of the world we both inhabit: on your screen and mine, as on the sensitive plate in the camera, is reflected that world. But we are at the same time projecting on to the screen our own needs and desires. In this sense then, we build what is for each of us a representation of the world and at the same time is to each other a representation of a different individuality, another self [1982b, first published in Jones and Mulford, 1971].

As we evolve our world representations we each construct a text for ourselves in which we are the main character. Each text is thus an evolving autobiography, filled with different versions of times, places, people and events. Each text evolves across the different spaces we occupy – school, home, work; across, therefore, the public and the private, the social and the personal. Each text evolves as an attempt to make sense of the discontinuities, the similarities, the certainties and the ambiguities. We construct our texts; we evolve our autobiographies; we learn. Schooling experienced is a sub-text within the text. Each student therefore is engaged in constructing many texts. This is a significant part of an evolving autobiography built upon the different contexts for learning in which each participates. The worlds of science, history, technical studies or geography are ripe for appropriation to each individual's story of learning.

What then of the role of English in the curriculum, in the experience of schooling? It is the one subject in which one's language is the focus of attention. Thus the English classroom is the one place in the school where the very *raison d'être* is the reshaping of one's world representation through talking, writing, reading, listening. It is the one classroom where one encounters the ways others have shaped their versions of the world through poetry, novels, essays, speeches, plays and so on. It is the classroom where the student is consciously and deliberately a writer and reader, speaker and listener. It is where the demanding work of crafting with words is the very business of student and teacher.

In the school the English classroom is specifically a workshop for writing, speaking, reading and presenting. Here, ideally, learning and teaching are scarcely separated so that all members of that classroom community are engaged in both learning–teaching and teaching–learning. Thus it is the place at school where particular ways of exploring (indeed, reflecting on) versions of lives lived, being lived and anticipated can occur. Here students can deliberately act on their versions of the world. They can anticipate future ways of acting in the world by the way they test their language as a personal and public tool for action and reflection.

English, the subject, is predicated upon ways of representing the world and of acting upon the world with words. There are particular ways of knowing in English. In *The Connecting Conversation* we articulated them thus:

The foundation of this charter is that there are particular ways of knowing in English, and the English curriculum in practice will reflect:
- the importance of the personal and reflective uses of language
- the centrality of active participation by students in the processes of reading, writing, listening, speaking, viewing, observing, presenting and performing
- language used for many purposes and in many contexts
- the significance of narrative and story in understanding and interpreting the world
- the power of metaphor and the imagination
- the nurture of the intelligence of feeling
- the importance of students and teachers working together as a community of readers, writers, speakers, listeners, viewers, observers, presenters and performers in a language workshop
[South Australia Education Department, 1987, p. 26].

In that document we call on English to help make the connections between the students' experiences within and outside school:

> The English classroom is thus a workshop for what we call *connecting conversations*. Conversations that enable all students, inclusive of race, gender, social, or cultural background to make connections between their understanding and knowledge and that of others.

> The English curriculum makes connections with other subjects: through the students' experience of learning and knowledge in those subjects and through the ways of learning by reading and writing, speaking and listening in those subjects [ibid., pp. 23 and 30].

We are mindful indeed of the need to have schooling as part of a continuum between home and the world. Britton has said it succinctly.

> We can no longer regard school learning as simply an interim phase, a period of instruction and apprenticeship that marks the change from immaturity to maturity, from play in the nursery to work in the world. School learning must both build upon the learning of infancy and foster something that will continue and evolve throughout adult life [1970, p. 129].

In the past twenty years English teachers have allowed the experiences of their students to take centre stage in their classroom and thus have enabled maintenance of the continuum. They have also begun to extend the range of texts they make available to students so that the writings of the cultures of all our students are seen as more acceptable within English. There is a long way to go in this regard. The worlds of immigrant or ethnic minority writers are not yet widely introduced in English classes. One day the wealth of literature – the heritage of the diverse cultures represented by the children (of whatever race or gender) in our classes – will truly be shared within the context of English. Then the continuum will be more obvious to all.

What of the other connections to be made within the subject English in practice? What is the evolving autobiography of the student in the rest of the school? What role is there for English and the English teacher in relation to the rest of the curriculum? All classes, all subjects should be an obvious link in the continuum of learning. We know they are not. Schooling is not. In English, however, the continuity should be made most obvious. It is in this focused time in the school day that children, students and teachers by the very nature of language at work are engaged in consciously constructing their own texts both literally and metaphorically. When you put your language out in front of you and when you announce 'I am a writer, reader, speaker and so on', you deliberately grasp your own text. Then it can be shaken, turned upside down for a time or refashioned. You also offer your narrative and its cultural contexts and meanings to others. The texts of others and thus of other ways of perceiving the world, can be shaken, questioned and interpreted too.

This is not easy. The English curriculum at work must recognize the realities of the world and at the same time the vulnerabilities of each individual. In the toughest and most sensitive way it must add to each student's repertoire of ways of acting in and upon the world. Its foci are the language and texts of spectators and participants. It must ensure that each student's voice has its own strength. It must ensure that students hear and discover the voices and texts of others.

It is my contention here that English teachers have a particular role in this which they have not accepted fully because they have not been bold enough to see themselves as constructors and interpreters with their students of a full range of texts where these reflect the world representations of different cultures and of different domains of knowing or knowledge. In *The Connecting Conversation* it is stated that,

The whole world of discourse is seen to be available for study in English: that is the texts with which we are surrounded, including conversations, stories, advertisements, films, newspapers, reports, television news, radio, comics, magazines, street theatre, poetry, novels, new fiction, sermons, scientific writing, children's stories and so on [South Australia Education Department, 1987, p. 30].

When literature, the traditional meat of the English table, is placed within the wider realm of discourse, and when the relationships of readers to texts and contexts of all kinds are open for exploration, then change will take place with the English curriculum in practice.

Since English teachers have not yet ventured into the texts or the stories of the scientist or biologist or the historian or the geographer, we have not been able to help students evolve their autobiographies of their schooling in anything other than a limited way. Similarly we have been loath to tread into the discourse and texts of the action of the world beyond school in any substantial way. And our forays into a diversity of cultural experiences through non-Anglo-Celtic literary resources have been but tentative.

With the latter we feel more comfortable than with the first two. Yes, we are required to shift our perspectives in order to add the literature of Turkey, Greece, Indonesia, Africa, the Caribbean or India to our resources for reading and responding. However, it is the world of literary texts. With these we feel at home even though the cultural contexts are different and alien to some of us. Making the shift to seeing the texts of the world of action outside and those of the other domains of knowing, of other subjects, as part of the work of English is for most of us difficult to accept. I want now to explore each of these with a view to rethinking what the doing of English might mean when we change and extend the range of discourse, texts, situations and purposes shared in an English class.

First then to English and the connections we need to help students make with the world of action. By this I mean the world of work and of community outside the school walls. How can we configure English so that this outside world is drawn more firmly into students' learning with and about language and so that they are supported in trying on the language of the world in action?

Many of our students will be parents, employers, workers in diverse fields within a few years of leaving school. With this in mind, one group of English teachers has established a senior school English course based on what we have called 'alternative texts'. They are so called because they represent materials which tend not to be included in English courses. The course still involves students in reading and responding to the range of literature, poetry, novels, adolescent fiction, drama and so on usually found in English. To these are added the alternative texts, which include oral histories, transcripts of peoples' accounts of their working lives (e.g. the Studs Terkel material or Ronald Blythe's *Akenfield* and *The View in Winter*), biographies of contemporary sporting heroes and heroines, non-fiction materials of all kinds and children's picture books, for example, those by Raymond Briggs or Maurice Sendak.

Students have the opportunity to investigate these texts, speculating on the authors' intentions, relating these to their own lives and responding in different ways to them. They are, for example, encouraged to read children's books to young children to discover the world of picture books, to discover how words, pictures and graphics are used to construct the text. These are the parents and workers of the future and the English course being developed with them (for they negotiate their path through the wealth of alternative texts) focuses on the way they may relate reading and writing to their own (and eventually their children's) lives.

Another approach to language in action in the world is to include in English the forms of discourse called forth when students are engaged in projects specifically aimed at discovering aspects of the world outside school. The writing might be of the kind described as documentary work and which Douglas and Dorothy Barnes (1986) have described in this way:

a group of young people identifies an issue – perhaps a proposal to begin opencast mining in rich farmland – and plan an investigation, interviewing interested groups, reading documents, and generally understanding people's perspectives as a way of shaping their own. The resulting presentation, whether in writing or as a tape-slide sequence, need not be a non-committal, pseudo scientific report, but can show those qualities of controlled passion that are essentially literary.

In one of the two final-year courses taken by half the candidates in English in South Australia students must undertake a project in which they work with an age group other than their own, either within or outside the school. Students choose their project – perhaps to work in a child-care centre, teach a primary-school class, do cross-age tutoring with specific children, carry out a project with the aged, explore a future place of work and so on – and must design the activities, conduct interviews, keep a journal, prepare written or visual materials, and present an evaluation and personal response to the experience. They must show that they have integrated a range of language activities into their work. The projects are somewhat akin to documentary work. However, they are not oriented to an issue but to particular experiences with other groups in the student's community. These projects call forth student enthusiasm and their independence as learners and users of language in a remarkable way.

In some other subjects such as technical studies or computing studies students now have the chance to undertake similar projects but with the focus being the investigation of a factory or industrial site or a manufacturing process. In these they are also required to move beyond the classroom and do more than simply write a traditional report; they must indicate that they have not only investigated thoroughly, but also that they have used language in a range of ways as part of that process. Here is an opportunity for collaboration between English teachers and other teachers to work with students on language that matters in the different learning contexts. It is a collaboration sorely lacking thus far in most schools.

A poster in many of our English classrooms reads 'The world is made of stories not atoms' (a line from the poet Muriel Rukeyser). In one school, the science faculty countered with its own poster: 'Every atom is a story.' 'Of course!' I say with surprise and not a little wonder at my own blinkers. 'Tell me,' I want to say to my colleagues, 'the story of the atom or of gravity or of force fields or of motion or combustion, or the Fibonacci sequence or . . . or . . .' I do not know many of these stories. Do our students? Do they see them as stories when they are sitting in maths or physics? How do they read the texts (I do not mean the textbooks) of the scientist? How have the scientists constructed the texts which represent their view of the world? What has this to do with English teachers anyway?

In order to answer this let me turn again to Britton and the distinction he has made between three major intentions for language used in school. The first purpose, he writes, is 'that of establishing and maintaining relationships' because 'learning is an interactive process'. The second purpose is what he calls Learning I, that is, using language in particular ways to learn in different subjects. Learning I involves the use of talking and writing as means of understanding and making one's own, new information. Learning II 'is the process of organising the subjective aspects of experience; of using talking and writing and reading to explore and shape our inner lives' (Britton, 1982a, p. 11).

English teachers have seen Learning II as a particular concern of theirs within schooling. They have certainly recognized the first two purposes of language and have seen the importance of other teachers understanding the implications of Learning I. They have assumed rightly that other teachers should adopt practices which allow for Learning I to occur. The aim for language and learning across the curriculum has been predicated upon this assumption. In some instances the English teacher has been able to fall back into Learning II as it relates to teaching literature, to teaching poetry, drama and writing, safe in the belief that other teachers are taking care of Learning I. At the same time it has not been generally possible for teachers of other subjects to feel comfortable with the responsibilities which are implied by Learning I even when they and the English teacher have collaborated to create units of work and include language activities which allow students to write and talk first about topics in language close to themselves. Language and learning across the curriculum is still a vision for learning.

Now the question again – what has this to do with English teachers? I want to argue that English teachers might best serve their students by working in a different way to mediate between Learning I and Learning II and in so doing support students as they learn in their other subjects as well as engaging with other teachers in the work of learning with and through language. In other words, they might collaborate with their colleagues in other subjects to bring students into a different relationship to the texts of schooling. In so doing they might change the way students evolve their autobiographies as learners.

The time has come when the English teacher (who draws students into particular relationships with texts, inviting them to read, respond to, generate and act through texts) should widen the range of discourse to include the texts, indeed the narratives, of other domains of inquiry and knowing. I choose my words carefully because I do not mean that the standard school textbooks of other subject areas should be included in English (although there may be a place for deconstructing them with vigour). Rather, if we accept that there are different ways of construing the world, then we should be showing students how the lens of the scientist or of the historian or the anthropologist allows for particular world representations. We should be helping students discover how, in their writings, scientists or anthropologists, for example, construct their worlds.

The English classroom focuses on texts, written, spoken, and visual. It invites students into the 'spectator' mode, just as it invites them to be 'participants' in using language. If the texts and narratives of historians or natural scientists are drawn into English, then the English teacher and her students as spectators can share something of the former's perspectives on the world. Students as critical and reflective readers can explore how these different texts work and, in trying to create similar texts for themselves, move from reflection to action with their language. What reading might we lure into English – popular writings about biology, economics, archeology, anthropology, political essays, social commentaries, the biographies of scientists and mathematicians, the autobiographical essays of Primo Levi or E. B. White, articles from *National Geographic* or *Scientific American*, journal observations of field naturalists or what? Can we invite other colleagues, teachers of science or geography for example, into the English class to help us and our students read these texts?

There is room in English for the reading of expository writing; writing that argues a case, describes, explains, defines, persuades, classifies and reports, that covers a breadth of contexts, situations and topics. Some of this writing might have an expressive function and some clearly serves the poetic. Other examples of such writing will fall into the kinds of informative and conative categories of the transactional. The consciously crafted essay, the specialist report in a journal, the diary observations of a scientist or explorer or a first-person account with technical detail of a motorcyle race invites particular engagement from students as readers and thence as writers. Such writing would be the models for many of the texts students encounter in their other subjects.

What writing might we find in English if we adopt a notion of the English teacher and students as discoverers and makers of texts? Obviously we would find writing of the kind just mentioned. We might also make the opportunity to work closely with other teachers; not to focus on a topic or theme in ways advocated by integrated studies or humanities courses but to help students to use their writing to learn.

Can the English class be a place for making texts of all kinds? A geography essay, a science report, a project diary in technical studies, a technical description of a geology excursion? English is concerned with students as writers and readers and with their being readers and writers for many purposes. We seek out different audiences for student writing. We talk of seeking the real purposes of writing and reading. Yet we have tended to ignore the real purposes and situations close at hand in the school, those in which students are engaged as writers and readers. Can the English class be a workshop where they read and reflect as scientists or geologists? Can they begin to see themselves as writers of science and of history in an English class where they are helped to make the connections between the texts of different subjects? What kind of reading or writing of texts do we encourage in English? We encourage our students to predict, to speculate, to reflect, to share through talking their current understandings. We encourage them to approach new material through personal and expressive language. We encourage them 'to shape at the point of utterance' as writers and as readers.[3]

Peter Medway (1980) sums up the distinction and yet underlying similarity between learning in other subjects and learning in English when he writes:

English at its best recognizes the validity of the knowledge that students bring to school with them, and provides means of expression – from informal conversation to consciously structured poetic writings – which allow it to be considered and made more of. Much of this knowledge falls within the fields of other school subjects – for instance children's knowledge of nature. Yet the other subjects tend to ignore this 'pre-disciplinary knowledge' and start from the assumption that students know nothing, or nothing that is 'real knowledge' – even though adult practitioners could not practise their disciplines without these unspecifiable awarenesses and sensitivities.

Medway comments that these 'awarenesses and sensitivities' or 'the personal and unstateable knowledge' of the different disciplines are similar to the kind of knowledge encouraged in English.

Yet these ways of learning with language which support such knowing have been difficult for most other subject teachers to recognize as valid and to adopt in their contexts. Language across the curriculum has foundered on this because what is demanded of teachers is a new conceptualization of who owns subject 'knowledge', of ways of knowing and thus of learning and of teaching. English teachers too have been unable generally to build the bridges between the processes of language and learning in English and other subjects. Often the differences between the intentions of the English teacher and those of other teachers have been insurmountable barriers in schools.

Two English language arts teachers who set out to tackle this problem in their school described it thus:

In most classrooms, it was very much a scene of the teacher – the giver of knowledge – using chalk and talk and textbooks as the main form of exposition, and the student – the recipient of knowledge – reciting it back through tests and written work to show how much had been learnt.

Teachers in many subject areas felt pressured to cover the course and institutionalised expectations of what constituted good teaching forced them to give priority to control rather than individual attention, and to focus their teaching on the content rather than the student.... .

Most of the specialist teachers in the various areas believed that they did not have the training or skills to teach reading or writing. They were unnerved by the prospect of being expected to do so, as well as to teach the content of their subject area. Some reacted by denying any responsibility for literacy development, although they remained concerned about students experiencing learning difficulties and wanted suggestions on how to cope with these students, especially those who were experiencing behaviour problems as well [Coggan and Foster, 1985].

These two teachers, Jennie and Vie, became resource teachers in their high school, with the specific task of working alongside subject teachers to support students' learning. They broke down the barriers by being inside classrooms where they could offer constant specialized support and by joining with teachers to design units of work which included quite specific language aims and language activities. The school recognized that subject teachers need specific professional development support to enable them reconceptualize learning and to promote active language and learning situations.

The resource teacher model is not possible in all schools. It requires the English teacher, in the role of resource teacher for learning and teaching across the curriculum, to enter the domain of the subject teacher. The suggestion in this paper is that, since generally we cannot do this in schools, we should investigate the texts of other subject areas within the context of English. Such texts, as I have noted above, might be student writing or the writing of historians or biologists. The possibility exists that, with cooperation from other subject teachers, students should bring to English the learning logs they write daily in their subject classes and use these as the basis for carrying their writing (and the talking which surrounds the process of composing) and reflecting on the world into other rhetorical forms. Encouraging the use of learning logs in other subject areas in a way similar to the use in English of the response journals students keep while reading can provide one bridge between the subjects for teachers and students (see also Mayher, Lester and Pradl, 1983; Fulwiler, 1986).

The barriers to the exchange of texts and processes across subject areas lie, however, not only with teachers but with students whose experience of education has led them to compartmentalize their learning. Medway notes:

The separation in the secondary curriculum of the scientific (in the broad sense) from the personal and intuitive ways of knowing fails to reflect the psychological realities of most of (the) students under 16 that I have known.

It does not correspond to any achieved differentiation in their thinking; few of them have come to regard objectivity and the establishment of impersonal truth as values in themselves. Arrival at that stage appears indeed to be hindered by teaching approaches which insist on the outward forms of objectivity and which exclude the larger part of the child's response [1980, p. 10].

Students recognize that subject contexts are based on different assumptions about learning. One teacher (who teaches English and biology) explained to me the difficulty she often has in involving her biology students in the process first of writing in the expressive and then of revising and reshaping their essays or reports. 'That's English!' they exclaim with confusion and indignation. They and other subject teachers need the opportunity to understand at first hand (not from the words of an expert at a conference) the learning that can go on through writing and talking in language close to self. 'It is only a step from this to the expected formal essay,' says Ruth (the teacher above) of a first draft from Domenico:

Heat is Molecole. When the molecole are moving sloo that mees it is iec. When the molecole are going a bit farsd that mees it is nomol weat vot fo the tap. When the molecule are moving farsd that mees it is hot weat. When the molecole are moving farsder that is gas. When you get the cert fool with weat and you get hot weat and the gas. the gas heatd the metol and the metlo gas hot and the metol heat the weat and the weat get the weat hot and it sdem and the molecole are moving rele farsd and that haon the wesel woock.

ond we daner sprenmet a bat molecole you can do this you get a block of iec ond a log pees of metlo. you put the metlo fredo the iec. you get A 12 vot bache you get to wiser ond you put the wier of the end of the metlo and you put the Ather wier on the Ather sid of the metlo. ond it weil spack and it shoud melit.

Ruth transcribes the attempt in this way:

[Heat is molecules (moving). When the molecules are moving slow that means it is ice. When the molecules are going a bit faster that means it is normal water out of the tap. When the molecules are moving fast that means it is hot water. When the molecules are moving faster that is gas. When you get the kettle full with water and you get hot water and the gas the gas heated the metal and the metal goes hot and the metal heats the water and the water gets the water hot and it (is) steam and the molecules are moving really fast that (is) how the whistle works.

And we done a experiment about molecules. You can do this you get a block of ice and a long piece of metal. You put the metal through the ice. You get a 12-volt battery. You get two wires and you put the wire on the end of the metal and you put the other wire on the other side of the metal. And it will spark and it should melt.]

She comments: 'This "experiment" was done at home. He was testing an energy transfer between electricity and heat. With so much evidence of competency in science shown here, despair at this student's progress is totally inappropriate.' Ruth's next step for this student was to suggest to him that he transcribe his work with help from her (see above), after which she discussed with him the nature of a science report and ways he could shape it into one.[4]

In English we can make connections through a focus on texts and on students as users of language in action, for we understand that language and thinking go together. We can make connections because we create a context in which students speculate and reflect as they read, write and talk.[5]

As English teachers, if we are to make these connections with other teachers, we need to learn more about the texts of other subjects. We need to learn what other subject teachers' expectations are for students as learners and in what ways they view and interpret the world. It is time perhaps, for us to be knocked off balance a little and instructed by different ways of seeing the world.

It may be argued that, by adding these things to English, the essence of the subject as English teachers have traditionally perceived it will be lost. I say to that, maybe it is time for us to be worried into a state of disequilibrium because we have chosen to reflect on an altered perception of what doing English entails and what we the English teachers do. We should reconstrue what English offers students. It is a powerful subject. Its strengths should be used differently to suit different times and different student needs.

Perhaps, as we include alternative texts, the writing of other domains of knowing the world, and help students into the language of action in the world and community, we will be forced to be learners again ourselves. For we will have to uncover the structures and insights of quite different texts and topics. We will see the world through new lenses. We might begin to wonder again, to be delighted by new reflections on the world. Why should we be trapped in a genre of English teaching because of the texts we have traditionally chosen? And in the ways we have traditionally *taught* them?

Often those ways have reduced texts to what have been called by Russ Hunt 'textoids' – texts taken out of context and used as exercises for the teacher's making of meaning. Garth Boomer (1987), writing of some classroom research he carried out in which he deliberately taught against his own best inclinations, commented of this sort of teaching in relation to texts:

This notion of textoids led me to recognize that I had treated the poem as a 'textoid' and that, at a higher level, the lesson itself was a 'textoid' in curriculum, rather than an authentic engagement.

Making connections across the curriculum with texts, with a view of our students as active and not passive text discoverers and makers, ought to minimize the chances for the 'textoid' syndrome (just as real in other subjects) to take hold.

In an article in which he challenges us to 'rethink our discipline', Robert Scholes (1987) opines:

> Our real subject – what distinguishes English from social studies or linguistic science – lies in a certain kind of textual transaction in which pleasure and power are exchanged. This happens in speech, it happens in writing, it happens in visual texts and the texts composed in mixed media. When it happens we experience what I will call *textuality*, and textuality – not literature as such – is our proper subject matter.

He then asserts that 'a concept of textuality offers us a way of rethinking and reorienting our enterprise so as to connect what we teach more fully to the lives of our students and the world they – and we – inhabit. It opens a path from the smallest and humblest of texts to the grandest and most complex'.

We can draw students into a wide world of text unconstrained by what Scholes aptly describes as 'arbitrary canons of inclusion and exclusion'. Thus, by focusing not on the notion of literature but rather on that of textuality, the way is open for English teachers and students to explore a wide range of discourse. We can offer our students the chance to develop power over and through texts and discourse. We can do this by enabling them to examine the metaphors, tropes, images and structures of the scientist's or anthropologist's writing or the television documentary or the picture book or the politician's speech. To do this is to offer students a way of reading, interpreting and thus commanding the world. English ought therefore be the place for 'authentic engagements' of the kind encouraged by a different set of activities relating to the world and its discourse and permitted by an altered range of texts. Thus students should be involved in reflection and action with their language.

An English curriculum reconstrued thus will have recognized what students know because of their backgrounds and experience. Their implicit knowledge about their social, cultural and political contexts will be specifically valued. The curriculum will also have recognized and anticipated where students are likely to be in two, five, ten or more years' time as parents, employers, employees and members of a community. English will be organized so that students' language and the language they need to learn to use in other situations is valued. They will be regarded as makers and as active receivers of texts. The English classroom will be the workshop for such making and receiving. The components of the curriculum can be depicted thus:

**ENGLISH CURRICULUM AND THE ENGLISH CLASSROOM,
WORKSHOP FOR MAKING AND RECEIVING TEXTS FOR**

A	B	C	D	E
Seeing the world through the lenses of other domains of knowing	Action and acting in the world	Discovering the inner self and the lives and thoughts of others	Using language to learn in other subjects	Emerging as adults and members of the community

In relation to all these components, students use language in reflection or contemplation as well as for doing and acting. As readers and writers engaged in making texts, students construct connections between, for example, reading scientists' essays (A) and being writers for learning in science (D); between this and ordering their personal world (through talking and writing) and responding to the world of fiction (C); between investigating workplace (B) and exploring children's books, including picture books, as texts (E); and between these and the exploration of texts and text making across the spectrum of discourse.

Let us recognize, then, that the personal-cultural narratives of our students are constructed from many experiences. Let us work with that knowledge and therefore support the evolving of the autobiography of each student as a learner in the classroom community. The last word here should be Jimmy Britton's, for so much of what he has taught has led us to new constructions of English to serve well our students in their communities:

As teachers, we are responsible for one important community – that of the classroom. Our role becomes that of seeing that that community, far from continuing as a captive audience for any instruction we care to offer, becomes a genuine learning experience for its members, a learning experience that draws upon and capitalizes on both their in-school and their out-of-school experiences.

So it remains as true as it always has been that all we know – about language, about learning, about literature, about life – is a potential source of information and assistance to the students we teach; yet its delivery will be structured by their needs, the activities on their part to which it is a response and with which it must articulate if it is to be effective. Don't let anybody suppose that this view of teaching and learning offers the teacher an easier option [Britton, 1986].

Notes

1. Long's story is in *Mosaic*, Findon High School, South Australia, 1985.

2. Pierina is a student at Thorndon High School, South Australia, 1987. This piece was written as a response to a unit of work on autobiography as fiction.

3. For a discussion of reading for meaning as 'shaping at the point of utterance', see Pradl (1987), pp. 66–9.

4. Ruth Trigg, South Australia Education Department, contributed useful points and examples of students' work to this paper, including that of Domenico, a student from Taperoo High School, South Australia.

5. A helpful discussion of reflection in learning is to be found in Creber (1987).

On Difference: Cultural and Linguistic Diversity and English Teaching
Tony Burgess

New sets of questions about language in a multicultural society have been addressed by English teachers in recent years. The issues which have multiplied in schools bring English new contacts and expose practice to different sorts of influence. Buried beneath the files and children's work on a head of department's desk – if s/he is lucky enough to have one – will be papers on topics unpredicted twenty years ago. They will include not just policy on talking and reading and writing (across the curriculum), but also provision for teaching English as a second language; provision for teaching community languages; policy on dialect, standard and written language; anti-racist policy, anti-sexist policy, records of working parties scrutinizing books, materials, schools and classroom practices; and language aware- ness, as a new and impending issue.

These issues are not unrelated. They will be seen as complementary aspects of the development of language policy overall, part of whole-school policies for education in a multicultural society. Nor are the reading and thinking on which an understanding of such matters depends unrelated. But each issue in this list reflects to some extent a different history, has been worked on by a different set of people, carries with it into the work of school different demands and interests and requirements. Their integration into a single perspective – the maintenance of a common developing vision of English teaching – grows harder.

It may be time for the attempt to be abandoned. I put the point seriously. Consensus, a common approach, may finish by excluding or trimming divergent or critical opinions. What may be needed, rather, is openness to different views. It is not just those who wish to dismantle public education who think so. Others have found English teaching to have had no special exemption from being too liberal, too white, too male. Language is an arena rather than a subject and has always been multidisciplinary. Perhaps, then, living openly with different groupings, different expertises, different in- terests, different points of entry may be preferable to seeking synthesis: policies before philosophy, an alliance, acknowledging differences as teachers, educators, linguists, feminists, anti-racists, activists, with no attempt to integrate perspectives bearing on language and learning and school.

Such a project would be different from the one which English teachers have inherited from James Britton, though different in only one respect. He would certainly have no difficulties with an alliance. There are no legislators in his work, no toeing the line of a point of view rather than thinking wholly, freshly, humanely, collaboratively from his own vision. But he has believed in the value of synthesis. Britton's concern has been for an integrated theory. He started where teachers and children were. He asked for teaching and learning to become research. He wanted practice both to contribute to and to be available to theory. But his thinking has offered to teachers not just a point of view but an attempt at summary. He insisted not just on innovation, or on policy, or on responsiveness to newly perceived demands and interests, but on principle.

It was not enough to have remade English teaching through the insight that language organizes learning. Recognition of diversity, conflict and differences in cultural experience had to accompany recognition of the general purposes in talking, reading and writing. The two principles are necessary and cannot be divided.

In the UK the recognition grew first in inner-city areas. The Bullock Report (1975) advised that language policies should be tailored to local circumstances. Belatedly, recognition of diversity became inescapable, as it had not been in earlier formulations of language policy. There, the policies had been for English. Language and English were interchangeable. For pupils who came into schools as speakers of other languages the curriculum began later. But in inner cities whole populations might be multilingual or bilingual and children in schools might be confident speakers of several languages. They might be literate in one or more of these. Thought about language policy needed to begin, then, from knowledge about the repertoires of pupils. Little was known. Diversity needed studying as a precondition for reconceptualizing policy[1].

But it was not enough, either, for diversity to be added on as a set of facts about the repertoires of some pupils. Behind the repertoires lay lived experience. To listening to what bilingual pupils said about themselves, it became necessary to recognize that bilingualism was not simply a quirk of linguistic competence, an additional facility. Bilingualism was a cultural experience. Bilinguals felt differently about their different languages. They had been acquired in different settings. They were not just used for different purposes. They reflected and offered different aspects of social identity. In their country of origin, in communities in British cities, in families, in schools, among friends and among brothers and sisters, the way languages felt and were used reflected patterns of cultural knowledge, a differentiated social history.

Recognition of linguistic and cultural diversity carried thinking about language and learning out of linguistics and psychology and into history. Linguistics might assist in describing pupils' repertoires. It debunked usefully notions that pupils were imprisoned in their languages and dialects. It laid out a plan of heterogeneity of language and languages as normal in societies. In a general way it mapped out power, social class, prestige and varieties of use. The importance of language to identity and to learning and thinking was well enough known. There was no reason to suppose that this was confined to English. But listening to bilingual pupils had also made social and political history, culture and differences in experience inescapable. Language had been inherited by these pupils within the history of their families' migration. They had discovered their experience and learning and language within the realities of post-imperial, post-war Britain. Suddenly it was not just bilingualism which had become visible. Britain itself, educational traditions, curriculum assumptions and classroom expectations became visible also.

English teaching has been as slow as any other educational tradition to take diversity, society, history into its central theoretical concerns. At the same time it has been different. Improving the quality of education for all children had been fundamental to the positions about language which were offered to teachers from the 1960s onwards. The paradox needs explaining. Is it just that the impact of new populations in schools came later? Or are there more fundamental points to consider in thinking about English in post-war years? Whether a new synthesis, incorporating diversity, can or should be created in the future revolves around the way the explanation is written.

The new positions about language and learning were disseminated at a specific moment in the transitions of post-war British society, the fifties and the early sixties. They were constructed to replace the dead hand of school learning. In them were rejected faded traditions of grammar teaching, rhetoric, exercises, copying, the ragbag collection of information about language rather than vitality and use. The power of literature had been learned from Leavis and Richards (their influence has been much less baleful and elitist than is sometimes stated). Making that power available for children in school was not impossible. A new schooling had also arrived in Britain in the post-war years, together with a new debate about equality. A changed map of English as a subject in the comprehensive schools, which many hoped for, was the immediate task. In establishing a new English the most promising direction seemed a conception of the range of language uses including literature, together with a firm and well-researched knowledge of language development.

So the new English emerged within initiatives towards a common schooling. It turned its back on selection at eleven and moved into different secondary routes; it prospered in the first bold attempts at comprehensive institutions and focused the energies of those in grammar schools looking to join within a common public system. In this first phase of the post-war equality debate in Britain the divisiveness of British educational traditions ensured that the radical impulse was towards general, universal understandings about language and development. It was these which offered hope of breaking with the partial, authoritarian, limiting, divided pedagogies of pre-war grammar and elementary schools.

New developments in linguistics and psychology offered the way beyond narrowing, restricted, specialized uses of language. Here, spoken rather than written language was emphasized. Grammar had been remade, both in its categories and in its conceptualization as a descriptive rather than a prescriptive study. A new, active, developmental psychology, part Piagetian and child-centred, part anti-behaviourist, mentalist, cognitive, ensured psychological understanding at the core of the new English rather than difference, diversity, class or power. What was missing was a sociology.

Much of this development is so deeply treasured and familiar that it is hard to suggest alternatives and other dimensions. The movement towards common schooling has been the most important development in post-war years. It retains its power and urgency, never more so than at present. Equally, the discoveries about children's learning by teachers in the course of repeated and continuing investigation of their practice have remade schooling for generations of children. Teaching has become a form of research and an instrument of social and cultural innovation. But even the most profound creeds and springs of action need to be revisited. It may be necessary to distinguish the power which lies for teachers within this tradition from the history of its realization. The continuing influence of a specific educational and political climate needs to be reassessed and reinterpreted.

The research programme of the newly formed Schools Council (1964) mapped out the directions of the new English decisively, marginalizing considerations of power, gender, race, other languages and social class. (*English*, Schools Council Working Paper no. 3, 1965). English as a second language was separated off from the main considerations of the English programme in research into the teaching of English to immigrants. Later, a small, separate research project on teaching West Indian children was also funded. Social class was left to the sociologists. Reference is made to the work of Professor Basil Bernstein in Working Paper No. 3, but there was no attempt at this stage to incorporate class into the central concerns of English teaching. There was no reference to gender or to languages other than English. Instead the way was cleared for a central core of research into oracy, writing, the role of linguistics in language teaching, children as readers. The concentration was on process. Hindsight is easy. But when a new equality debate broke in the later sixties and seventies, the concentration of this programme meant that the very strengths of English teaching had to be rethought in examining what it had to offer to the new awareness of institutionalized racism and sexism, of ethnocentrism and divisiveness retained in the heart of even progressive practices.

The debate about equality altered before the end of the sixties. A sociological critique forced a transition from equality of opportunity to equality of outcome, raised the question of positive discrimination and educational priority. Despite attempts of Halsey and his associates, this critique stayed in line with earlier tradition (Halsey, 1972). There was a new particularity, however, in the challenge mounted to deprivationist theory, for this initiative selected, as its target, definitions, ideology and ideas which had permeated the educational mainstreams, and not just provision. Social class was re-exposed.[2] As the experience of racism also surfaced, following the 1966 Immigration Act, and as women put new questions about discrimination, exclusion, institutions and opportunities, pressure on inequality and schooling was redefined. Equal opportunities direct quite different demands at institutions from equality of opportunity, equality of outcome, and reflect different sets of anger, a different debate.

But the Bullock Report was still in some ways heir to earlier decisions. The report's especial strength is to bring together the two fundamental principles. Chapter 4 formulates the role of language in learning. In the chapter on children from families of overseas origin, the importance of the culture of the child and the principle of multicultural education are firmly stated. What the report does not do is reconceptualize English in the light of both these principles equally. Gender does not figure, nor bilingualism, nor other languages, nor English as a second language other than marginally. Language and literacy are not conceived, in general, against the background of difference, cultural diversity and various traditions. There is no picture of society.

Many but not all these gaps have been closed in recent years. Teachers have come to appreciate bilingualism. The research into England's other languages has been undertaken. Teachers of English, English second language teachers, community language teachers and modern languages teachers are closer now than previously. There are signs of a new integrated conception of a language and languages curriculum. Under pressure from the EEC there is talk of pupils' language rights.

But ironies and inconsistencies remain. This movement among teachers has diverged sharply from the new political directions which were initiated in Callaghan's 'Great Debate' (1976) and which have accelerated recently. Teachers have reached a conception of language and languages in multicultural society precisely at the point when the attempt to dismantle this consensus by the Department of Education and Science and the political right is at its sharpest. Also, even such a consensus around bilingualism is a long way short of a reconceptualization of language and learning theory. A focus on languages, without deeper connections being made, without a shift of recognition towards difference as fundamental, without a shift of awareness into culture and history, will again leave conceptions of language and learning shorn of a fully social account.

I hope I have been clear. If I have seemed to be saying no more than that languages other than English should be attended to in the curriculum, then I have failed to make explicit my meaning. I have not been saying just that bilingualism, other languages or diverse repertoires should be recognized. I take these points for granted, debates about provision, practicalities and finance apart. Racist arguments aside, there can be no arguments against such provision. There are clearly important qualifications about how it may or should be done. But I have not been making this argument here. I have been attempting to stake out ground beyond it.

Instead I have been focusing on difference in language, languages and culture. It is a focus which is difficult to establish in educational discussion, less because of any particular conceptual finesse than because difference, within majority culture, is not easily accepted or admitted. In my own work with postgraduate students, seeing the difference for young people entering teaching now is often hard, just as it is sometimes hard for them to see the different paths taken through such problems by men and women, and the different experiences which await them. Thinking about bilingualism alerted English teaching to difference as a principle, a principle which is necessary to thinking about gender, race and class.

What has been difficult about the arrival of this principle in English teaching? Good will has not been lacking, nor real concern for children, pupils' language and experience. But difference is constructed historically; more than individuality lies behind it. Placing difference at the centre of its picture of teaching and learning has required that English teachers pass out of the search for timeless and universal understandings and into history.

Maxine Hong Kingston's autobiographical novel, *The Woman Warrior* (1975), describes the formation of a Chinese American.[3] The account covers girlhood into young womanhood, though it is told in flashbacks, episodes, asides and, above all, stories. Gradually gender, childhood, language, schooling, family, a sense of the past, a struggle for identity are pieced together. The story transcends simplified divisions and stereotypes and shows an experience which is not free from history, which is lived within traditions, family and wider beliefs and ideologies, contradictions, confusions, but a life which struggles, criticizes, compromises, looks for change. I introduce this story into thoughts about diversity here because it has a lot to offer English teachers, I believe. Perhaps it is only through story that language, culture and difference can be seen concretely and not abstractly, fully grasped as shaping and shaped by experience.

As much as the experience of living between two cultures, what matters, as she grows up, are the disabling versions of what it is to be a woman. Back in China her father's sister has drowned herself and her newly born illegitimate baby in a well when the village rises up against the family in anger at her pregnancy. The sister is never to be spoken of to her father. Her mother's sister has been given in marriage to a man who then leaves for America, where he marries again, bigamously. Later, when the sister finally makes her way there too, he will have nothing to do with her. She is destroyed by a combination of this rejection and an inability to adapt to the rigours of immigrant life. But these are only the most touching and revealing of many episodes. A favourite uncle will take only boys shopping, 'No girls.' In her mother's story of the war a mad woman is stoned to death. In China they expose girl babies, don't they.

Through it all her mother tells stories. These stories arrange the past for her mother as well as presenting Maxine with difficult and confusing glimpses of a world which she has no other means of constructing. At the impossible contradictory centre of these stories is one about a girl who is selected to be more than just a girl, who becomes the saviour of her village and achieves heroic feats of courage and endurance, the woman warrior.

The book offers only glimpses into schooling. The real centres are in the family, in the family laundry, in relationships, with her mother, at home. The prizes and achievements which she ultimately brings back, her compensation, count for nothing against the perception of her girlhood and her destiny. *The Woman Warrior* is told as counsel against such successes. But her first years of schooling are depicted memorably in a further, remarkable, resonant episode.

She attends for a time both a Chinese school and an American school and it is possible to watch the transitions between them, made by herself and other children. The Chinese school is rough and rowdy. In the American school she does not speak for a year. There are other Chinese children who do not speak either. But there is only one who does not speak for longer than Maxine. Later, when she has given up her silence, she confronts the other girl in the toilets. She screams at her to give up too and in an appalling, terrifying encounter beats her in uncontrollable frustration and rage.

As readers, we have been left to infer the reasons for her silence in the face of the American school. But the later episode makes these plain. Her anger is with a rival, the rage of the weak at their own kind. As girls, Chinese girls in the land of the Americans, they recognize and compete with each other. Silence has been the course of resistance and opposition; and the power which the other still claims for herself, shamefully as well as defiantly, a last rag of refusal, is a power which she, Maxine, fears to have given up.

There is a straightforward sense in which not ignoring history is important. Diversity is not a single phenomenon; nor is it timeless. The portmanteau noun can be confusing, just as it may be mistaken to talk, as I did earlier, of a single principle of recognition. Sexism and racism have different histories in British society. Policies constructed in parallel may be necessary now, but are no substitute for a deeper understanding which acknowledges a different past and present. Just as important, the experience lived by children – inside/outside classrooms – is specific, historical, different, not typical, prejudgeable, able to be assumed. That is different from saying that it is simply individual. History lives in particulars as well as in great movements, large laws, general events.

Such a history involves more than just a cultural tour – an introduction to Sikh customs, a guide to the West Indies – even if, in the UK, we have much to learn. Part of that learning must be a history of British society that can be lived with. Such a history must include its long story of racism, as Crispin Jones (1986) and others have argued. It must learn from the historians of gender and from the major historiography of class which has been developed in the post-war years. The goal is not impossible. Just this route has been followed in the seventies by teachers who embarked on rethinking the curriculum in response to new populations in their schools. I stand on their shoulders to make here only a broad, procedural point. History counts as much as language. History needs debating equally on the road to constructing a practice.

History has not been popular as a starting point for thinking about language. Jonathan Culler (1976), writing about Saussure, makes a now familiar point. He argues that the great gains in linguistics, sociology and psychoanalysis all derive from a similar recognition. Somewhere in the last quarter of the last century the founding figures of twentieth-century thought all turned from explanation through and origins of phenomena and looked instead for understandings through the exploration of structure. The claims for necessary idealization, for scientific limitation of the object of study run through twentieth-century linguistics, psychology and sociology. Be that as it may, in the transfer of academic theory into classroom theory it is necessary to reject some aspects of that inheritance as well as to learn from it.

In Maxine Hong Kingston's family's mythology ghosts are the 'other'. Threatening, intangible, not known, they lurk everywhere, needing to be fought or shunned or appeased. Western psychology's individual/ universal child is no child either. Removed from history, experience, traditions, practices, this construct of ages and stages, divided into three parts (cognitive, affective, social) has loomed too long in classrooms. The ghost scares out of mind the real, gendered, competing, conflicting, actual, different children, made and making, shaped by and shaping cultures, living in time and of their times. Ghosts may illuminate by their simplification of the real. But there is a price in distortion, paid by classrooms and children and teachers. Loss of the social and historical, loss of the sense of cognition as engagement with materials supplied by the particular culture have to be set alongside the gains in knowledge about thinking, intention and interaction.

Language is more than a system, more than the possession, for good or ill, of the individual, private child; it cannot be separated from cultural traditions and questions of power. Maxine Hong Kingston grows up amidst traditions, practices, discourses, idioms, stories. She does not just invent language, however active she may be in determining its rules. Language precedes her. It lies between people. She is inserted into it, both making and made. It is more than her individual possession. Neither individualist psychology nor the sense of language as à systematic, even a sociolinguistic system, catches at her experience in negotiating languages, cultures, power. That experience lies in history as much as in language, is both constructed for her within culture and permits creativity, is involved in language but involved in much more.

Again, an anthropological identification of different linguistic and cultural traditions does not catch her experience if these are regarded as separate, normative, clear in their boundaries, equal. The half-imagined, half-real sense of how Chinese culture and language are perceived within American society penetrates her sense of herself and her family's sense of their past and of how to conduct themselves. Stories are changed in meaning – for her, for her family – by being told within the American setting. Her life is shaped by more than uncrossed boundaries, more than just different traditions misunderstood by adjoining cultures. Rather, she has to deal with ambiguity, with conflicting and contradictory versions of what is possible for her within the ambiguous, interpenetrated, unequal social history which she is living. Her critical achievement is to come to make her own selective choices within the ill-considered and uneven sets of opportunities which are on offer.

Inequalities exist. Individualist assumptions, even sociolinguistic notions of appropriateness and communicative competence, even anthropological portraits of communities can come to disguise conflict in culture. But conflict is not necessarily confrontation either. In sharply exposing institutional practices, anti-racist and anti-sexist positions can also oversimplify experience, can come to be more about policy than practice, can come to be about something or somebody else: about white self-criticism rather than black realities, about anti-sexist struggle in a male version of militancy, not about women's strengths and the ambiguous ways in which these are both inserted into the world and excluded and suppressed. Conflict is also present in ambiguity, uncertainty, unevenness, ghosts and false imaginings, as well as in explicit and excluding stereotypes, in opportunities and in versions of identity which beckon and linger confusingly.

'It is confusing ...', says Maxine Hong Kingston of her family when the Chinese revolution came, ' ... it is confusing that my family were not the poor to be championed. They were executed like the barons in the stories, when they were not barons. It is confusing that the birds tricked us' (Hong Kingston, 1975, p. 52). In learning difference, English teaching needs more than anti-racist and anti-sexist positions grafted onto existing universal understandings. Fundamental questions need posing freshly: about the place of culture and history in a theory of language and literature, about the historical construction of difference, about conflict and paper.

History is the forgotten side of Vygotskian thought, rediscovered in *Mind in Society* (1978) and in the recent new edition of *Thought and Language* (1986 [1962]). As well as confronting behaviourism, Vygotsky's thought was equally poised to counter abstraction of language from history and the individual/universal explanatory duo in which society is set apart from mind. Alongside policies, recovery of the full historical project in Vygotskian (and Bakhtinian)[4] thought offers English teaching a way forward which is continuous with its own traditions.

Practice has moved ahead of theory. In the UK the counterpart to the description of cultural difference in works such as *Functions of Language in the Classroom* (Cazden, John and Hymes, 1972) or *Ways with Words* (Heath, 1983) has lain predominantly in initiatives by teachers and by curriculum teams working closely with them. It is teachers who have responded to new classroom populations, to the children living through, not just testifying to, the tangled, difficult history of inner cities in post-war years.

Classroom work of this kind should be better known nationally and internationally. Typically, though, it has been local, informal, completed in the doing, not written up widely. However, a common attention to language and languages, not just to English, has informed innovative work by teachers in London, Leeds, Bradford, Coventry and Birmingham. In London the initiatives of ILEA's Centre for Urban Educational Studies provided the practical strengths for Neil Mercer's *Language in School and Community* (1981). The English Centre's *Languages* (1981) and *Our Lives* (1979), a collection of student autobiographies, have been a powerful and precisely judged influence (ILEA English Centre). More widely, the teaching of English as a second language, through the continuing efforts of educators such as Josie Levine, Hilary Hester, Jean Bleach and others, has moved beyond its origins in teaching overseas and been renewed as a central (not peripheral) practice in British schools (Levine, 1981; Brumfit, Ellis and Levine, 1985). Increasingly, links are made in schools between

English, English as a second language and community and foreign languages.

Joan Goody's work pioneered a multicultural practice in classrooms, the necessary base for any anti-racist policy. The significance of her classroom work lay in listening to children as much as in doing and, as importantly, in encouraging children to listen to each other. She paid attention to difference within a classroom process. As she describes in her article, 'Classroom interaction in the multiracial school' (1977), her work recognized a class's internal social relations and children's awareness of each other as being fundamental to what became of the interpretation of curriculum meanings.

John Hardcastle has documented, over four years, the growth of discourse in a multicultural classroom. His class is shown returning to themes which have been accumulated through the years: about West African culture, bias, balance in versions of British imperialism, slavery. The pupils reinterpret these themes in the light of increasing differentiation and growing specificity about their own cultural experience and cultural history.

In a memorable example Hardcastle analyses one striking and moving poem in which a pupil's recognition of his past accompanies his contribution to a particular stage in the wider classroom debate which has been developing. The pupil perceives, suddenly, the paradox that West Indian history was not taught to him in his early schooling in the West Indies. He then makes a link with the class's discussion of what history should be taught which rests on a deepening identification of his own differentiated history, a history which it has now become possible to make common with other pupils and to share (Hardcastle, 1985).

Generalization is difficult but necessary. Such examples of practice have had overlapping concerns but have developed in specific, local circumstances. Particular interests and particular configurations of diversity have shaped them. Such initiatives (and countless others to which I have not referred) mirror the fragmented ways in which difference has forced its way into national attention. The new equality debate from the 1960s onwards has been conducted within particular constituencies for the most part. Where difference has been considered theoretically, it has been at the margins and therefore been considered separately. Isolated and rarely communicating bodies of work have explored bilingualism, dialect, gender, anti-racist education and social class.

Meanwhile in the UK the new, post-Bullock, theoretical orthodoxy has stressed description not theory, phonology and grammar of English not languages in contact, language not history. Crystal's (1986, first published 1976) critique of pre-Bullock work on language and learning led the way.

He argued for closer attention to the description of English in the central theoretical orientations of those interested in language in education. Taken up by others (Gannon and Czierniewska, 1980), the case has been a central influence in the brief given to the current Kingman Committee (1987). But the project is too little and too late. The diffusion among teachers of descriptive understandings about language only ('a model of English' as the Kingman Committee's terms of reference have it) falls far short of being adequate to the linguistic and cultural diversity which is at the heart of contemporary experience.

Difference, ethnicity, class, gender, traditions, social practices, cultural dominance and subordination need to be primary not secondary considerations. The history lived in classrooms presently requires linguistically competent theory which attends to more than language. What is needed, in Deborah Cameron's phrase, is an 'integrative' theory (Cameron, 1985) or at least, as Michael Stubbs has argued, an interest in description which is matched by equal attention to institutional and pedagogic levels (Stubbs, 1985). Instead, the new descriptivists have set out to speak of that whereof they are competent to speak. The fine work on spoken English by Gillian Brown (1977) or by Katherine Perera (1984) on children's reading and writing (for all her teaching background) has been innocent of speculations about learning or culture or social practices. The task of integration is left to others, elsewhere, in sociology, in classrooms. But how do teachers come to give attention to difference, culture and history if these are not heard within the theory which they are offered?

I have argued elsewhere for a renewed attention to classroom discourse, guided by a social view of language and development (Burgess, 1984, 1985). Alongside such a Vygotskian project, autobiography and fiction have much to contribute to an integrative stance in classrooms: Hong Kingston, Achebe, Steedman, Toni Morrison. For difference is a point about cultural experience. To attend to it is to attend fundamentally to people's experience in time, across cultures, across languages, as these are given, unequally and unevenly, in history.

Notes

1. A first attempt to describe the languages and dialects of London school-children was made in a DES-funded research undertaken with Harold Rosen. (Rosen and Burgess, 1981.) Teachers emphasized the need for such description at conferences on Language in Inner City Schools, a collaborative enterprise run from the English department at the London Institute of

Education and successively chaired by John Richmond, Eve Bearne and Denis Pepper, and Tim Hall. The social and cultural nature of bilingualism was taken up by Jane Miller (1983), a colleague and collaborator in this work. National work on bilingualism in the UK has since been done by the Linguistic Minorities Project, directed by Verity Saifullah Khan (see Stubbs, 1985a).

2. William Labov's essay 'The logic of Negro non-standard English' made a strong impact in the UK and influenced critiques of compensatory education and of deficit accounts of working-class language (in Labov, 1972). It is perhaps worth noting this reinterpretation of the essay in terms of class, indicative of the British setting. Attention to Caribbean languages, to bilingualism, to issues of gender in language arrived by different routes (see Bernstein, 1971; Rosen, 1972).

3. Jane Miller has written about *The Woman Warrior* in both *Many Voices* (1983) and in *Women Writing about Men* (1985). Her linking of bilingual and women's experience in an account of alternating inclusion and exclusion in cultural traditions has influenced my argument here.

4. Bakhtin's work has been taken up by feminist and literary scholars in the UK, though not by many linguists. His analysis of 'utterance' in the late essay, 'The problem of speech genres', provides the best short introduction to his thought about language (Bakhtin, 1986). It should be read alongside Volosinov's *Marxism and the Philosophy of Language* (Volosinov, 1986 [1973]).

Reality, Play and Pleasure in English[1]
Peter Medway

I start from a very familiar standpoint, a twofold proposition which now seems so self-evident that we are likely to forget that, not so long ago it had to be patiently argued for and insisted on against a quite different orthodoxy. The proposition is that, first, language develops best in the course of motivated use and, second, that one use, yielding satisfactions sufficient to power the most intense struggles with words, is for making sense of the world, organizing experience and constructing knowledge. It is perhaps Jimmy Britton's greatest contribution that this standpoint, essential to the claims of English as a serious and worthwhile human pursuit, has come to be taken for granted in the thinking of so many English teachers, even if it does not inform all practice.

When I look at some recent English practice in England with the expectations these convictions induce, I find myself critical of four features which I identify especially in the *writing* curriculum experienced by the younger secondary age range.[2] In this chapter I start by indicating what these worries are. Taking seriously the principles I referred to above leads me then to suggest an alternative programme in terms of which English might more effectively contribute to the development of students' power in language and to their making sense of the world. That line of thinking, though, leaves unresolved questions about the place of English work centred around literature. As a result I find myself in the latter part of this paper heading off in a different and unfamiliar direction.

The first characteristic that I identify in current English curricula is *fragmentation*. Far from bringing experience into order, English curricula convey a message that the world is a lot of disconnected bits. The message is implied by the way one topic follows another and one extract another without apparent connection, the grave and the trivial indiscriminately thrown together. It is also implied by the way teachers and the texts they use to stimulate writing tend to concentrate on the surface of things – on the parade of phenomena, on anything that is immediately accessible to the senses: what it's like, how it feels, the 'itness' of individual phenomena in their specificity. English seems to have no interest in causes and structures, in underlying but invisible realities which lead to things being the way they are. It is as if, for instance, society and social tendencies do not exist, but only innumerable particular face-to-face interactions. The prevailing mode of operation is not in fact *ordering* and *organizing* but *savouring*, not making sense of the world but re-enacting the feel of this or that specific experience.

My second feature is related to the first. This is *subjectivism* or individualism. The empirical world, in so far as it gets addressed by students in English, tends to be seen from an individual's standpoint. The object of attention is, in fact, less the world and its workings than the responses of an individual centre of consciousness to the world. Reality is of interest only in so far as it produces flickerings on the writer's own dials, and not for any significance it has on less personal grounds.

In English courses of any period and any country there are criteria, rarely made explicit, whereby phenomena, states of affairs, ideas and so on may be judged worthy of inclusion in the curriculum as writing topics. In the classrooms on which I am basing these comments one of the main criteria is the *personal significance* of the topic: thus events may be written about which are of no public importance but which are significant in the writer's own biography. There is a focus on what is unique and different about each individual's experience. The adoption of such personal criteria of significance was one of the changes which marked the English of the 1960s. It involved a rejection of the criteria which had counted for most in the 1950s, when topics were admitted because of the *publicly ascribed significance* already attached to them – as with festivals, school occasions, birthdays and seasonal changes. To allow the private significance of an event in an individual's life to determine its inclusion as a subject for writing was felt to be, and was, a liberation from a stuffy and conventional formalism. Jimmy Britton is one of those we chiefly have to thank for this important transformation of the possibilities.

Yet *formalism* is the third feature I ascribe to the English courses I have analysed. This seems contradictory in that we associate the personal criteria I have mentioned with a new purpose, that of 'personal growth', of helping students *by means of* writing, talking, reading and drama to 'come to terms with' their experience and order their worlds. But personal writing in many contemporary classrooms is not in fact about personal growth. It is there because personal topics have been found to give rise to vivid and detailed writing, and it is the production of the latter, and not the students' development, that is experienced as the imperative. Personal topics from the sixties have been added to the English teacher's stock-in-trade simply as additional options in the repertoire.

Formalism means that what students are required to do is less to engage with a substantive content than to practise a form, to turn out a particular sort of approved writing product. It is part of this that the 'experience' they engage with is an idealized, abstracted construct. 'Experience' in English is not the range of what people in fact experience. It excludes not only those items in consciousness which derive from the media but also all that life around them which meets neither the criteria of public conventional significance (for these are still commonly operative) nor those of special personal significance, even though amongst that life there is much that is interesting and would repay being reflected on in writing for what it might reveal about the way the world works.

So now we have three of my four characteristics: fragmentation, subjectivism (or individualism) and formalism. Their effect is that the potential of language to probe and penetrate reality, and to enable shape and order and meaning to be found in it, is not strongly developed.

When we think of the place of English in the education of less advantaged groups – the poor, the socially marginalized and the alienated – we have in mind, I take it, their access not only to forms of language but to an understanding of and hence some control over their world and their destiny, so that they do not see these as magic, arbitrary and opaque. My belief is that writing and talking in English could make a difference to students' grasp of the world and their own situations, if only we directed activity onto topics which would yield useful insights and in the detail of our practice placed the achievement of such insights above *literary* criteria.

For my fourth feature is *literariness*. Why should this be a worry? Literature is indisputably part of what English is about, so in that respect at any rate what else would English be but literary? The literariness of English, however, goes far beyond what might follow from the circumstance that English deals with literature. English is *pervasively* literary. In the first place I found that the topics about which children were called upon to write were drawn more from imaginative literature than from life – so the *writing* curriculum was all about literature too. Secondly, most of the writing was modelled on clearly literary types, though some of the types were those of popular or 'airport' literature such as horror, adventure and crime.

What I find most unfortunate, though, is that *literary* criteria and values tend to be dominant not only when the students are exploring literature or doing literary things but also when they are purportedly addressing the world. Only those aspects of the world are written about which will lead to a piece of writing which stands well on its own, which is internally coherent and which displays a satisfying closure. The emphasis on redrafting and 'conferencing' can amplify this tendency: in the course of successive drafts I have seen students move further away from the attempt to capture reality as they experience it and towards what they see as an acceptably shaped piece of writing. Concern for the writing as writing displaces concern for truth and insight. Literariness has in these ways been a drag on the development of the full possibilities of learning in English.

It is considerations like these which have led me to think English ought to orient itself towards *learning* rather than language for its own sake: learning about oneself, certainly, but above all *social* learning. Just as once, led not least by Britton, we discovered how to exploit young people's perceptiveness about their own feelings and responses, so we can build on their resource of implicit social knowledge, knowledge of what is going on in the social world around them. If language were treated in the course of our practice as a *means* to social learning rather than as an end, I believe it would actually be more, not less, effectively developed.

Learning English as part of learning about the world, then, is one way forward I have come to see. I have learned another partly from observing the Technical and Vocational Education Initiative in operation. Alongside learning English as part of *learning about* the world, I now want to add learning English as part of *participating in* the world. One realization of this is the requirement in the South Australian year 12 school-assessed English course that students engage in dealings with people of a different age group, older or younger, in situations that will give rise to a variety of language uses. It is the development of an English of *participation* that is perhaps the most crucial in securing access for those presently denied it, since what such students often find most hard to tolerate as they approach the age of adulthood is the sense of marginalization and exclusion, of dribbling their lives away in classrooms while the world, which they are big enough and old enough and clever enough to contribute to, carries on out there without them.

Now I am far from clear how in practice one can achieve such a programme but, rather than go on to explore practical options, I want in the rest of this paper to look at an important issue which my argument so far fails to address. In what I have said above I have portrayed the *literariness* of English as an unnecessary burden, preventing the subject from making the contribution it might. Given the views I have expressed, it will be no surprise that in the past I have been happy to associate myself with the efforts of certain social studies and history teachers, and of those adult literacy tutors who teach literacy *in the course of* helping their students set up a playgroup or get something done about their housing, and have wished to dissociate myself in some embarrassment from those who take a predominantly literary approach to English. The implication would seem to be that in my conception of English I do not consider literature to be important. This is not, however, how I actually feel. It is true, though, that the account I have given does not give expression to the value I actually place on literature. In fact, I think that here there is an unresolved problem for the theory of English in general. There appears, at any rate, to be a contradiction, between the socially engaged English which I have been advocating, and the need for which I take to be established, and the importance most of us intuitively ascribe to literature in practice. The problem, then, is to construct a rationale for English which will integrate the reading and writing of literature with the pursuit of social learning and social action through language. Putting it another way, what has *literature* to do with access? At the present stage of my efforts to resolve this difficulty I have done little more than identify considerations and arguments which somehow need to be taken into account, and some of these I now want to present.

I have recently discovered that I like opera. The most recent production I saw was Richard Strauss's *Daphne*, performed by Opera North in Leeds. I am going to tell you not about the opera but about the programme notes, which I read while waiting for the show to start. It is the experience of this reading that I am interested in.

In the Greek myth on which Strauss's opera is based, Daphne is, at her own wish, turned into a laurel tree, to escape the embraces of the god Apollo or Phoebus who has fallen in love with her. Here is what I found in the notes.

Synopsis

Time and place: the classical world

After a short pastoral introduction, and heralded by the sound of their flocks, the four shepherds appear and discuss the forthcoming feast-day in honour of Dionysus, which is traditionally the time for lovers' mating. Evening falls as Daphne enters. She reveals her love of nature and identification of herself with the trees and flowers around her; the prospect of the festivity gives her no pleasure....

As light dies away, Daphne's father, Peneios appears.... He points to the light which still shines on Mount Olympus; the day will yet come when the gods will return amongst men. In spite of murmurs of protest from the shepherds, he affirms his belief that Apollo will come to them and suggests they prepare a great feast to receive him worthily. Peneios laughs and is answered by a mysterious echo. A stranger appears – Apollo dressed as a herdsman – and greets the company. He tells them his cattle had run wild, and he has only just succeeded in rounding them up.... [T]he shepherds laugh at Peneios for this mundane realisation of his prophecy that Apollo would visit them. He answers by sending for Daphne and bidding her look after the stranger.

When Daphne appears, Apollo is amazed at her beauty, and calls her 'Sister'. Although she is taken aback by the compliments he pays her, she feels an affinity with him, and asks him his true identity. In enigmatic language, he explains that he saw her from his chariot. ... She sinks on his breast, and rejoices in his promise that she will never again be parted from the sun. For a time she is hidden in his cloak, but suddenly tears herself free. Apollo declares that he loves her, and tells her to listen to the distant chanting; it is the voice of lovers. But Daphne is full of fear; Apollo told her he was her brother, and now he talks of love.

I continue in the words of another text which I found when I turned one page back in the programme. This explains that Daphne turned to flee and Apollo pursued her. It then continues:

> Fear gave her Wings; and as she fled, the wind
> Increasing, spread her flowing Hair behind:
> And left her Legs and Thighs expos'd to view;
> Which made the God more eager to pursue.
> The God was young, and was too hotly bent
> To lose his time in empty Compliment.
> But led by Love, and fir'd with such a sight,
> Impetuously pursu'd his near delight. ...
>   She urg'd by fear, her feet did swiftly move;
> But he more swiftly, who was urg'd by Love.
> He gathers ground upon her in the chace: ⎫
> Now breaths upon her Hair, with nearer pace; ⎬
> And just is fast'ning on the wish'd Embrace. ⎭
> The Nymph grew pale, and in a mortal flight,
> Spent with the labour of so long a flight:
> And now despairing, cast a mournful look
> Upon the Streams of her Paternal Brook:
> Oh help, she cry'd, in this extreamest need.
> If Water Gods are Deities indeed:
> Gape Earth, and this unhappy Wretch intomb;
> Or change my form, whence all my sorrows come.
> Scarce had she finish'd, when her Feet she found
> Benumm'd with cold, and fasten'd to the Ground:
> A filmy rind about her Body grows;
> Her Hair to Leaves, her Arms extend to Boughs:
> The Nymph is all into a Lawrel gone:
> The smoothness of her Skin, remains alone.
>   Yet *Phoebus* loves her still, and casting round
> Her Bole, his Arms, some little warmth he found.
> The Tree still panted in th' unfinish'd part,
> Not wholly vegetive, and heav'd her Heart.
> He fixt his Lips upon the trembling Rind;
> It swerv'd aside, and his Embrace declin'd.
> To whom the God, because thou can'st not be
> My Mistress, I espouse thee for my Tree.

I have cheated slightly here. The Dryden (which was from a translation of part of Ovid's *Metamorphoses*[3]) did not follow straight on in the notes but was on a separate page which I discovered after reading the synopsis to the end: here I have switched halfway through in order to heighten the effect. I have also included eight lines of Dryden which were not in the programme booklet (and have ungarbled the lines that were). But I really did experience a luxurious, almost sensual pleasure when I came upon this rich and crafted language after the turgidity of synopsis prose. I am hoping you had something of the same experience. There is the stateliness and dignity of the language, the 'wiry bounding line' (to misapply Blake's phrase), the sudden concreteness of words like 'rind', the satisfying sense of closure when Dryden simultaneously brings off an awaited rhyme and drops the second block of an antithesis neatly into place. There is a pleasure also in the strange and magical reality we are presented with.

This, I think you will agree, is an aesthetic experience. The nature of the pleasure seems to have nothing to do with receiving a new insight into the world's workings, with 'organizing our world' or 'coming to terms with experience'. Our pleasure is not in learning, in the satisfaction of a curiosity or the solving of a puzzle or the discovery of a regularity in arbitrary-seeming phenomena. It is more like rain coming on a parched summer day. It is like suddenly getting out of a confined position and using limbs and muscles which have gone dead. We have a sense of being more alive.

Now I can make a point that is relevant to our concern with access and our search for ways of making the curriculum relevant and satisfying for non-academic students. This is that the pursuit of aesthetic experience is one of the most obvious and dominating drives in the lives of vast numbers of young people. I am referring to their insatiable thirst for music. I have in mind not those who are obsessed with pop stars or who never turn off the pop channels on the radio, but those who buy LPs of 'serious' pop and rock which do not necessarily get in the charts, who listen to them actively, attentively and repeatedly, singly and in company, who develop fine discriminations about groups and techniques, and who talk and read about music. To be cut off from their music would for many people be a deprivation analogous to having no conversation, never being able to take a walk or never being able to read, and would lead to a desperate dissatisfaction: part of them would wither.

When we worry about making English more obviously meaningful to students we tend to think in terms of social relevance, of providing useful maps and showing ways to exert leverage in the world. But here we have staring us in the face a phenomenon of vast significance, that what lies at the centre of the lives of innumerable students is a quest for *aesthetic* experience. Now literature is not music, I know, and aesthetic satisfactions are less readily available from books than from records, tapes and performances. Nevertheless it seems to me a consideration we should not lose hold of that pleasure in the organization of formal elements, in the creation and resolution of tensions, in lyrical expression, in the neatness and closure of rhyme, far from being an alien set of concerns towards which we must gently draw our students, are already serious business for them. Maybe, then, it will be through the *pleasure* of the text and not the *lessons* of the text that our students may best be brought into motivated engagement with reading and writing.

The thirst, cramp and numbness I mentioned earlier are sensations I have experienced after my own teaching, and would doubtless experience also after the English I have been advocating. Certainly I *have* exposed my classes to literature; but often it has been poetry and fiction which 'related to their own experience' and to the nature of the wider society, texts that, pondered, chewed over and talked about, I thought would yield valuable awareness. Often, though, I would want to slip in texts that seemed to have nothing to do with such purposes – texts like the Dryden. Such texts intuitively seem important: I want kids to be exposed to them. And I think they can be justified simply in terms of pleasure. The problem is to fit them into a programme that takes social learning and social participation seriously, without producing again the lang/lit divide we have worked so hard to get away from.

It is true, of course, that some literature is a valuable source of social and personal learning, so that we can easily accommodate it to an English that pursues those purposes. Some texts do provide us with maps, often a kind we cannot find anywhere else. Psychology, of course, *sounds* as if it ought to provide that sort of enlightenment for us; but for, say, a young adult who has led a hitherto sheltered existence, and who wants some answers to questions like 'How long does being madly in love last?' or 'What's different about an affair between a younger and much older person?' then psychology is a let-down. Advice columns can be good, but it is novels that will be most help. We read them voraciously because they throw light on our continuing questions and life themes. But other texts clearly are not maps. Kafka's *Castle* is not a National Trust guide to any identifiable institution – and particularly not to any institution that was around when Kafka wrote it. What do we *learn* from Dryden's Daphne story?

I do not now think that the notion, adapted by Britton from D. W. Harding, of spectator and participant roles succeeds in accounting for these texts within the same model as 'transactional' ones. It is true that the differences between some texts can indeed be seen in terms of two different stances which may be taken in relation to reality, those on the one hand of participating in the world's affairs and on the other of being an onlooker, or perhaps, rather, of *having been* an onlooker and now savouring and reshaping the experience for one's own satisfaction. Other texts, though, are not appropriately characterized in terms of a stance towards reality. It is not their attitude towards reality that is distinctive about them but the fact that they can hardly be said to have a relationship to reality at all. To put it epigrammatically, being about reality is not what they are about, unless in such an indirect way that the concept of 'aboutness' becomes useless. Rather they are about just being, as artefacts. In other words, there are other roles to be taken besides participating and spectating. You can join in the fight or watch it from the sidelines. Either way you can go home and tell the folks about it. But you can also put it out of your head, shut yourself in the shed and knock something up on the bench.

I want to say that literature must be in, and that it must be in in ways that do not evade what is distinctive about it or attempt to assimilate it to everyday speech and storytelling. I want to include texts that we do not necessarily learn from – not, at least, in any specifiable or statable way – and that do not purport to provide maps. I want texts that reveal their own constructedness, that do not dissemble about their own textuality or pretend to be transparent windows onto the world; texts that draw attention to their language and to the artificiality of the realities they show, realities which we may nevertheless find ourselves entranced by and involved in. I want students to register on their pulses the sheer textuality of poems, for instance – their 'textility' or textileness, if you like – their phonic substance, the dance of sound, all those seemingly gratuitous elements that are over and above the formulations of views of the world, and that constitute, as it were, the *singing* of the text.

In giving full play to these elements I am aware that I am making the integration of English – the merging of aesthetic with social and cognitive purposes – that much more difficult. But we paid a price for the unity – language and literature – that we had before, from the 1960s. I said earlier that in allowing literariness to pervade the curriculum we put a drag on our uses of language for learning. As the other side of the same coin, by trying to assimilate literature into personal development, learning about the world and coming to terms with experience, we cut ourselves off from exploring what was most distinctive about literary texts. We denied the students the experience of texts as 'semantic playgrounds' (David Lodge's phrase; see Lodge, 1981, p. 68). We did not encourage a sense of playfulness, of the ludic possibilities of 'doing things with words', of manipulating and rearranging verbal structures, of trying effects. There was little *jouissance*. In writing we encouraged *only* the authentic, sincere, monovocal 'own voice' of the writer himself or herself. A big advance on the conventional posing of the fifties but offering no opportunity for the fun of 'ventriloquism' and plurivocality, of trying on voices and discourses and seeing what they get you to say.

In enjoying and analysing with our students texts which are not obviously about the identifiable world but which revel in their own textuality we may help students to see that *all* texts – and not only literary ones – are constructed and are not simply 'read off' nature, and that they could have been constructed differently, in which case what they 'said' would have been different. We need to do this for the reason which Robert Scholes (1987) explains: texts may bring us great pleasure, but at the same time they are capable of exerting power which we may be unaware of. Students need to be helped to understand what is going on when texts work on them. We want them to have the pleasure while retaining the capacity to resist the power. Literacy should not just mean that you are available to be worked on by a text. The ability to slip out from under the control of a text must be part of what we mean by access.

It is possible to imagine the sort of practices we need. Indeed, we do not entirely have to imagine them since some are in operation, I believe, certainly in some Australian classrooms at tertiary level. With other people's texts I would like to see students climbing in and taking over the controls, making the text go off in a different direction, changing the register and generally taking liberties. Scholes wants classic texts to be treated 'not as frozen masterpiece, austere and untouchable, but as . . . something to be admired and affectionately tinkered with, like a classic car'. He wants students to 'see the textual apparatus from the inside and learn how to pull the strings themselves'.

So what might we do with something like the Dryden? I am not suggesting that many students would find that particular text appealing, but let us take it as an example. Leaving aside for the moment the consideration that the story is told in verse of a particular kind, what is the appeal of such a myth? Perhaps it is that what in our own experience are simply desires and feelings get amplified in the Greek myths into physical actions: desire becomes a chase; a wish to escape takes the concrete form of a metamorphosis. Could the students write the realistic story of which the myth might be an emblematic enactment? Could they take a realistic short story and write a parallel Greek myth? How about converting Dryden's story into a ballad or a pop-song lyric? Kate Bush's lyrics are often on equally strange themes.

But I want this textual experiment to be carried out on the students' original texts too. These texts may themselves originate from a playful impulse or an attempt to tackle a form, but I still want much of their writing to be a means of addressing the social reality they live in. Let us suppose a girl has seen an incident – a row between a gentrifying incomer to the district and a neighbour whose family has lived there for years. We would start by eliciting an account – the student's own recollection of the event. Then we might work to make the point that her version is not reality but a construction of it: so let us discuss what the original inhabitant's mother is like, who lives there too and who also saw the incident – and let us write *her* account. Ventriloquism.

Then let us read other accounts of similar incidents – from novels, from newspapers, from court transcripts. (I know that in reality we do not have all that stuff readily to hand, but for the sake of the argument I will imagine ideal circumstances.) Maybe some generalizing writing about the phenomenon of gentrification.

Now let us get her to distil what she sees as the essence of each of the participants' stances and positions and ways of seeing the world. Let us formalize: they are going to be on stage, in masks, and they will speak alternate lines. At this point ventriloquism moves towards art, to express a type of social insight that cannot be propositionally stated. We move away from a mimicry which simply simulates the real person, like a forgery, towards the simplification, density and power of poetic language. What does the student gain? Rhetorical power: her view of this event, or perhaps rather, now, of this *type* of event and of the underlying social relations, is communicated to others in a powerful and memorable way. Maybe music could be added.

In general, maybe: make what starts off as factual, found, mundane into something formal or ritualized. Combine social observation with the fulfilling of formal requirements: introduce a ritual counting, put everything in threes. Switch into different discourses: legal language, eight-year-olds' slang. In the multicultural classroom use more than one language.

In ways like these it may be that we can reunify English around the notion of textuality, as Scholes indeed suggests. As a further justification, it may in any case be that even for an ability to write clear and simple transactional prose a rich experience of other sorts of language is the best preparation – including language which is extravagant, metaphoric and textually intricate.

Let me make one thing quite clear. I do not want clever crafting or detached manipulation to be a substitute for students' having strong intentions which impel them into language. The recognition that children and young people have something to say and that giving them the chance to say it is the best way to get them to stretch themselves linguistically was an immeasurable step forward. What I am talking about is not a retreat into arid metalinguistic cerebration. Rather, I want us to recognize that students' powerful intentions may be not only intentions to express themselves or to construct new understandings, but also to make, to build, to fabricate; and that the self and all its energy and passion can be poured not only into the direct affirmations and self-exposures of personal writing in which there is no apparent distance between the 'I' of the text and the 'I' of the writer, but also into other voices, alternative personas. Even as artificial a medium as the opera has been a vehicle for satisfying realizations. To write in modes remote from those of one's naturalistic everyday speech is not necessarily a form of Alexandrian academicism: it is an extension of what little children do when they play with words, talk nonsense and impersonate nurses, kings, aliens, ghouls and teachers. And not only little children. The conversation of fourteen-year-olds I know and indeed of many adults is full of passages of mimicry, pastiche and fustian: such intertextuality or playful allusion to other discourses is a common feature of many people's spoken language. 'Doing things with words' seems to be a motivating purpose in its own right, and fostering it seems an important part of bringing young people to mastery and confidence in language.

This fostering is a subtle business, difficult to plan and manage in the classroom. You can begin from a *form* rather than from a message you want to communicate; you can start from words, shapes, a rhythm in the head, a remembered phrase – as some poets attest they do – or from an image of a scene: some people in a setting, say – as some novelists do. Now what starts in this way, as a formal exercise, may remain that. But it may also become infused with meaning and intention and become a means of realization of something the writer is beginning to know or feel. Why English teachers have to be skilful and sensitive is that they have to watch over that oscillation between expressive intention and awareness of how the words are working, so that the student is locked neither into sterile formalism nor into blind and unaware expressivism. (I am in little doubt, by the way, that the former is the danger more to be feared.)

The way I am provisionally seeing English, then, is in terms of separate starting points and converging activities.

First there are the purposes of social and personal learning and social participation. Curiosity about the world and the urge to get stuck into it will give rise to the production of texts and the reading of texts. Some of these texts will be literary and will yield a high degree of textual pleasure. Examining the texts as discourse, for the way they construct pictures of the world, will be an aspect of the pursuit of social understanding – a logical continuation of social inquiry. (An interest in society implies an interest also not only in the texts we find in it but in the texts we see it through.)

On the other side there are purposes of pleasure. These will lead to the reading of texts, many of them literary, and the production of texts, in a playful, disinterested, irresponsible, exuberant sort of way. The texts produced and the texts read will be enjoyed and their textuality studied: sometimes they will be played with and experimentally altered. It will often happen that these texts turn out also to say interesting things, to offer insights and perspectives which are illuminating: social and personal learning may result.

That is the sort of criss-crossing text or tapestry that I think I would like to see English becoming, one in which activities arising from distinct starting points end by connecting through a unifying interest in textuality. I see access as being at the same time access to understanding, to pleasure and to control over the texts one produces and is exposed to, and I see the separately originating pursuits as mutually confirming.

Notes

1. A version of this paper was presented as a keynote address to the annual conference of the Australian Association for the Teaching of English in July 1987, and was published in *English in Australia*, 82, Nov./Dec. 1987, pp. 12–22.
2. The research, made possible by a studentship from the Economic and Social Research Council, is reported in Medway (1986).
3. John Dryden, The First Book of Ovid's *Metamorphoses*, lines 711–55, quoted from J. Kingley (ed.) (1958), *The Poems of John Dryden*, vol. 2. Oxford: Oxford University Press.

Doing Things with Language: Skills, Functionalism and Social Context
Mike Torbe

'Make sure,' wrote sixteen-year-old Jason, remembering the farmer he worked for during his work-experience placement, 'make sure you ask any questions you think are relevant, because he won't tell you otherwise.' And Leigh, reflecting on her time in a graphics office, advised other students, 'Try not to be shy. They settle you in there very well' (National Writing Project, 1987).

They were writing their comments in a manual which would help students in future years to check on different workplaces and learn from the past experiences of people like themselves. They may have thought they were giving advice on something more tangible and relevant than language – behaviour, perhaps, and what other young people could do to make the most of their own experience in work places. They certainly do not separate 'behaviour' and 'language behaviour': justly, because it is a total experience they reflect on. Before the work experience, they had a commonsense knowledge about language use in the social contexts they were familiar with, but the contexts may not have included adult workplaces. Now that knowledge is extended, generalized and made subtler, which is one of the best outcomes of a work experience for school students. During and after the work experience students can test out their existing ways of talking and relating to people and have to develop more complex modes of relationship in adult environments which make new social demands on them.

The language exchanges implied by Jason and Leigh are part of the total social context of their work experience. They could not have encountered them in school, because they simply do not exist there. Had what they learned about language at school, then, prepared them for the work experience? One of their friends thought so, after her time as a hotel receptionist: 'Setting out letters and good spelling are useful things from school,' she remarked. These are familiar items from the traditional list of 'basic skills' which give her a way of thinking about her experience. But she also indicates a wholly different dimension of the experience and of her learning by saying, 'Don't expect too much responsibility because you won't be able to cope with it.' Her conscious knowledge may perceive that those familiar 'skills' of language are relevant; but she has another, as yet inexplicit, understanding related to her encounter with a wider world which requires quite new personal and social capacities, which she is not certain she has. Nor has she a way of talking about them in language terms.

She is not alone in that. The ideas about language that have currency in discussions of education, training and industrial experience can easily ignore those social and personal capacities and fail to recognize the kind of experience Jason, Leigh and their friends had. I want to examine in this essay, therefore, what lies behind the ideas usually expressed as 'basic skills' in language and 'functional literacy'. Because these are formulations especially associated with industry and preparing students for the world of work, and with an inexplicit politics of language, I want to investigate that politics and relate it to the cultural contexts of language in society. This means asking some very simple questions, like: what are 'skills' and can language ever be described as a 'skill'? If we discuss 'functional literacy', who determines the necessary functions and uses of language? And what do young people gain and lose by having an education or training which sets out to impart skills?

The views I want to explore first are the 'commonsense' ideas of basic skills and functional language. These are that there are certain straightforward language competencies, namely reading and writing; that they have to exist as 'basic', that is, a kind of foundation for all other language of a more complex kind; that the more complex uses are less 'relevant' and practical and often frivolous – like poetry or fiction – and that contemporary schools favour those instead of the yeoman virtues of the basics. In addition, 'commonsense' people who inhabit the real world of industry are impatient with the otherworldliness of those in education who concern themselves with the frivolities, when it is quite clear that what one needs to do is to make explicit to young people how important the basic skills are and to drill them as one would practise piano scales or marching.

I will be questioning these commonsense ideas, and so I must clarify one important point now. I believe that it *is* important for young people – and older people too – to be able to write with clarity and conviction, to be confident and competent spellers, to be articulate talkers and attentive listeners, and to be able to read and understand whatever they have to, or want to, read. I write that firmly for two reasons: first, because I believe it; and, second, because it is common for anyone who makes critiques of certain systems and the language patterns and ideologies associated with them to be accused of being subversive and of rejecting the importance of correctness, competent performance and conventions. This accusation of subversiveness is made particularly when the systems in question are closely associated with the distribution of power and access to positions of influence.

Well then. A 'skill' is a practical knowledge in combination with ability. It is something we learn to do in collaboration with the more capable (Vygotsky, 1978), but may not need to be taught explicitly. And when we are taught it – when a parent or friend teaches us how to ride a bike or to swim – it is by engaging with the experience which is purely itself. Once we can perform the skill, we have achieved something the subsidiary parts of which may be, in Polanyi's term (Polanyi, 1958), 'unspecifiable': we may be able to do something, but not be able to explain what it is we can do: 'What the pupil must discover by an effort of his own is something we could not tell him. And he knows it then in his turn but cannot tell it.'

A skill is always a way of achieving something of which the skill is a part and never an end in itself,[1] and it is generally physical and practical. It is a strategy for now, for using these physical abilities in a particular way for a particular outcome, and it will need to change if the process changes. Woodworking skills with hand tools are very different from those needed with power tools: planing, jointing, even cramping become very different operations when done by machine. Skills are still needed, but they have changed as the process has changed. So too with cooking and microwaves, arithmetic and calculators, handwriting and fibre-tips rather than ink dip-pens.

Physical skills are very different from language operations, which are not at all about physical activity, and inhabit a different cognitive domain. The difference primarily is that active use of language is a way of *discovering*: by talking and writing we find out what we think and what we have to say. It is through the use of our language that we actively create a world, which, in a sense, does not exist until we have spoken it. Babies as they begin to talk learn how their native language works, but they also develop and discover a way of looking at the world; the experience is qualitatively different from learning to walk or use a knife and fork or switch on the television, which are intensely physical achievements.

'Skill' applied to language implies that thoughts exist, feelings exist, and all that is needed is the skill to choose the right words to produce an appropriate sentence. But language, as all human experience show us, primarily *discovers* the thoughts and feelings. We express and discover, and 'shape language most effectively at the point of utterance' (Britton, 1967). Myra Barrs (1983) remarks that 'writing even about something you are very familiar with can lead to new realisations: you end up with much more than you started with'.

My first major point, then, is that the metaphor implicit in the term 'basic language skills' is misleading. Using the word 'skills' implies that, like physical skills, language contains discrete components that can be isolated, described, practised in isolation and mastered. Once the initial premise is made that using language is like deploying physical skills, then what follows with specious logic is the attendant intellectual structure of drills, practise and testing. Physical skills, however, are very different from language abilities (Hammerston, 1984) and an examination of the differences will be rewarding in the context of this argument.

The most subtle and persuasive analysis of skills and their acquisition is by Polanyi (1958). He makes the distinction between *focal awareness* and *subsidiary awareness*. Taking the example of driving in a nail with a hammer, he says we attend to both nail and hammer in the hand,

> but in a different way.... The feelings in our palm and the fingers that hold the hammer ... are not objects of our attention but instruments of it.... We watch something else while keeping intensely aware of them. I have a subsidiary awareness of the feeling in the palm of my hand which is merged into my focal awareness of my driving in the nail.

He also points out that when focal attention is given explicitly to the subsidiary elements, the result is a self-conscious clumsiness and also a failure of achievement. His example is the pianist whose attention shifts 'from the piece ... to the observation of what he is doing with his fingers while he is playing', and therefore gets confused and may have to stop'. I will return to that idea of giving attention to subsidiary elements later, because its significance in a discussion of language use is great. Polanyi himself makes that link: 'when we use words in speech or writing, we are aware of them only in a subsidiary manner'.

Given this subtle analysis of 'skill', it is hard to see how language can in any way be either a skill or a composite of separate skills. Yet the idea of basic language skills has a tenacity and a quality of survival which suggest it has a greater importance than ought to be associated with matters of reading, writing and spelling. What could its attraction be?

First, it has a pleasingly simple and persuasive charm. The linguistic deficiencies of young people can be put down to their failure to practise simple, easily defined 'skills', like playing scales on the piano. Second, it has an attractive political dimension. A description of language as skill or tool predicates a political view of human relationships in which the implicit metaphor is of production and instrumentality, fulfilling technical imperatives and involving the structures of manufacturing – product, systems, management. It implies a linearity of process which is that of production and not at all of language in social interaction. Third, it touches deep feelings about social identity and belonging to groups, because in this view skills are the signifying marks of an elite group who possess something not widely available, and who permit others to join the group only by passing on, selectively and piecemeal, the skills that allow new people membership.

'Skill', then, is seen as static, fixed, permanent, symbolic as well as actual, there to be acquired as an initiation symbol into the group. There is no easy recognition in this model of the dynamic nature of industry, as it necessarily changes to produce new productions or introduces new technology to do old things. What is needed to acquire the appropriate skills, according to the model, is a set of abilities and political values which are seen to be clearly articulated, easily visible, universally shared and accepted, and socially of high status, though the skills themselves are low-level. There is, it seems, no need to articulate the values, because they are 'known', in a taken-for-granted way, as universal truths.

To return, then, to one of my questions about who makes the definitions: those who define language in these ways feel that they are personally beyond the need for such basic low-level skills, and that they are in touch with a value system which is unspoken *because* it does not need to be articulated. The definitions are then presented not as theirs, constructed ideologically to support their position, but as what is publicly realistic. Any alternative, as Fred Inglis (1987) points out, is described, and dismissed, as unrealistically utopian. The definitions of appropriate and proper usage are political claims because anyone who claims to be able to define what is appropriate is speaking out of a power position.

As for defining language as a tool, the metaphor is imprecise and revealing. What sort of a tool? we have to ask. Tools are precise and limited in their uses: a saw is for cutting timber, not for driving screws. What tool, then, is language? It is hammer and nail, saw and chisel, plane and paintbrush. It can do everything with equal and unlimited facility. No tool is so protean in its flexibility. Language is also, and above all, about identity and about relationships. Whatever we say or write expresses, conveys and gives us away, whether we will or no. No tool does that.

Functionalism in language is as slippery an idea as 'skills'. The idea of 'functional' language indicates a culture in which what is valued about language is its unique value as a labeller – for people to label for each other things, operations and events – and as an important aspect of the necessary task of 'getting things done'. A term like 'functional literacy' is generally used in relation either to an occupation or to some more generalized idea of survival within society. It is implied, but rarely stated, that society broadly agrees that such and such are the necessary literacy requirements of living in present-day industrialized civilization. There is an unspoken assumption in that definition that there is universal acceptance of the unarguable meanings of language, with no uncertainties in understanding.

But definitions of 'functional literacy' must always be seen in a political context (Street, 1984), and politically this implication of broad social agreement is disingenuous. People do not, in some idyll of pastoral innocence, collaborate happily to construct and support a mutually accepted social order, platonic in its perfection. Behind many of the definitions of functional literacy lie attempts to define how *other people* ought to be literate in order to do their job better for us (ibid.). Completely missing is any suggestion that the primary reason for literacy should be that the individuals want to use it for their own purposes, any notion that being more literate can help a person to understand the world better and gain some control over it for their own personal reasons, as Jason and Leigh have in the examples quoted at the beginning of this essay. The importance of literacy and the sometimes exaggerated claims for its benefits are not always convincing enough to persuade people to commit themselves to it. 'Literacy may decline if ... the goals it has been thought to accomplish are not achieved,' remarks Shirley Brice Heath (1986), and she continues, commenting on the experience of people in 'emerging' countries like New Guinea when their literacy needs are defined for them,

> When the population recognised that they remained poor despite their sons' learning to read and write, they withdrew from literacy and maintained it only for select purposes in religious ceremonies.

It is only when people consciously or unconsciously accept the political value system of the literacy givers that they will also accept the definition of themselves as deficient in literacy performance. In the same essay, Heath lists functions of literacy current in 'Roadville':

1. Instrumental. Literacy provided information about practical problems of daily life (price tags, checks, bills, advertisements, street signs, traffic signs, house numbers).
2. Social interactional. Literacy provided information pertinent to social relationships (greeting cards, cartoons, bumper stickers, posters, letters, recipes).
3. News related. Literacy provided information about third parties or distant events (newspaper items, political flyers, messages from local city offices about incidents of vandalism, etc.).
4. Memory-supportive. Literacy served as a memory aid (messages written on calendars and in address and telephone books; inoculation records).

5. Substitutes for oral messages. Literacy was used when direct oral communication was not possible or would prove embarrassing (messages left by parent for child coming home after parent left for work, notes explaining tardiness to school).
6. Provision of permanent record. Literacy was used when legal records were necessary or required by other institutions (birth certificates, loan notes, tax forms).
7. Confirmation. Literacy provided support for attitudes or ideas already held, as in settling disagreements or for one's own reassurance (advertising brochures on cars, directions for putting items together, the Bible).

It is striking that when a community defines in practice its own needs and uses for literacy, the list does not include the usual 'high-value' functions – critical, aesthetic, organizational and recreational – which an external definition might well use as ways of defining literacy attainment and therefore psychological ability. Roadville is literate in ways that suit its community needs perfectly; what 'schooled literacy' (Cook-Gumperz, 1986) would require as evidence of achievement is not part of this community's culture. When literacy is externally defined without acknowledging a community's existing uses of literacy this can be damaging, for then 'ordinary people have much less control over their own cultural products' (ibid.). Brice Heath's analysis of real uses of literacy derived from a community's own living energy is evidence that when a sensitive observer asks what those uses are, the answers are different from any simplified ideological response.

Shirley Brice Heath affirms the significance of social and cultural contexts and all the messages carried by context in its fullest sense; and that notion of *context* must be applied to any discussion of literacy. 'Functional literacy' must never be exclusively defined in terms of the static decontextualized literacy demands of a particular occupation, especially when social, political and economic mobility characterize Western society. Like all phenomena, literacy can only be fully understood by placing it in its actual social and cultural contexts (Watzlawick, Beavin and Jackson, 1967). Yet some of, for instance, the Unesco definitions propose a view of literacy which separates it from any cultural context, and sees it exclusively from the viewpoint of Westernized industrialized society (Cook-Gumperz, 1986) and appears to approve of acquiescent acceptance of information and political passivity (de Castell, Luke and Egan, 1986).

Social context bears upon the language users in its community in complex ways; and all of us are members of different communities, with varying degrees of allegiance to them. People in a society and in communities communicate with each other through shared meanings, and a large workplace generates its own speech community. Within that general culture of industrial activity there are subcultures and corporate views of language which differ subtly from each other within a framework of largely tacit and inexplicit agreement. When those differences are explored, they begin to call into question the surface simplicities of that 'getting things done' description. For language can do many things, and what else does it do, what else are its functions that the simple view of basic skills and functionalism leaves unrecognized and unexplored? The bluff practicality of the view can only be maintained by averting intellectual eyes, so to speak, from what human beings know about the wider uses and significances of language that they know by virtue of living and surviving in a culture.

A recent ethnographic study of literacy and writing in the workplace (Brown and Herndl, 1986) considers what are apparently matters of 'skill' and removes the neat solutions that are so comforting. It demonstrates the complex human, social, political and extralinguistic functions that writing carries within an institution. The authors considered a familiar problem that is generally dealt with pedagogically and linguistically: able middle managers in industry persisted in using two common writing behaviours – superfluous nominalization (saying 'undertake an examination' instead of 'examine') and narrative structure in unacceptable contexts like executive reports, recommendations and proposals. Why, the authors wondered, do these able people refuse to adopt style conventions which their supervisors considered should characterize effective professional writing?

They identified groups defined by upper managers as the best writers and communicators. Having found two groups, one of 'Central Peers' – respected good communicators, 'who often turned out to be the best product managers or grain traders as well' – and the 'Other Guys' – good-to-adequate workers – they analysed the original professional writing of the two groups and discovered that both groups used superfluous nominalization, the Central Peers less than the Other Guys. But then they asked another apparently unrelated question – which of the managers were secure in their jobs, and which of them felt that they were in jobs that were volatile or vulnerable? And, behold!, the Other Guys in the volatile group were markedly less effective in their writing.

Now it could be argued that *because* their writing was less effective, *therefore* their jobs were vulnerable. But Brown and Herndl looked more closely than that:

Writing for the eyes of upper management or for powerful people outside of the corporation was more heavily nominal-consistent.... . When writing up the corporate hierarchy, nominalization goes up. When writing down, nominalization goes down.

And they show what they mean with a telling anecdote:

> Our most insistent nominalizer was a black male manager reporting to a white
> female. His most nominal texts were those sent or copied to her. When writing to
> peers or subordinates, his tendency toward superfluous nominalization decreased.
> In an interview with one of us, his speech was formal and hypercorrect – at the start.
> Over the course of an hour's conversation, he became comfortably informal and
> lucid, perhaps realizing that he was not meeting his old English teacher and that his
> ability as a market analyst and manager was recognized.

Insecurity, in other words, produces writing that is overformal, cautious
and seeking for approval. Re-embed this in your own biography, and
remember the notices, the letters, the memos you have read (and written)
that came from an anxious writer – someone anxious about his/her position, about his/her level of education, about how readers would respond,
about his/her efficiency, his/her security. And consider how often that
writing was overformal, pompous, self-protective and meeting some unspoken definition of educated public language. 'Speakers and writers under
stress are less fluent,' remark Brown and Herndl. Of course. And under that
stress attention is directed, to return to Polanyi's analysis, to the subsidiary
matter of language instead of the focal matter of the task in hand: the
language ceases to be transparent and becomes the centre of attention. The
pianist becomes incapable of playing the piece and thinks only of what the
fingers are doing. The anxious writer thinks not of what is to be said, but of
the significance of the way of saying it and the messages that carries. Thus
the conventions of language, because attention is drawn to them in this
way, are overvalued and interpose themselves between the writer and the
writing: subsidiary matters receive the focal attention and become the
dominant issue.

   This is a convincing analysis, but sensitively they do not leave the matter
there, though that is already a long way from simplistic notions of skills and
self-evident functionalism. They look further. Why is it that a particular
feature, superfluous nominalization, shows up like that?

> Nominalization is ... a favoured means for achieving semantic density, a sign of
> syntactic maturity, a formal trace of literate cognition, a feature of published writing
> and spoken language in academic cultures.

Because of its perceived public status, the Other Guys overvalue the
feature: they *hypercorrect* their prose. So we have four motivations for the
Other Guys' use of this feature: lesser professional stature, job insecurity,
dysfluency under stress and hypercorrection. Is this all we need to know to

understand what is happening? No, for they pursue now a significant new direction.

All language structure 'signifies' (Barthes, 1967), and if authors choose to use superfluous nominalization or narrative when a reader – even if it is a supervisor – advises differently, this indicates the multiple functions that language can have for its users. The Other Guys were doing much more than being indifferent or bad writers, and the problem could never be corrected by approaching it as a matter of easily defined skills which should be taught in a transmission style so that the indifferent writer, by practising the skill, becomes better. They were choosing identities and declaring allegiances. If nominalization is a marker of academic and corporate language, then it is not surprising that people who feel insecure would try to mark themselves as members of the dominant group:

> Their need to communicate 'group' solidarity was often primary, especially when their roles in the organization seemed in jeopardy. Narrative structures ... allow writers to take roles which match their sense of themselves and their favoured functions in the corporate environment: task-centred, impartial, orderly, non-directive.

Any attempt, by supervisor or teacher, to correct the writing as though it were quite separate from the identity of the writer will seem like an assault on identity itself, like opposition to the cultural affiliation of the writer, who is trying to create a sense of identity by the very act of writing. Reject a feature of writing – or, in a wider context, of the whole language – of a group, and you reject a sign of group affiliation and therefore signal your rejection of the group itself.

'What is good [writing] is what meets the complex needs of the language culture,' say Brown and Herndl; and, as we all know, errors and hypercorrections are often signs that the user is growing and trying on new and not yet fully internalized forms – 'the roots of hypercorrection are aspiration and uncertainty'.

I want to return now to Jason and Leigh, who had the opportunity of working with a sensitive and thoughtful teacher to make important generalizations by reflecting on their experience. If someone were to ask, 'What was the importance of basic language skills in the education of Jason and Leigh?', what sort of answer is possible? It seems from the brief example of their language use shown here that they are competent; but what matters, to them and to us, is what they say, not how they say it. Their comments illuminate the relationships between everyday life and school learning, between identity, personality and day-to-day living, between school competence and survival. It is clear that they have learned from their experiences out of school, as they ought to; and that they can articulate and make generalizations about what they have learned. But the expression of what they have learned, the life generalizations, are made *because* they are expressing and reflecting upon their experiences for other people to read. That process, of experience reflected on, leading to generalizations articulated for others, and then affecting future action, is a neat version of the business of living, of constructing constantly adjusting schemata by which we operate (Kelly, 1955).

Jason and Leigh might not have been able to articulate their own life generalizations if their teacher had not invited them to talk about their experiences and then to write about them in ways that would be helpful to future students. They have learned to ask questions of reticent farmers, to respond to sympathetic offerings, and to move from the necessary writing of autobiography, with its remembering and anecdotes, to informed analysis, by being in a position where they know that other people like them will want to know these things, and that the only way to tell those absent, future readers is to write like this. They are, in other words, generating real uses of language and discovering the real basics – not externally defined, imposed notions about spelling and handwriting masquerading as politically neutral, but energetic expressions of their views of life and themselves. We could also say that they possess useful competencies in writing and have learned other new language competencies, though not those usually defined as 'basic skills' in the way I outlined above. What they have now learned involves social operations in which people use their language resources to control social situations so that they are able to express themselves, feel capable and comfortable, and grow a little as a result.

We are in a position now to say different things about Jason and Leigh and their language performance. We can say that the way they use writing to express their views shows them confident, assured, secure in their understandings and in their roles. Their experiences, the way they see themselves as a result of everything that has happened, including how they have been taught, and the opportunities they have had to reflect on themselves and their experiences make them feel they have something to say.

In these ways they are very different from the Other Guys. Where Jason and Leigh know that they have valuable information to give to other people who want to know it and feel a power and control in the language transaction, the Other Guys feel little power, and the result of their insecurity is an apparent linguistic incompetence. That is the force of the social context in its effect upon language performance. So, although the idea of 'basic skills' carries, as I have suggested, the pedagogic implications that language competence can only be learned by an individual struggling through drills and practice to reach mastery, and that individual mastery is what is called for, it is now clear that the social and cultural contexts in which language is used have a major influence upon the language outcomes. Reflecting on the changes in his own position about learning, Bruner (1986) defines the issues elegantly:

My model of the child . . . was very much in the tradition of the solo child mastering the world by representing it to himself in his own terms. In the intervening years I have come increasingly to recognise that most learning in most settings is a communal acitivity, a sharing of the culture.

That activity applies not just to young children, but to the learning that students do about language competence and functionalism.

What then can we say finally about the business of basic skills, functional literacy and identity? I am arguing that young people will learn how to operate effectively and comfortably with their language if they feel confident and in control of the social context they live and work in. I am arguing therefore that definitions of 'basic skills' and 'functional literacy' must grow out of a shared, negotiated view of what the language is *for*. If functional literacy is defined for people externally, by those in power, then it inevitably involves a range of unarticulated political positions whose effect, intentionally or unintentionally, is to maintain the power position of those making the definition.

To illustrate what I mean, take the idea I discussed earlier of the importance of students being confident and competent spellers. I believe that spelling does matter (Torbe, 1978), but there are very different ways of reaching competence and the differences matter enormously. They matter because there is a difference between learning and being taught, because different processes of learning will support different political ideologies of education. Some of the ideologies are about openness, collaboration, equality and personal ownership of learning; and some of them emphasize obedience to superiors and practising skills in ways determined by other people. In this latter view, achieving a capacity to spell proves that a person is worthy of gaining access to the system; in the first view, gaining control over the spelling system is a way in which the learner discovers how to make autonomous decisions and choices.

Both ideologies agree that it is not enough to achieve competence. Competence in spelling, despite its real social importance, is also symbolic; it is what the learner *becomes* in learning how to spell that matters most. To those committed to the ideology of 'basic skills', some ways of achieving competence are seen as subversive because, for example, they offer the learner independence and autonomy. Even if the result is effective spelling, the political cost would be felt to be too high by those who are wary of systems which give power to people who are usually denied it.

Cook-Gumperz (1986) suggests that the result of many definitions of functional literacy is an education which seeks 'to control rather than expand the life experiences of the working class'. Jason, Leigh and the Other Guys attest, in their different ways, to the importance of workers, new and experienced, feeling that their social context values their experiences and gives them the opportunity to grow and expand. The true basic skills are about social dealings where language expresses and realizes individual identity in the context of shared community intentions.

Notes

1. When detached from its proper context, it becomes something quite different and often celebratory. It is competitive, like ploughing or log rolling; or decorative, like topiary; or therapeutic, as basket-weaving can be.

Stories of Stories: Footnotes on Sly Gossipy Practices
Harold Rosen

Going over past events in our minds must occupy us for a great deal of our spare time, and might be called the typical form of mental activity for many old people.... 'memory' as we usually think of it, takes a narrative form. It may well be that the stage at which narrative speech becomes possible to a child is the point at which memory in this sense begins [Britton, 1970, p. 71].

James Britton touches here on an aspect of narrative largely neglected in the literature. And the literature is huge. It is not as though, when looking at narrative, we find that the field is undeveloped or that studies are sporadic or that they are conducted largely within one discipline. On the contrary, scholars from almost every humanistic and social science discipline (psychology, psychiatry, cognitive sciences, sociolinguistics, history, anthropology, discourse analysis and, above all, literary theory) have turned to examine narrative. We have a name for the study of narrative on which so many diverse endeavours converge – narratology. Gerard Prince, whose book (1982), a kind of users' manual, is called just that, set about outlining its goals.

Narratology examines what all narratives have in common – narratively speaking – and what allows them to be narratively different. It is therefore not so much concerned with the history of particular novels or tales or with their meaning, or with their aesthetic value, but with the traits which distinguish narrative from other signifying systems and with the modalities of these traits. Its corpus consists of not only all extant, but also all possible ones [p. 5].

These goals are ambitious but yet extraordinarily narrow, for they exclude concerns which any educator would regard as central – meaning, narrative thinking, the motives of narrators, culturally specific narrative styles, narrative within spoken discourse and, of course, *memory*, which for James Britton is a starting point. Prince's examples, liberally scattered throughout his text, are all drawn from written narrative, though he claims 'much of what I say is applicable to any narrative regardless of the medium of representation'. The reader will look in vain for any reference to narrative memory or the slightest concern for the thought processes of the narrator. The same is true for many others who attempt comprehensive studies of narrative (see, for example, Chatman, 1978). For James Britton narrative is best looked at, first and foremost, as an act of the mind, the remembering mind, the mind which is for ever sifting the past in order to celebrate, to mourn, to confront its riddles, to rewrite it – in a phrase, to wrest meanings from it. We transform raw events and actions into causes, consequences and point.

If memory does receive attention, it is not at all in the way James Britton had in mind. For, as we might have guessed, it is based above all on *short*-term *recall* of stories which have been read or heard. The tradition goes back to Bartlett's classic (1932) study of retelling. But whereas Bartlett was interested in how narrators interpreted and changed stories, current work puts its main emphasis on how close children and others can come to the original or retain what the investigator believes to be its essential features (plot or 'story grammar'). This has nothing to do with memory as art, our capacity to transform past experience and thus to make our own stories or, like Chaucer and Shakespeare, to make new stories from old ones. I have met people who were shocked at the suggestion that children might be encouraged to change stories in whatever way they wished. They were steeped in curriculum practices which confront the student with the unremitting demand to hand back what has been handed out in the teacher's words, the textbook's words, the blackboard's words. Success is measured by how close the student comes to the original. More sophisticated methods of judging recall have developed within cognitive science, in particular within schema theory (Mandler, 1984).

From this program has emerged the insight that in addition to knowledge about concrete plots and actions people have a more abstract understanding of what happens in stories. From an early age people develop expectations about the overall form of traditional stories: they learn that these stories involve protagonists who have goals and who engage in attempts to achieve these goals, and that goals and events cause other goals and events in predictable ways.

The work is full of interest, yet it is flawed both by the experimental conditions under which it is carried out and by a total disregard for how people, including of course school students, change stories when they retell them, not because of faulty memory of either form or content or specific narrative features, but because that is what creative storytellers, strictly retellers, do everywhere, reworking what is given in the light of other memories of other experiences, of other stories, of other language. The reteller works to his/her own double sense of goodness of fit, that is, both to the original and to his/her own sense of rightness. To read the studies described in Mandler is to be informed by some discoveries but also to be strongly aware of how the self-imposed limitations have taken us a long way away from really motivated storytellers, what they do and why they do it.

Nowhere are memory and narrative more closely intertwined than in the autobiographical story, par excellence in the story which insinuates itself into conversation, which is tendered as a fully valid contribution to that conversation, in pursuit of its evident intents. Indeed, once we are alerted to the presence of autobiographical narrative in everyday conversation, we cannot avoid the impression that it is a powerful and often dominant feature of all such encounters, that we cannot talk freely and informally without drawing on our narrative competence. For we are always testing ideas and motives against our memories. Such narrative, significantly, tends to be eliminated only by special social constraints which announce, 'No stories here', in the seminar room, for instance, or certain religious gatherings. On the other hand in many cultural settings conversation would be defined by the stories which bind it together, the tales of personal experience, the anecdotes. Conversation without stories is impossible to imagine: it would be the banishment of life itself.

It makes sense therefore when we come to look at narrative in school to begin by turning to a careful examination of its most modest and ephemeral moments, performed without benefit of clergy, sanctioned by no hierarchical authority, uncanonized, even despised as some low order activity. We should beware of dismissing 'anecdotes' (e.g. Stahl, 1983) simply because anybody can compose one, which would be like dismissing speech because we can all talk. We need to turn away from those narratives which have won themselves a comfortable and secure place in the curriculum, the great novels, children's literature and even traditional tales, the latter transformed, as Zipes (1983) has shown, into sanitized printed versions in the nineteenth century. We should do this not ultimately to ignore them but so that in returning to them we should do so with a deeper understanding of the narrative impulse. More than this, we would come to respect the skills and complex competences of the everyday storyteller. But that means we come to perceive some new possibilities for the classroom by liberating and extending children's narrative powers to enrich classroom discourse. This is simply to extend what we learned a long time ago from James Britton when he made us think again about that simple activity, talk.

Conversational storytelling fuses memory and autobiography. Michel de Certeau (1980) goes so far as to assert that memory, emerging as oral narrative, is a special resource enabling us to resist institutionalized power and its oppressive discourse: 'It is the strangeness, the alien dynamic of memory which gives it the power to transgress the law of the local space in question' (p. 41). What he calls 'the intense singularities' of storytelling he counterposes to scientific discourse, which, he says, 'eliminates time's scandals'.

> Nevertheless, they return over and over again, noiselessly and surreptitiously, and not least within the scientific activity itself: not merely in the practices of everyday life which go on without their own discourse, but also in the sly and gossipy practices of everyday story-telling.... a practical know-how is at work in these stories, where all the features of the 'art of memory' itself can be detected ... *the art of a daily life can be witnessed in the tales told about it* [p. 42; italics added].

The idea that everyday anecdotal storytelling is an oppositional practice occurs too in Ross Chambers's book (1984), where he argues that the storyteller gains authority without power and thus is able to convert '(historical) weakness into (discursive) strength' and become 'a major weapon against alienation, an instrument of self-assertion'. Everyday storytelling then derives its power from being outside the legitimized operation of institutions and wriggles its way into the interstices of those same institutions.

The extensive literature on narrative has its rewards and frustrations. The adventurous search by scholars for invariant taxonomies is seductive. To read Barthes's *S/Z* (1975a) or Genette's *Narrative Discourse* (1980) is to be challenged and enriched. Yet all the time, with the eye fixed on storytellers who are not thin and elusive spectres hovering behind written text (always scrutinized strictly within its pure white frame), one is conscious that stories are communicative acts committed in particular situations by known and knowable people. Although we might look at certain texts in the classroom in this way ('reading', 'literature', 'comprehension'), it is quite impossible to participate in storytelling as tellers and listeners and not be intensely aware of who is telling, who is listening, the shared history of the group and the particular circumstances of the telling. This is only to do with narrative what we have learned to do with all discourse – put it in context. It is anthropologists and ethnographers to whom we have to turn for a thoroughly contextual approach, for it is they who have shown the significance of *performance*, the very act of storytelling, which is

> a way of speaking, the essence of which resides in the assumption of responsibility to an audience for a display of communicative skill, highlighting the way in which communication is carried out.... From the point of view of the audience, the act of expression on the part of the performer is thus laid open to evaluation for the way it is done, the relative skill and effectiveness of the performer's display. It is also offered for the enhancement of experience, through the present appreciation of the intrinsic qualities of the act of expression itself. Performance thus calls forth special attention to and heightened awareness of both the act of expression and the performer [Bauman, 1986, p. 3].

Here at last I begin to recognize the storytellings in which I have participated, from the unexpected tale which captures conversational space and is readily accorded a larger than usual measure of it to the recognizable storytelling event where by tacit or overt agreement storytelling is the business in hand. For storytelling belongs with conviviality and trust and flourishes when people are comfortable with one another. It both arises from a sense of social ease and also creates it. It confirms and extends social relationships, in the renewal of acquaintanceships, in intervals at work, at street corners, wherever knots of people gather to become spectators of their own lives, as Britton has put it. The stories exchanged on these occasions not only emerge from memory of others but are available for retelling. Memories of the memories of others. It is Bauman who seems to have the keenest sense of what the anecdotal tissue of conversation means.

Because these stories are about known and familiar people and constitute part of their social biographies, they are deeply indexical in a concrete social sense. That is, part of their meaning derives from the indexical associations they evoke – the people portrayed, other known aspects of their lives and characters, including those present at the storytelling event, with whom they are linked by the kinds of social and communicative ties that give cohesion to the conversations in which the stories are told [ibid., p. 76].

After examining in great detail different kinds of Texan oral narratives, he concludes,

When one looks to the social practices by which social life is accomplished one finds with surprising frequency people telling stories to each other as a means of giving cognitive and emotional coherence to experience, constructing and negotiating social identity ... investing the experiential landscape with moral significance [ibid., p. 11].

We are very familiar with the great claims made for the value of studying works of fiction in the classroom and can hear echoes of them in Bauman's analysis of the functions of storytelling. It makes good sense to see in both activities similar forces at work. Fiction writers certainly have always drawn on the resources of the oral storyteller and an unbreakable thread has always linked the two together. But what is being said here is that the oral storytelling has particular potency because the human disposition to narrative experience makes available unique methods and means for creating by themselves ways of achieving in one and the same act the most ambitious of acts – cognitive, emotional, social and moral. Storytelling, then, taken in all its forms, is a curriculum. To isolate a single anecdote by a child and invest it with such huge significance would be to invite ridicule, though closer scrutiny usually reveals a richer meaning than a hasty glance. It is the web of narratives, the storytelling culture, which must be weighed. Narrative both in and out of school is best regarded as a complex set of social practices rather than as isolated texts to be appraised in isolation from each other. It is the narrative culture of classrooms which we should be debating, what it is and what it might be.

I am making no attempt in this paper to draw on all the diverse literature on narrative from which we might derive illumination and develop a full educational theory and practice. I have started on that agenda and some sketches of the possibilities I have expressed in other papers (see Rosen, 1984). Suffice it to say at this point that my own explorations have led me to conclude that we have most to learn from those scholars who have rejected the notion of the autonomy of the text and those who do not see narrative as simply a cultural mirror but rather as a means of actively re-creating and changing culture (see, in addition to Bauman, Hymes, 1981; Polanyi, 1982; B. H. Smith, 1981; Stahl, 1977 and 1983; Tannen 1982 and 1984; Heath, 1983). Wherever we turn in the literature, no matter what its stance, sooner or later we encounter a phrase which suggests an awareness of the deep meaning of narrative in human life and in the human psyche: 'the central function or instance of the human mind' (Frederic Jameson); 'the interpretation of reality is radically implicated in the narrative process from the very beginning' (Jeremy Hawthorn); 'a primary and irreducible form of human comprehension, and article in the constitution of common sense' (Louis Mink). These ideas (there are many similar ones) are usually proposed almost parenthetically when other business is in hand or as an aphoristic reflection generated by a particular study. They are never elaborated, developed or lingered over. For mere writers never seem to ask the question, 'What do I have to do to read a story?' (in Wolfgang Iser, for example). It is an axiom of narratology, which we owe to the Russian formalists, that one must distinguish between actual events which have or might have happened and the discourse which presents them (*histoire* and *récit*), the actual street accident I witnessed and the story I tell about it. This crucial distinction has made it possible to create very refined analyses of the transformations made by narrators of all kinds. Genette (1980) shows with great subtlety the differences between real time and story time. We need, however, to show what exactly even the humblest, youngest storyteller does which reveals the process of the narrative act. Suppose I were to tell you about my frustrated endeavours to fix to the garden door a hook for holding it back in the wind and how I broke two drills in carrying out this simple task. Actually it is quite a long story. For the door-hook events to be rendered into a story, I must do at least the following:

(i)   I must confront the increasing flow of events and actions and, by cutting into them, create 'a beginning', which need not be either an event or an action but might be a way of signalling that I am about to begin a story or a general comment on my life as a handyman or many other opening gambits. This will be my first step in constructing a verbalized demarcation of the events. I am building boundaries with my words.

(ii)   I must then proceed with my boundary building so that what was inchoate, interpenetrated with a multitude of other events, is foregrounded by a process of selection, emphases, silences, evaluations, indications of causality, digressions, reflections, accommodation of the listener.

(iii)   The boundary must be completed with an 'ending' which in reality was no such thing. Life, as we say, goes on. The ending-ness of the final comment or event has to be composed.

(iv)   In telling the story of the door-hook I must draw on all those resources which I have learned from encountering the narrative events of my culture.

That is but the bare bones, sufficient, I hope, to indicate that storytelling calls for an active, exacting attention to the world, the very kind of attention which should be at the heart of learning. An invitation to narrate should be seen in the classroom as a call for this high-order attention. Since narrative draws on any language resource that suits its turn, plundering every kind of discourse, especially through representing the speech of its protagonists, it digs deep into the linguistic resources of the narrator. Indeed, the teachers with whom I am working are persuaded that narrative, more than any other mode, produces the highest levels of linguistic performance.

Deborah Tannen uses the idea of frame in one of her papers on narrative ('What's in a frame?', 1984). She notes the widespread use of terms in many disciplines to deal with patterns of expectation (frames, scripts, schemata, scenes and so forth) such as the typical buyer–seller exchange in a shop. There are two ways in which patterns of expectation can enter narrative activity. The first would make it necessary to modify Tannen's description. Because we develop a rich experience of hearing and telling stories we see one experience rather than another as having narrative potential. Thus an experience in a shop when the normal frame operates, that is, the purchase is effected without a hitch, is scarcely worth the telling. But if I have suffered because of incompetence and incivility, I find myself telling the story. The story will still be framed by the conventions of the buying–selling episode, though I am free to disrupt them both in the actual event and in the telling. But beginnings and endings are naturalized by the culture. Football matches begin with the kick-off and end with the final whistle, but a storyteller, who might be one of the players, is under no obligation to be constrained by that frame. He might begin with a quarrel in the changing room or his thoughts while packing his kit. Nevertheless it would be interesting to know more about events in which we immediately perceive a compelling and dramatic story, ready made. Thus is the stuff of journalism, good and bad. A second refinement which I would add to the narrative-composing process I have outlined above is particularly relevant to the account of personal experience. I was writing briefly the other day about my grandfather handling a piece of cloth from which I wanted a suit made. At the time the scene was, as Tannen suggests, framed by recognition of it as having narrative potential, of matching other scenes in which the craft expert carries out his inspection techniques and his judgement. A half century later around this frame another is constructed. Instead of a structure of expectation derived from similar experiences and relating to a present experience (i.e. a form of memory), we now have the intervention of memory in a different way. The form of presentation (narrative) still conforms to the notion of frame, but this distant scene is now filtered through intervening relevant experience represented in my memory and in particular by the frequent and increasing evocation of my grandfather in my thoughts. This gives autobiographical narrative a fascinating complexity – a new and bigger frame is placed around the original one, which at the same time is definitely not discarded. The autobiographical narrative speaks with a double voice, the voice of then and the voice of now indissolubly fused together. At this point the frame metaphor becomes an encumbrance. I linger over this speculative point not only because of its intrinsic interest, which I could have lingered on (perfectly 'remembered' conversations, for example), but also because it reminds us once again of how complex are the processes by which some stories, easily taken for granted, are composed.

Jerome Bruner has for a long time been a leading participant in seminars on narrative theory and practice at the New School for Social Research in New York. In his most recent book, *Actual Minds, Possible Worlds* (1986), there is a chapter called 'Two Models of Thought' which is a bold attempt to assess the role of narrative in human thought. Bruner starts without compromise by proposing that when we speak or write we have two quite distinct ways of thinking which each give rise to their own kind of discourse.

> There are two modes of cognitive functioning, two modes of thought, each providing distinctive ways of ordering experience, of constructing reality. The two (though complementary) are irreducible to one another. Efforts to ignore one at the expense of the other inevitably fail to capture the rich diversity of human thought [p. 11].

Note first that Bruner is talking about language as a way of 'ordering experience'. One of the two modes is narrative; the other is 'paradigmatic', epitomized in argument, of which scientific thought and discourse are kinds. I immediately find myself objecting. Why are there only two modes of thought, not three or ten? To be sure, Bruner wittily explains that scientists have their stories to aid invention and discovery but these are under-the-counter, non-legitimated ways of going on.

That is surely beside the point, for formal scientific discourse abounds in narrative of processes, descriptions of experiments and case studies. Indeed, it is these narratives which, once freed from the constraints of conventional language and policed style, point the way to a wider role for narrative right across the curriculum – the stories of all kinds of learning experience. Bruner's apparent neglect here is more easily understood if we notice that, although he begins by talking about all narrative, the kind of narrative he has in mind is essentially *literary* narrative. Herein lies the essential weakness of the argument, for he cannot by this approach show us what links all narrators. It also absolves him from the necessity of giving close attention to the ways in which everyday stories enter the fabric of society and would do so if not a single written story existed. He tells us: 'I shall want to concentrate on narrative . . . at its far reach as an art form. . . . The great works of fiction that transform narrative as an art form come closest to revealing "purely" the deep structure of the narrative mode in expression' (p. 15); and 'one does well to study the work of trained and gifted writers if one is to understand what it is that makes good stories powerful and counselling' (p. 15).

None of this is argued, and it certainly does not bear close inspection, coloured as it is by cultural snobbery. It takes nothing away from the great works of fiction to note that they are a particular narrative phenomenon arising from a European historical context, that narrative also exists as a highly developed oral art and, finally, that it is necessary to demonstrate rather than assert that great works of fiction come closest to revealing 'purely' the deep structure of the narrative mode. This would be like saying that the Royal Ballet Company would best reveal to us the deep structure of dance throughout human culture. Bruner writes: 'Anybody (at almost any age) can tell a story.' Any young child can speak but that did not lead Bruner in his studies of early language development to choose star performers. Nor is it any surprise that he chooses to apply his analysis to a classic short story, James Joyce's 'Clay'.

Flawed though this chapter is, we would not expect so profound and adventurous a scholar to fail to provide us with many insights into narrative, though even here he concentrates on the quality of written texts, not on the narrative mode of thought we were promised at the outset. The most promising set of ideas deals with what he calls the subjunctivization of a narrative text, an elaboration of some ideas in Todorov's work. This enables us to see precisely what features in a story change it from a set of mere assertions of fact to an engagement with psychological process, transform 'pure information' to a world of presuppositions, possibilities and predicaments. The whole chapter is richly informed by every strand of narrative scholarship; a better introduction to it could hardly be found. For all my reservations it puts narrative in a context which makes for immediate educational relevance.

Take retelling. Bruner sees how much can be learned from a student's retelling of a short story. His focus is on how the student picks up the subjunctivization of the original story and also strives to preserve its point and maintain its genre. 'Genre seems to be a way of both organising the structure of events and organising the telling of them – a way that can be used for one's own story telling, or, indeed, for placing the stories one is reading or hearing.' All stories feed greedily on other stories in many different ways. Children can soon learn how to compose a particular kind of story. From the retellings I have elicited and examined it is clear that we can go beyond Bruner and say that, given the encouragment of a teacher, pupils can switch in a retelling from one story genre to another. Betty Rosen's book on storytelling in the secondary school contains many examples of students doing just this. If one thing stands out in that text it is that retelling is a profoundly creative activity. For stories do not offer single isolable meanings. They formulate interlocking sets of meanings, and listening to a story is a search for these meanings through the meanings we already possess. In retelling we both repeat the words of others and also change them. Even in the retelling of our own personal intimate stories (for we do retell them!) we change them in new contexts, carrying forward some of the old and with certain reworkings shifting however slightly the meanings of the story. We are incorrigible reworkers of our own and other people's stories. I tell not only my own stories but reworkings of my family's and my friends' stories.

It is worth lingering on this point. We have come to believe that creativity in language consists in the creation of a novel text as distinct from the reproduction of an existing one. And what higher praise can we offer than to say a story is original. Such a view runs counter to all we know about narrative practices. To retell with changes a story we have received is only to continue what we did as little children. The teacher can put richer resources at the disposal of pupils, other stories which propose new strategies, and can provoke students into taking liberties with the original. We might say that this is to turn time-honoured practices over their heads. The schoolboys in Betty Rosen's book are liberty takers of this kind. They elaborate, compress, innovate, discard. None of them is a mindless mimic. They act as all good storytellers do, taking what they want, shifting nuances, even turning the story upside down. These changes repay study for they reveal the creativity of retelling and the delicate tension between reproduction and invention. The traditional storyteller was never a mere echo of an accepted version but a creative performer putting his personal stamp on a traditional tale. The role of the teacher emerges clearly. It is first to emancipate students from the incessant demand for recall and then to set them free to take over the story and bend it to their purposes.

I am intensely aware at this point that in my pursuit of certain themes I have failed to set before readers the kinds of stories which might through their own force have made my points more powerfully. Nor have I sketched out in some detail what is possible in schools. My apology can only be that this will be forthcoming in the publication of work of the London Narrative Group. An American teacher, Valerie Polakon, one of the few who believe totally in stories, including the teacher's stories, argues that the teacher's stories are a valid kind of research.

On every story there exists a dialectic between teller and listener and at some moment the horizons of listening and telling fuse . . . and as our lived worlds merge, engagement begets reciprocity and participation in the world of the other and evokes from us a call to act. The educator–researcher as storyteller is a metaphor for engagement, a call to action.

For narrative truly to penetrate school culture, teachers will need to tell each other the stories of their stories. From that repertoire of metanarrative the best narrative practices will emerge.

The Enterprise We Are Part of: Learning to Teach
Arthur Applebee

Though most of us who work in schools of education in university settings spend much of our professional lives training teachers, we have paid surprisingly little attention to the enterprise we are part of. As educators concerned with language and learning we study how young people learn to read, write and speak, but rarely how our teacher-education students can best learn to teach.

In this chapter I argue that this lack of attention to the process of learning to teach has left the field of teacher education open to theories and approaches that do not blend well with our own beliefs about language learning. Further, that we already have some very powerful models of learning that apply very well to learning to teach if we only take the time to apply these models to teacher education in a systematic and intellectually rigorous way. If we do so, we can better protect the gains we have made in the teaching of English in recent years, and can give our teacher-education students a more powerful and consistent framework for approaching their classrooms.

Teacher Education Today

In the United States today teacher-education programmes are caught in the midst of a variety of conflicting directions and goals. Teacher education as a field of study has concerned itself primarily with the generic skills of teaching: classroom management, lesson planning, discipline and the setting of goals and objectives. Given the history of educational research in general in the USA, and of research on teacher education in particular, this work is often framed in a behaviourist tradition, focusing on the development of particular 'skills' and 'competencies', which must often be 'certified' before a teacher is allowed to teach. At the same time there has been in the past few years a growing emphasis on subject-matter preparation, realized most sharply in the Holmes group recommendations that teacher education should always be a post-baccalaureate enterprise. That, in other words, a teacher should be, first, an expert in a particular discipline and, second, a teacher. In the field of English the practical result of such a recommendation is that teachers train first in traditional literary criticism and then come to a school of education for a year of additional training in classroom skills.

These two traditions, coming together in the training of teachers of English, are at heart antithetical. The classical, humanistic, elitist tradition of the college literature curriculum has little in common with the be-haviouristic, reductionist, management-oriented tradition of teacher education. The usual result is an almost universal disdain for 'education courses', both among beginning teachers and among our colleagues in the university community. (The preparation in literary studies, on the other hand, usually survives unscathed, since it represents 'real' scholarship and a long academic tradition.)

But our reliance on these two traditions to shape teacher education reflects our failure to think carefully about what a teacher must know and do, and to base our teacher-education programmes on the conceptualiza-tion that results. Both traditions foster dangerous misconceptions about the nature of teaching, misconceptions that our beginning teachers will take with them into their classrooms.

Teaching as Management

The misconceptions fostered by the teacher-education programme itself usually have to do with a view of teaching as a variety of skills and behaviours that can be 'trained' and 'improved'. In this image of teaching the skilled teacher is a technocrat, possessed of a variety of teaching technologies that can be deployed to control the classroom and to stimulate learning. In different versions, this image of teaching has led to management-by-objectives, to teacher-proof curricula, to mastery learning programmes, and to teacher-training programmes that emphasize such skills as 'redirecting questions', 'wait time' and 'asking higher-order ques-tions'.

The problem with such approaches is that they are overly simplistic. They emphasize isolated components of a good teacher's behaviour and lose sight of the fact that what distinguishes a good from a poor teacher is the ability to utilize those skills effectively, as part of a larger conceptualiza-tion of the teaching process. Good and poor teachers alike already 'redirect questions', 'ask higher-order questions' and 'wait for student responses', and simply increasing the frequency of such practices without providing an understanding of the contexts within which they are effective will not produce a better teacher.

As teachers of language, we should recognize the problems immediately.

They are directly analogous to those we have long recognized in language programmes that focus on the subskills of reading, writing or speaking without providing real contexts for use. The examples from our field are many, ranging from the long tradition of unsuccessful teaching of the rules of formal grammar, to reading programmes that have been preoccupied with phonics, to spelling and vocabulary drills conducted in isolation from our students' own uses of language. We know that such skills-orientated programmes are easy to construct and easy to monitor; we know too that any improvements they generate in our students' reading and writing ability are minor and short-lived. Why then do we not react more quickly to similar problems in teacher-education programmes?

Teaching as Scholarship

The other image of the necessary preparation for teaching stresses the importance of knowledge of the content field, in our case usually literature. On the face of it, arguments for the importance of such knowledge are unassailable: we can hardly teach a subject we do not know something about, and as English specialists we all cringe at stories about the coach or the maths teacher who is given an English section because 'anybody can teach English'. The problem here is of a different nature; it concerns the role of such knowledge in school teaching.

When we start to teach a new subject, one of the most powerful influences on what we do is our memory of how we were taught. In the teaching of English this has usually manifested itself in a tradition of literary study in which the high-school course mimics (with a sometimes sizable time lag) recent developments in linguistics or literary criticism. Thus at various times in the last hundred years American high-school teachers have concentrated on philology, on literary history, on folk lore and oral interpretation, on the study of semantics, on the new criticism, on deconstruction and on reader response theory. Young teachers have brought these movements straight from their college curricula, with little thought and less understanding about how the approaches might or might not relate to the developing abilities of adolescents.

These approaches may or may not have been appropriate. But what is clear in all of them is that they carry with them a definition of the teacher's role that is shaped by a conception of scholarship in an academic field, rather than by an understanding of the teacher-student relationship. As long as we leave our beginning teachers to rely upon the content of their college curriculum for their understanding of the content of English instruction, we are reinforcing a tradition of what Barnes (1976) has called 'transmission' rather than 'interpretation'. We are inviting teachers to tell students what they should know, rather than giving students an active role in making sense of new material.

An Alternative View

But if there are serious problems in the two major conceptions shaping teacher-education programmes, where can we turn for an alternative view? The best source is in contemporary scholarship on language and learning, a rich body of scholarship which we have used to examine how schoolchildren learn but which we have yet to exploit fully to help us think about the problems of teacher education.

The past twenty years have been a particularly fruitful time for language studies, as indeed they have been for the study of child development in general. The theories of Piaget, Vygotsky, Bruner and others have become widely known, and with them has emerged an image of the child as an active participant in the process of the construction of knowledge. Approaches to reading instruction and to writing instruction have been transformed as teachers and scholars have become aware of the complex processes of comprehension and understanding that go into a reader's or writer's approach to a text. Rather than focusing on the accuracy of the final product, process-oriented approaches to instruction have sought to provide support for the young learner still in the process of solving the problems posed by a particular reading or writing task. 'Prereading' and 'prewriting' activities have become part of the conventional wisdom about effective instruction, as have multiple drafts, peer response groups, small-group discussion and other techniques designed to give students a more active role in the negotiation of meaning within their classrooms.

These are now familiar (if not always implemented) notions to most teachers of English, in large part because of the work of Britton, Martin and their colleagues at the University of London Institute of Education.

As we have learned more about the processes of language and learning, we have also been developing a third body of knowledge to compete with generic teaching skills and traditional literary scholarship for a place in the teacher-education curriculum. This body of knowledge might best be thought of as *subject-specific knowledge of teaching*. In the field of English teaching this subject-specific knowledge is based on scholarship in a variety of fields, but the form it takes is rather different. In its most useful form subject-specific knowledge of English teaching is practical knowledge of the nature of children's English skills, the directions of growth these skills will follow, and the contexts that foster such growth. It is knowledge, for example, of the kinds of literature twelve-year-olds are likely to find difficult, how they make sense of specific works when they read them, and how teachers can structure classroom activities to develop new skills and strategies that may make initially difficult works easier.

In this form subject-specific knowledge of teaching looks very different from knowledge of traditional subject matter. The concerns of the scholar – whether those concerns focus on theories of literary criticism or structures of language – are different from the concerns of the classroom teacher. The universe of scholarship is not irrelevant to the universe of teaching, for the scholar and the teacher are likely to draw on the same texts and have, ultimately, shared goals of understanding those texts better. But the concerns of scholarship must be fundamentally reconstrued before they become relevant to the classroom. It is this reconstrual that should be at the heart of teacher-education programmes.

Principled Practice

What should such a construal look like? One typical approach to defining content for teacher training has been to focus on the performance of expert practitioners or model programmes. Such a concern with identifying and promulgating examples of good practice underlies many popular movements in education. In the United States it is at the heart of the work of the National Diffusion Network, which requires evaluation studies of programme effectiveness; it forms the core of the National Writing Project, which is built around the expertise of successful teachers; it provided the rationale for the Project English curriculum centres in the 1960s; and it underlay the eight-year study of the Progressive Education Association earlier in this century.

These attempts exemplify one seemingly very sensible approach to the specification of good practice. Each relies upon the provision of model approaches, validated against some external criteria (evaluation data for the National Diffusion Network, peer and supervisor recommendations for the National Writing Project, the basic tenets of the discipline of English in the Project English centres, ongoing experience of participating teachers coupled with extensive evaluation data in the eight-year study).

Though seemingly sensible, each of these attempts has failed to have a widespread impact on educational practice. Such failure may be due to the entrenched nature of current approaches to schooling, to the inability to reach a wide enough audience or to some fundamental flaw in the newly advocated approaches themselves. But I want to suggest another and more far-reaching reason for the failure of these reform movements: we have allowed our understanding of teaching and learning to focus on *what* we do when we teach – the activities and curriculum – rather than on *why* we do it – the principles underlying instruction in general and our subject in particular. We need the kind of shift in our thinking that we made in our understanding of reading and writing processes during the past two decades: from a focus on the skills that students need to a focus on the general process of making meaning, from *what* to *why*.

What difference would it make? Current attempts to promulgate 'good practice' give us careful, often enthusiastic, descriptions of new or reborn activities, activities that work beautifully in their original contexts, and that often continue to work well when transported by first-generation disciples. In the enthusiasm for defining good practice, these approaches are often codified in elaborate detail – a detail that describes very accurately exactly what goes on in the successful model classrooms. In turn, these codifications make their way into our methods course, either in encyclopedic methods texts or in collections of readings designed to introduce our students to a variety of successful techniques.

The trouble comes when the approach must be transferred to other schools and teachers, facing a different combination of student needs and experiences. In such a circumstance no set of materials and approaches can successfully be introduced 'as is'; they must be adapted and modified to fit each new context in which they are used. Teachers will take from the new materials what they need for their own classes. This process of 'taking from the new' approach often – perhaps even usually – preserves the form of the approach, but is equally likely to subvert the original purpose, *unless the original purpose is well understood*. If we truly understand *why* a particular approach is working, on the other hand, it is quite possible it will be successfully implemented in new contexts without incorporating any of the 'model' activities at all – if the functions of the original activities can be better served by other activities in the teachers' repertoire.

We can take as an example Marva Collins's Westside Preparatory Academy in Chicago. In her classrooms students study the great masters of the Western tradition – Shakespeare and Sir Walter Scott, Plato and Chaucer. If our teacher-education students were to build upon this approach in a traditional fashion, such works would surely play a central role in the classroom activities they would devise. And just as surely, if these activities were widely adopted as the way to educate children who have repeatedly failed to learn to read, they would fail in the majority of classrooms in which they were introduced. The programme would fail not because it is a poor programme, but because the implementation would have focused on the activities rather than on the principles underlying them. (To speculate, those principles probably have a great deal to do with high expectations for all students, strong role models and an atmosphere in which success is expected and praised warmly when it occurs.)

Where does this leave my concern with the content of teacher education? It suggests that our approaches to teacher training should focus on the development of *principled practice*. Rather than the teacher-proof models of good instruction, models of principled practice would rely on developing the novice teacher's understanding of *why* a particular approach was chosen, and on developing his/her expertise in creating his/her own solutions to the unique problems that a teacher faces in every classroom. Rather than focusing on particular activities that teachers should use, such an approach would focus on principles for orchestrating activities, for choosing what should happen next and why.

Much of what we do in education, even in the most forward-looking programmes, is still at a considerable distance from this image of principled practice. Thus recent work on process-oriented writing instruction has been very successful in specifying a range of useful activities that teachers can introduce into their classrooms, but we have been somewhat careless in developing and clarifying the rationale for those activities. The result has been that in some classrooms (and many composition textbooks) the activities have been introduced for their own sake: all writing activities begin with prewriting, involve a peer response group and require one revision, with no consideration of the particular problems that any given task may pose. Activities that worked well when embedded in purposeful contexts of use lose their power and appeal when stripped of those contexts.

Shifting our focus from knowledge of content or of activities to knowledge of the principles of good practice is thus a critical step in rethinking teacher education. It is not, however, an easy step, because so much of our thinking has focused on activities rather than on principles. We need to reorient not just our teacher-training programmes, but the whole context of professional discussion, research and scholarship that flow into teacher training, to emphasize the principles underlying successful teaching rather than the outward form of good practice. (The shift is analogous to that we have already gone through in thinking about writing: rather than focusing on the outward shape of the final product, we have shifted our attention to the processes that give the final product the shape it has.)

Where does this leave us in terms of the knowledge that beginning teachers of English need to have? It leads towards a conceptualization in which subject-area knowledge of the type provided by an undergraduate specialization in literature must be transformed before it can be utilized effectively. Such a specialization is an important base, introducing prospective teachers to the broad universe of material with which they will eventually deal in their own classrooms. Without this base the curriculum is likely to lose its sense of direction, with no standards to guide selection of the important rather than the trivial. But by itself it will be an inappropriate base for classroom practice because it will be oriented towards the issues shaping the discipline of literary studies rather than those governing the processes of language learning.

The Process of Learning to Teach

So far I have focused primarily on the content of teacher-education programmes, on the question of what beginning teachers should know. But issues of content are not really separate from issues of the process of teaching: what we know is conditioned by how we have learned it.

Here again, our approaches to teacher education have lagged far behind our understanding of children's learning. Our studies of learning have increasingly emphasized the importance of learning in context, of allowing children to take ownership for what they do, of engaging them in an active process of problem definition and problem solving. Our approaches to teacher education, on the other hand, have continued to emphasize knowledge *about* teaching, gained primarily through reading about what others have done. Classroom instruction in teacher-education programmes all too often focuses on introducing students to a potpourri of accepted techniques, sanctified by tradition and by their place in the methods texts. Practice in teaching comes separately, usually in the guise of 'student teaching' done under the supervision of a 'master teacher' at a local school site. Conflicts usually emerge, as the techniques espoused by the university come into conflict with the practical realities of the classroom, and the students find that the techniques they have been introduced to do not work when they try them. Their master teachers confirm that they did not expect such practices to work anyhow, and the tradition of the irrelevant methods course is reinforced once again.

Though the scenario does not always work itself through this bleakly, we should not be surprised when it does. What teachers choose to do in the classroom is shaped by a variety of complex factors, ranging from the demands of a particular curriculum to the needs of particular classes to the time of day and state of the weather. The art of teaching involves the ability to respond to these complex and interacting forces, selecting an approach that will provide the best balance at a given point in time, an approach that will look different on another day or in a different classroom. If we have taught our teacher-education students that the world looks otherwise – that there is a solution they can rely on day in and day out – they are in for a rude and usually painful awakening to the realities of classroom life.

What is our alternative? To use our teacher-education classes as places to introduce students to a range of real problems that they must face as teachers, clarifying principles of good practice as they struggle to find appropriate responses to the problems that we have introduced. If the problems are real, they will have no answers – only a range of alternative approaches that may be valid under different circumstances. As experienced professionals we can provide informed criticisms of the suggestions that our beginning teachers come up with, pushing them for justifications and helping them recognize unanticipated problems, just as in another context we react as more experienced writers to our students' early drafts.

Ideally such a methods class would operate in interaction with our students' first classroom experiences. Such experiences provide the most authentic sets of problems to discuss and the most effective test of the appropriateness of the solutions which have been arrived at. But that in turn requires cooperation and mutual understanding between the school site and the university, rather than the separate territories they presently usually represent.

Principles of Effective Instruction

Much of my argument so far has been based on the assumption that much that we have already learned about language teaching can be applied, in turn, to the problems of learning to teach. I want to carry that argument one step further now, and to claim that the most effective teacher-education programmes will be governed by the same principles that govern effective teaching of oral and written language. The principles of practice that we teach our beginning teachers, in other words, should also govern how we go about that teaching.

Judith Langer and I, in a series of articles and reports, have argued that many problems in instruction can be traced directly to conceptualizations of teaching that reduce it essentially to a process of diagnosing what students know, teaching the missing information, testing to see what they have learned and reteaching – in a never-ending cycle (Applebee, 1986;

Applebee and Langer, 1983; Langer, 1984; Langer and Applebee, 1986, 1987). This model of teaching fits well with 'transmission' views of instruction, but is fundamentally incompatible with process-oriented approaches in which error is expected as part of the process of learning, and in which constructive response and final evaluation are very separate (and necessarily separated) processes.

To provide teachers with an alternative way of viewing their teaching, we have developed the metaphor of *instructional scaffolding* as a way to think about the teacher's role in effective instruction. In this metaphor the teacher's role is one of providing appropriate support as students engage in new and more difficult tasks. This support should be structured to help students internalize new and more sophisticated problem-solving strategies which they will eventually be able to use on their own; at that point the scaffolding will no longer be needed and the teacher's attention can move on to new tasks.

We originally developed the notion of instructional scaffolding to describe effective teaching of reading and writing (Langer and Applebee, 1986), drawing for our arguments on earlier studies of the development of young children's language skills in interaction with adults (who provided appropriate scaffolding to support early language activities). But the model can be generalized, and provides a good way to think about our work with beginning teachers. The five criteria follow:

1. Ownership. Activities that we ask students to undertake must provide room for them to make their own contribution to the task; activities will be less effective if students complete them simply by reciting the teacher or text. In our methods courses this means that the problems we pose must be open-ended, not simply contexts for testing whether students have learned a technique or approach that we may favour.

2. Appropriateness. Activities should be too difficult for students to complete on their own, but not so difficult that they cannot complete them with help. Vygotsky put this best when he noted that 'instruction should be aimed not so much at the ripe, but at the ripening functions.' This implies a careful staging of the problems we introduce, beginning with activities which teachers-in-training can engage in by drawing upon their own experiences as students, and gradually introducing tasks which also require them to reflect upon their new experiences as teachers.

3. Structure. Instructional activities should model an appropriate sequence of thought and language. This will ensure that in carrying out

the task students will also be given strategies and approaches which they can eventually use on their own. A corollary point is that the techniques that are introduced need to be highlighted as the strategies they are, making students aware of the tools that are available and the ways in which those tools can be used. Put another way, as we introduce students to new approaches, it also helps to cultivate the metacognitive skills necessary for them to use the approaches most effectively.

4. Collaboration. The teacher's role in the process of learning should be collaborative rather than evaluative. Evaluation also has a place in instruction, but the process of assessment needs to be separated from the process of teaching and learning. When the two are confounded, we test but do not teach.

5. Transfer of control. As students learn what we are teaching, the scaffolding we have provided needs to be removed so that they can take full control of the activity for themselves. Our attention as teachers can then move on to help them develop approaches to other, more difficult, problems which they cannot yet cope with on their own.

Reflective Teaching

If we approach teacher education in the ways I have been suggesting, we will transform not only the teacher-training programme but also the vision of the teacher as professional. Teachers who emerge from such a programme will be teachers who have a way of thinking about and reflecting upon their experiences that will help them continue to grow, improving their own teaching and, ultimately, helping them contribute to a continuing professional dialogue about the principles of effective practice. They will have seen this process at work in the discussions and activities that constitute their teacher-education programme. And they will have begun to practise applying it as they develop approaches and activities to use with the students they themselves are teaching. Just as Britton (1970) and his brother developed a gradually elaborated map to introduce them to a new childhood neighbourhood, these new teachers will be guided by a consistent map of the processes of teaching and learning, a map that should stand them in good stead as they journey down the path that their own careers will take them.

Part Four   Implementing Change

The concerns which preoccupy the writers up to this point have been essentially those involving the teaching process itself and the theories which underly that process. Between those concerns and the dissemination and implementation of change there is a host of further processes through which messages need to travel. There is the in-service training of teachers, the competition for resources, the managing and orchestrating of teachers with similar concerns, both locally and nationally, and there is the interface with the formal political system and with the media. These are complex processes, if only because they involve new kinds of actors: administrators, advisers and inspectors, academics, journalists and politicians. It goes without saying that this implementation can block or seriously modify what eventually happens in classrooms. English teachers have more reason than most to know this: because we all speak language and it is recognized as a fundamental skill for operation in the world, there is an intense public focus on what English teachers do.

This section contains three accounts of the process of implementation – from Canada, Australia and the UK. What is notable about Don Rutledge's article on the Toronto experience is the sustained administrative attempt to place language and a language policy at the centre of the educational enterprise. Toronto's schools, like those in most Western urban centres, have been challenged by intense pressures, from multiculturalism, community involvement, gender considerations and political controversy. It is clear that to sustain through such pressure a conviction of a more fundamental analysis of the educational process requires vision and considerable administrative energy, persistence and powers of persuasion. The Toronto case study contains both encouragement and warning: with the right kind of leadership, administrative and political, an education system can grow and learn, but it is hard work and a slow process.

Garth Boomer would agree. He begins his account of developments in Australia with a remark of James Britton's to the effect that we need 'to learn how to make better and better compromises'. Not of course that compromises are not needed; they should be better. In seeking to implement a policy of a 'negotiated' curriculum the same slow process is evident and the same degree of energy is needed to sustain momentum. And yet – and here Garth Boomer echoes some of the appropriating motives of writers in the previous section – adverse movements and opposition can be channelled into constructive purposes.

Are there similar lessons to be drawn from the UK? Slowness of change, certainly, and the necessary energy is at least comparable. But the context, Martin Lightfoot argues, is different. No parallel to the kind of committed administrators the Canadian and Australian systems can produce has been seen in the 1970s and 1980s in the UK. He suggests some of the reasons for this and outlines some of the effects. The UK system has divided its energies, and its administrators have been deflected by political necessity into protection of resources and an overwhelming concern with the structure of the system. The effect of this, he argues, has been to place a greater emphasis on local associations of teachers, together often with their English 'advisers', and on the National Association, while at the same time removing them from the main sources of official power. It is in this sense that he sees teaching as a 'rehearsal of politics': English teachers must seek to organize among themselves and persuade, in the absence of the kind of focused administrative direction described so strikingly by Don Rutledge and Garth Boomer.

Institutionalizing Change: The Problem of System Belief
Don Rutledge

This article is about change in curriculum, about the realities of classroom practice, about the inevitable and often useful impact of politics on teaching. It describes a sustained effort at curriculum change lasting more than a quarter of a century, an effort only partly successful and by no means completed, but a real effort in a real place by ordinarily imperfect human beings. This article will acknowledge the partial truths of the current literature of curriculum implementation, but will also point to the enormous gap between intelligent professional analysis and action in the boardroom and at the polling booth. If there is anything different about this description, it will be its argument that change in schools must accommodate and eventually transcend political currents, and that it can only do this, in the end, by producing demonstrable results. The trick is to buy the necessary time so that real change can produce real improvement, assuming, of course, that the desired change is gradually identified and gradually made possible.

The Board of Education for the City of Toronto is a large urban board at the centre of a metropolitan area of about 3 million people. It is one of six regional boards serving metropolitan Toronto and, for purposes of financial planning and some staffing arrangements, these boards come together in the Metropolitan School Board. Otherwise the boards are largely autonomous. Certainly they take various approaches to education. The Toronto Board operates 163 schools and has about 65,000 students, with a teaching staff of about 4500. Since 1950 the population served by the board has become more and more heterogeneous, so that now more than half of the students come from homes where English is not the first language. Most of the board's publications and communications for parents are printed in nine different languages: English, Polish, French, Spanish, Chinese, Italian, Greek, Portuguese and Vietnamese.

Over the last twenty-five years the board has made radical shifts in its policies concerning multiculturalism, race relations, affirmative action and community involvement. These shifts do not make the board unusual, although most would agree that the board has been unusually enlightened and certainly a leader. What is unusual in Toronto is the unifying nature of its linguistic policy and the political and popular approval that policy has won.

There are several chronic difficulties in creating, sustaining and attempting to implement a consistent language policy. Teachers must come to understand it and believe in it or they will not make the difficult efforts required to change classroom practice. Politicians must be persuaded that it is effective and therefore worthy of financing and staffing. Parents and the general public must understand that it answers their anxieties about usage and rigour. Committed subject specialists must see it as enhancing the teaching of literature, physics, mathematics or whatever they care passionately about. Senior administrators must understand it well enough to make it simple and to see its implications for all the other policies being developed. (When system-wide curriculum implementation plans or teacher performance reviews are being devised they must have the language policy at their core.) Most important of all, when accountability is invoked and a system-wide evaluation of pupil progress is ordered, that evaluation scheme must not violate the language policy and its teaching practice.

In short, what is needed is what the curriculum theorists call a 'system belief'. It hardly needs saying that such a belief can be a dangerous and limiting orthodoxy. If it is to be sustaining and systematic, it must deal with the roots of learning theory, and it must have wide practical implications and applications. The language policy adopted by the Toronto Board in 1982 is not merely a rhetorical statement but a lengthy document which articulates most of the now commonly held principles for developing linguistic competence. It did not arrive full-blown, but grew out of fifteen years of learning and debate among Toronto teachers, administrators and trustees. The story of that policy evolution is perhaps worth telling.

One hot August day in 1965 James Britton spoke to the Inspectoral Board of the Toronto Board of Education on 'Language and Learning'. He began by rejecting the traditional literacy criticism-cum-grammar view of English teaching, and he also disagreed with the basic premises of the project the United States Defense Department was funding at that time in Oregon, with its division into language, literature and rhetoric.

They've looked at literature or the work of literature and they've looked at the grammar and they've structured these things and they are now attempting in their curricula to teach these structures.... My objection to any of these facts as a starting point is that they take a fact and they examine that and then they ask how to teach it. They haven't asked the earlier questions: what is language? How does it work? What use does a boy or girl want to make of his mother tongue? ... What we've got to do is to look at linguistic activity in children, in ourselves ... and that is the structure to operate on.

Britton went on to explain Cassirer's view of the human being as unique among animals in his symbolic system. He then took the somewhat bewildered audience through the function of language in creating both prospect and retrospect, and how this creates man's inevitable social nature. 'If man symbolizes experience, the representation is something which lasts in time, which doesn't disappear when the phenomena disappears, and therefore can be worked upon. And since it lasts in time and can be worked upon, it can be worked upon jointly, and this seems to me to be the key to it.'

Before he was finished that afternoon Britton had gone on to deal with early language acquisition, with the spectator/participant distinction and with the relationship between every-day conversation and literature.

I think the whole function of working upon our representation of experience through talk and literature is to preserve the faithfulness and the shapeliness and the unity of our representation of the world.... In other words, our picture of the world is only maintained as active, unified and harmonious by strenuous attempts to come to terms with experience, using language as the instrument for doing so, structuring experience by talking and reading and writing, both in the role of participant and in the role of spectator.... English teachers above all are concerned with the role of spectator, concerned therefore with the kinds of literature that the children write and the kind they read, concerned with the unity of those two processes.

To many these ideas now seem merely received wisdom, so it is difficult to imagine how eccentric they seemed to some at the time. To the inspectors it was an astonishing speech, and the inspectors were duly astonished. But they were also impressed, and senior administrators at the board began immediately to think of the implications all this had for teaching practices. They were not naive. They realized that radical changes in classroom practice could not come quickly, and they saw how essential it was for teachers to be introduced to underlying linguistic theory. And thus began a change in direction which the Toronto Board of Education has stayed with: the evolution of a language policy which was eventually endorsed by the board formally and in considerable detail. The application of linguistic theory to teaching and learning has been the central focus of the Toronto Board for almost a quarter of a century and it remains the focus in 1987.

Britton's influence on this has been important. Every year since 1965 he has visited the classrooms and done in-service work for the Toronto Board. He has lectured, demonstrated, lived in 'project' schools for weeks at a time, collaborating with staff. He has offered seminars short and seminars long on all aspects of language. In 1977 he joined the staff of the Ontario

Institute for Studies in Education, and from that nearby base he served as mentor and teacher to many Toronto Board teachers. His growing influence after the Dartmouth seminar gave him a strong voice when the Ontario Ministry of Education published new provincial guidelines in English and other subjects. In fact, it is impossible to separate his impact on Toronto from his part in the general growth of the language-and-learning movement, which also affected Toronto as it did many other cities. Others who are part of that development have visited or lived in Toronto and had their influence as well – Nancy Martin, Geoffrey Summerfield, James Moffett, Harold Rosen, Douglas Barnes, Jerome Harste, Michael Halliday, Frank Smith, Yetta Goodman, Myra Barrs. But for Toronto the most powerful force has always been James Britton. And for Britton Toronto represents one major educational system which has consistently worked to give his ideas about learning a practical application. Why? What particular congruence of circumstances has made this consistency possible?

The timing, for one thing, was exactly right. The Toronto Board had in 1962 created a Language Study Centre, dedicated to involving teachers in the improvement of language instruction. (That such a centre could be created and not made either an English department or a language arts department indicated the board already had some broader vision of language than was general at the time.) In England complex factors, including the growth of interest in Vygotsky and other linguists, were leading to the debates at the Dartmouth seminar of 1966. The Toronto Board was searching for an informed and coherent basis for the improvement of instruction. And Dr Z. Phimister, Toronto's Director of Education in the early sixties, had the wisdom to invest authority and resources in the new learning venture. From the beginning the Language Study Centre enjoyed status, and for many years it could draft promising teachers and principals to its staff. Two-way traffic with the schools has been important. A score of practising principals and superintendents in Toronto's schools today have worked as consultants in the Language Study Centre. For the last five years the first qualification listed in advertisements for school superintendents is knowledge of linguistic theory and demonstrated skill in its practical applications.

All of this evolved gradually and as part of a general shift, of course. Toronto for many years was going with the stream, not against it. Britton could have been talking about Toronto – and perhaps to some extent he was – in his address to the Third International Conference on the Teaching of English in Sydney in 1980 (Britton, 1982a):

But the recognition that learning is always an interactive process is a crucial first step: its implications – that talking and writing may be modes of learning, that a curriculum must be negotiable, that in-school and out-of-school learning should be inseparable parts of one pattern – the working out of these implications constitutes an area of active innovation in secondary schools today.

These were the ideas that blossomed in the 'sixties, a heady and dangerous decade. I see it as a 'grand processional' from the Dartmouth Conference in America to the Bullock Report in England. It was heady to have ideas that had germinated in quiet processes and small circles suddenly come out into the open; and dangerous in the way that an institutionalized orthodoxy is always dangerous.

In Toronto the blossoms have changed a little over the last twenty years but they have never wilted, so the questions remain. Why did the new ideas take root, leading to new frames of mind and new patterns of teacher? And, equally interesting, why has Toronto persisted with this approach to language in spite of political vicissitudes? Part of the answer is that senior levels of authority have supported the changes. The Ontario Ministry of Education has endorsed a language-in-use policy and given it practical application in its authoritative provincial guidelines. The senior administration of the Toronto Board of Education has also understood the depth of the changes required, the length of time necessary and the inevitably uneven nature of classroom reform.

Yet the process has been strenuous and its continuing a perennial feat. In fact, the institutionalizing of change has been as difficult in Toronto as elsewhere. Conservative teachers for a long time scoffed at a passing bandwagon and refused to change. (Some still do, but not openly. The new orthodoxy is now powerful.) The anxieties about grammar and literature continue, although *among teachers* they are less acute. New immigrants to the city must be persuaded that a frontal attack on spelling and grammar is not the best approach for their children. Public understanding of the new methods must be fostered and the results must be reassuring. The role of language instruction in fighting racism and stereotyping must also be understood and demonstrated. Politicians naturally and properly need reassurance about performance levels. System-wide evaluation must be sensitive and intelligent. It must not dictate outmoded teaching practice as poor evaluation techniques tend to do, yet it must deliver an accurate reading of student achievement. In summary, the new linguistic theory and practice must suffuse and inform every aspect of the board's activities. Eternal vigilance is needed in shaping policy, and some depth of understanding is therefore required in senior administrators.

But all this continuing support from the top would not have worked unless it had been accompanied by something crucial to Britton's approach

– respect for teachers' opinions and experience. There is no doubt that the new ideas and methods were introduced *to* teachers in Toronto, not *by* them. But teachers were presented with the new ideas as possibilities, not as dogma; not as lesson structures. Britton summed it up in 1980 in a speech in Australia.

I think there are great opportunities for people like me – in professional development, initial and in-service training, whatever you call it – provided we see that interactive learning applies to teachers as well as to those they teach; provided we see our role as helping them to theorize from their own experience, and build their own rationale.

What has been happening in Toronto has been the active involvement of teachers in their own learning. Not all have been involved, and those involved have learned varying amounts. Old practices have by no means vanished. Grammar is still taught in formal isolation by some teachers. Socratic lessons on the literary devices in Shelley's 'Ode to the West Wind' can still be observed, although increasingly rarely. *Grouping* of students working individually is still as common as genuine *group work*. But for many of Toronto's teachers the basic arguments of the movement were and are persuasive. Some practices began to have intellectual respectablity – more opportunity for talk in small groups, more use of writing to learn in all subjects, more concern for the language in which presentations are made to children either orally or in textbooks. As for reception of students' spoken language, that was seen as crucial.

Emphasis was also placed on how the student's written work was received. It was not to be constantly evaluated and graded with reference to its comprehensiveness, accuracy and freedom from solecisms. Only on rare pre-arranged occasions was that to happen. It was, instead, to be seen as part of an evolving thought process which would both influence and result from the student's linguistic growth. The cumulative writing folder became important. The teacher's job was to deepen both thinking and language by entering into a discussion concerning what is written; clarifying, enlarging, rejecting or questioning fallacies or wrong information, pushing the student to think and write better, and dealing with form only as a means to that end.

So the changes in teaching practice in Toronto have been uneven, but they have been substantial. It would not be too much to call them a revolution. The security and energy afforded by administrative and political enlightment were put to good use – and that enlightenment would not have been present had less coherent and intelligent reforms been proposed.

It may not be clear from the account above that the language-teaching revolution in its particular emphasis in Toronto has been a little different from that in the English-speaking world generally. It has stressed the child's expressive language in the classroom, and that has led to the other side of that coin, an emphasis on great literature – especially poetry in the primary years. From the beginning it promoted the active use of language by the learner, and that created an upsurge in early student writing long before the influence of Donald Graves became strong. Through the years Toronto has worked hard to promote the idea of a continuum of language with the expressive at the centre. (As Britton once said, ' "Hey diddle diddle" leads inexorably to *The Critique of Pure Reason*.') This idea, it seems to us, is crucial to an intelligent understanding of the 'language across the curriculum' movement. There is a growing understanding of Sapir's (1961) dictum that expressive language is the language closest to its user, and is the foundation on which even the most apparently impersonal discourse must build if it is to avoid a sterile anonymity.

Toronto attacked the poetry question in the primary years first. Britton stunned some teachers by reading Rossetti, Blake, Shakespeare and other great poets to very young children – and finding enthusiastic listeners. From the beginning he advocated fostering this response by opening doors, not closing them; by building on the student's genuine responses with little attention to formal analysis or even, initially, to explicit comprehension. Perhaps his greatest contribution to the teaching of poetry to young children in Toronto was his demonstration that you do *not* teach great literature, but present it consistently. (As Northrope Frye says, 'You can't teach literature. You can just keep them at it.') Teachers became accustomed to having him visit their rooms for a quiet ten minutes to read 'The Chimney Sweep', 'Space Travellers' and 'The Forsaken Merman', then to sit quietly for a while if the children wanted to talk. Teachers got over looking for the lesson plan, eventually. They learned two or three things – read good literature; read it consistently; let the articulation of the student's response come only if it is important to the student.

A few more observations about Britton's effectiveness in Toronto and his part in the total effort at change may be useful. His total message is complex, and current wisdom in curriculum implementation theory would judge it as unlikely to affect classroom practice on a large scale. But one reason for Britton's success with teachers is his consistency, which teachers begin to realize springs from conviction. In May 1986 Britton gave a talk on literature to a large audience of Toronto teachers. He was anxious to distinguish literature from daily discourse, yet to make it part of the language continuum. It was not a simple talk, but once again he demonstrated that his latest ideas rise naturally from his thinking of twenty years ago. Teachers respect the integrity and the consistency, so they strive to understand the approach and its implications for their classes.

In all of his Toronto work Britton has not only championed the teacher but preferred to work with the individual teacher or with small groups of teachers in the school. When Toronto initiated its version of 'effective schools' in the inner city back in 1975 Britton soon became a familiar figure in them. In particular he worked in Toronto's first 'project' school – Dundas Public School, a primary/junior school in the heart of one of the city's poorest and toughest neighbourhoods. Here he began a dialogue with the teaching staff which has lasted ten years and more. Some teachers accepted his views readily, but some did not, opting for basal readers, 'remedial' exercises, decorum and rigid discipline. The school was assigned extra staff because of its inner-city status, and some of these were used to provide spare periods for teachers to discuss, reflect on and perhaps modify their teaching practices. Arguments were often long and heated, and James Britton was at the centre of them, usually calm and patient, but sometimes irritated. Never patronizing. (A startlingly large file containing transcripts of some of those staff discussions over a two-year period sits in my office today. Were resources and money available, these transcripts would merit examination. They might help reveal some of the real reasons why teachers alter their practices. Most teachers at Dundas *did* change their opinions and their methods – but some of them took a long time to do it.)

The value of his being on site for long periods of time was enormous. He formed lasting friendships with many of the staff, and his willingness to admit difficulties and yet demonstrate the power of his convictions produced many a convert. The practical nature of his work in the 'project' schools also won credibility for many of the practices he advocated throughout the Toronto system. He showed that he was willing to live according to his own (and George Kelly's) description of the best human behaviour, conducting life in the nature of an experiment, confirming or rejecting hypotheses in the light of experience. His wide background knowledge in many subject areas made it possible for him to demonstrate one of his basic tenets – that the teacher must bring to the interactive learning experience a rich input. He demonstrated what he wrote elsewhere – 'that teaching consists of moment-by-moment interactive behaviour, behaviour that can only spring from inner conviction.' (Britton, 1982b)

Britton's personal and continuing involvement in those inner-city Toronto schools was important to the acceptance of change. It was unusual for teachers to have a person of such stature with them for practical teaching involvement over weeks and months. It was perhaps equally unusual for such a person to have the desire and the chance to prove his own pudding. The dangerous experiment worked, on the whole.

Throughout Toronto teachers are increasingly willing to try new methods, and the notion that the language-and-learning movement is just another passing fad has pretty well disappeared. Which is not to say that the day is won. There will have to be many more years of trial and error, and the long-range results will have to vindicate the practices.

The difficulties that persist were predictable, and they will probably persist for some time. The biggest difficulty, as the teachers know, is that the new approach requires much energy and some wisdom. The paragon teacher needs the inner conviction, the depth of experience and knowledge that makes it possible to shape at the point of utterance. She must also have an acute sensitivity to what the students need next, the ability to discern the cutting edge of student competence and keep feeding it appropriately.

Many good teachers feel sadly aware of inadequacies. And even those who believe that they *can* teach in this manner worry about 'covering the course', dealing with the topics outlined in provincially or locally assigned curricula. They are often torn, knowing that reverting to content-covering impositions may allay their anxieties temporarily but will be destructive to real learning. What remains to be demonstrated for many teachers is that the student's increasing autonomy as a learner can eventually make the learning both swift and deep. Teachers know that is how their *best* students learn – independently, energetically, voraciously. Some teachers are still sceptical about producing such results among the *majority* of students. But as the nature of learning becomes clearer to them, they are convinced that nothing else really works.

It is surprising to some that the new emphasis on active learning is gaining ground in the secondary schools. The subject specialization and the heavy course content would seem to be problems, and for quite a while they were. But in Toronto the new methods are now being attempted in the secondary schools. The spearhead group are English teachers of some experience, many of them now department heads. (A few are now vice-principals and principals.) They are honours graduates in English, many of them with graduate degrees, many of them disciples of Northtrop Frye at the University of Toronto. They were trained as Socratic teachers in teacher's college, so they are good questioners; they have Frye's vision of literature as a prime means of educating the imagination. They are well read, passionate, intelligent, sceptical of most educational reform. Yet in Toronto they have gradually come to be the best informed and most vigorous proponents of language-in-use. Partly they are products of the general shift in teachers' consciousness about language during the past decade, including the growth of the cooperative learning movement. Partly they are influenced by the theorists who visit the Toronto Board. They have formed their own council, which flourishes, inviting speakers and sponsoring discussions. Because they are respected by their peers, these English teachers are beginning to make teachers of all subjects consider language use and its relationship to student learning. Their influence is much more powerful than official pronouncements. And the desirable effect is to foster intelligent discussion among teachers within a school and across the system.

All of this owes much to Britton, of course. Linking language, life, learning and literature consistently and coherently, Britton also interested many teachers in the theoretical giants on whom he draws to produce his rich synthesis – Vygotsky, Luria, Piaget, Kelly, Polanyi, Langer, Sapir and Chomsky became familiar names through the seminars and through the years. So gradually a considerable number of Toronto teachers have become knowledgeable about the underlying ideas which inform Britton's vision, and they have come to appreciate its compelling coherence. For many of them this vision and the reading they have done in coming to understand it have altered their own view of life and generated their new enthusiasm. They are the people who provide leadership to other teachers now.

Each year in Toronto a course in 'language theory' is offered. The calendar description reads like this:

This series of five seminars will provide a *brief introduction* to some of the most powerful ideas concerning language that have developed during the last century. So that the conduct of the course will embody the learning principles outlined in Ministry and Board policy concerning language, all participants will be asked to do preliminary reading assignments and to be involved in the presentation of material during the seminars themselves. Two books will be provided in advance to all participants: *Prospect and Retrospect* by James Britton, and *Children's Minds* by Margaret Donaldson. In addition, printed materials and bibliographies will be circulated at appropriate times.

Most of the reading is Vygotsky and Piaget. Readings from Bruner, Britton and Donaldson draw out implications for teaching. The course is always offered in the spring, often offered in the fall. Registration is limited to twenty-two for each session and there are, therefore, about forty graduates each year. A waiting list of applicants remains a happy problem, since the list remains long six years after the course's inception. How much of this continuing interest arises spontaneously and how much results from a desire to be promoted is impossible to say. Some of those who are doing the right deed for the wrong reason are surprised by their own enthusiasm once they begin the reading. Nobody finds the course easy. Everybody participates. Gradually most relax. Some administrators do as well in their presentations as some classroom teachers.

The description continues as follows:

Students will not learn to speak, read and write well unless they are speaking, reading and writing to learn all their subjects. So the *use* of language is what produces good linguistic and academic results.

Of course language across the curriculum does not just happen. Teachers and their principal share in the development of a school program which involves much active use of language by the student. In schools where language across the curriculum is really happening students will have a considerable amount of written work in their files, and this work should become increasingly complex and accurate as the student moves up the grades. In addition, the teachers will always be introducing new words and concepts related to the subjects they are teaching, and they will continually be helping the students to improve their control of both speaking and writing.

A good language across the curriculum program requires patience. It is always a temptation to put the teacher's words or the textbook's words into the student's notebook without being sure that the student really understands. But to give our students a firm base for future work, we have to be sure they have moved *from information to understanding*. Since we have all had the experience of trying to explain something complicated to somebody else, we know that explaining an idea in your own words is the best way to understand that idea. As students get used to recording events, experiments and ideas every day at the earliest grades, their writing and their understanding improve. They are put in control of their own intelligence.

Public reaction to the interpretation of the new language teaching has been quite positive – partly because the emphasis in schools really is on reading and writing. But results must be reassuring. During all the years of attempted change, the threat of system-wide standardized tests has hovered. In the spring of 1987 the political arm of the board demanded some form of system-wide accountability and a new evaluation policy. In anticipation of this demand, a small group of staff had been preparing an evaluation scheme which provides appropriate monitoring of system achievement through random sampling, without imposing standarized tests and without ranking schools. After hot debate, a list of principles was approved and a variation of the staff plan formed the basis for action.

The specific implementation of this evaluation policy is now being worked on by committees of teachers who will attempt to meet the acknowledged need for public information about achievement in general while still honouring the professional function of the teacher in making judgements concerning individual students. If this total solution works, the results will be a reconciliation of political and parental needs with teachers' professional responsibilities. So far there is evidence that the 'new teaching' will meet the new accountability demands without any loss of integrity.

So the changes in Toronto continue. Only a careful documentation of classroom practice would reveal the extent and nature of the changes and only the newly planned monitoring of student achievement will reveal the extent of the improvement – if any. There is no doubt about the reality of the change, however. Most teachers have seen to it that talking and writing by students have sharply increased. Since language-in-use is official board policy, even the most obdurate of teachers have been persuaded to try some changes as part of their teacher performance review.

In the end it is up to the individual teacher, as it must be. We would not believe in uniform learning any more than we would believe in legislating teacher behaviour. Sometimes, even so, we feel that Toronto's commitment has been a little doctrinaire, a little impatient, a little 'administrative'. But perhaps Toronto has been as stable and enlightened as can be reasonably expected of a large board. That stability is necessary to quiet work and political acceptance.

The chief learning from the Toronto experience is that both an enlightened administration and intelligent theorizing by teachers themselves are needed if teaching is to improve. Teachers, parents and politicians are like students, they must make the new ideas their own. Everyone involved is now familiar with one of Britton's favourite sayings, from Rufus Jones, the American Quaker: 'I pin my hopes to quiet processes and small circles in which vital and transforming events take place.'

Negotiating the System: A Letter to James Britton
Garth Boomer

Dear Jimmy,

Back in 1978 when you were in Melbourne doing consultancy work for the Education Department of Victoria, I asked you a question about strategy. It was at a time when, after a period of development and growth in education in the early seventies, the shades of the prison house seemed to be closing in again. I was impatient to be pressing on. A national task force on the role of language in learning, of which I was a member, was working 'across the curriculum' to test the effects of negotiation as a means of securing the intention that unlocks tacit powers. The results were exciting. Cumulatively, teacher inquiries in subjects as diverse as mathematics and home science, at both primary and secondary levels and even in classes with severe disabilities, attested to the power of student intentionality. Members of the task force and the teachers with whom we worked knew that you and Polanyi were right.

The book, *Negotiating the Curriculum* (Boomer, 1982b) eventually chronicled the learning which we did at that time. It was written by teachers, both primary and secondary, on subjects as disparate as mathematics and outdoor education and even work on documents in a special education class. The tenets of negotiating the curriculum are directly related to the principles of language and learning which underpinned the influential book *Language, the Learner and the School* (Barnes, Britton and Torbe, 1986). If, in Vygotsky's terms, schools are to effect productive connections between the rising spontaneous concepts of learners and the formal concepts of subject disciplines, then students must be invited to help shape the curriculum journey so that it takes account of their present store of experience and language and allows them to use language and thinking exploratively as they move into new territory. The personal construct psychology of George Kelly sees deliberate learning as an experiment which must be in the control of a learner who has intentional designs. Linking Kelly with Vygotsky, as you have done in your own work, we in Australia developed a strong and clear conception of learning and teaching which required a co-curriculum planning relationship between teachers and students. Until such a regime and such a process was at the heart of classroom activity in all subjects, we saw that efforts to introduce theories of language learning would tend to result in cosmetic surface changes but little fundamental change.

As I say, I was anxious to bring on the learning revolution I believed was necessary. And so I asked you, 'What is our greatest challenge over the next decade?' Do you remember your answer? You said, 'We need to learn how to make better and better compromises.' I don't know whether you sensed my disappointment. There was I, uncompromisingly sure of what we needed to achieve in our classrooms, and you counselled compromise. I've thought about your counsel often ever since.

In a recent note, you said you tend to think of me as misemployed as chairman of the Commonwealth Schools Commission in Australia. This has set me to wondering just what we have achieved since I saw you last and, in particular, what being a bureaucrat of a kind has led me to see and to think about what strategic gains we have made.

This letter is by way of reporting back. The decade is over and your advice to me is now, retrospectively, brimful of meaning. I'm almost ready to write the sequel to *Negotiating the Curriculum*. I think I'd call it *Negotiating the System: Struggle and Compromise in Education*.

You know, I should have made better connections back in 1978. After all, what is negotiation of the curriculum but a process of mutual compromise between teacher and learner, an agreement to work together on certain tasks in certain ways? Of course, it is a negotiation between unequals, in that teachers have the positional power, the experiential power and the power of sanctions (of pass and fail). Compromises are therefore likely to be strongly loaded in the teacher's direction. The student's negotiating territory is likely to be constrained, contained and, given the persuasive power of teachers, colonized, even if ever so gently. This kind of analysis has led some of the critics to label negotiation in schools as a confidence trick.

My rejoinder is to talk about the intention and the learning theory of teachers who engage in negotiation. If the teacher's intention is solely to lure students into learning what he or she has decided will be on the menu, then the negotiation will be a power play that diminishes students. Such strategy will lead in schools, as in life, either to gullible capitulation or to cynical rejection by those who have twigged the hypocrisy. I don't see how someone with a well-developed learning theory based on intentionality and the personal/social construction of meaning could indulge in this kind of subterfuge. Therefore I am led to assume that such a teacher is likely to be a crypto-behaviourist, a transmission wolf in sheep's clothing.

In contrast, the teacher who has a deeply internalized view of the learners as scientists, pushing their present constructions into new territories, will negotiate to empower, to ensure, as far as possible, that the students are not participants in the teacher's script but *bona fide* planners and writers of their own script.

And yet I have come to see how even the best-intentioned teachers must fall short of their ideals. First, there are the witting compromises which they must make in order to live to fight another day, based on judgements about the personal energy that would be spent in tackling an issue now, about the short-term and long-term consequences for the cause and about the penalties which would befall the teacher, and indirectly the class, if a certain controversial course were pursued – the stigmatization of the different or the disruptive.

Then there is what I dramatically call institutional contamination. We become so used to living in institutions that, no matter how vigilant we are, we carry with us and perpetuate certain habits, values and metaphors ingrained, naturalized, in the fabric of institutional life. Even something as seemingly innocuous as ticking and crossing student work carries with it vast and powerful assumptions about teacher authority, motivation and the reciprocal roles of teacher and learner. The very way that the curriculum is timetabled in blocks and fragments predisposes schools and teachers towards a factory metaphor of education.

You may be pleased to know that today, having seen many fine teachers reach the point of despair (resignation or illness) through trying to be too pure in an impure medium, I counsel compromise and the abandonment of guilt.

I have known teachers who were able to read their students and themselves well, but lacked a theory about how schools, the system and society works. These teachers bore enormous burdens of guilt because, try as they might, they could not seem to secure what they knew to be right. Once they had realized that schools and classrooms are framed in various ways and understand how this framing shaped their work, they became liberated compromisers, working long term to change what needed changing but relatively guiltless about what cannot be changed at once.

Meanwhile, explicitly where possible and tacitly always, they continued to work in the direction of their ideals. They became strategic both within their classrooms and in their systems. They had learned how to make good compromises.

One of the other things you said to me, years ago, concerned perspective. We need to view our efforts for change over a ten-year time span or else we are likely to go mad, you said, or at least that is how I have put you into my own words. Well, I have heeded this advice and I can now see some progress. I shall leave it to others to attest to my sanity.

Since 1978 I and many other Australians interested in language and learning have been negotiating within the system of education, and I thought it might be useful and interesting if I reflected a little on what we have learned. This will also help me to report back to you on what has been happening in Australia.

By the way, 1978 seems to have been benign in comparison with the bleak winds of 1987. We are in considerable economic difficulty. Along with reductions in resources, there is a concerted devaluing of public education and the prevailing mood amongst parents is fear that their children will not make it in an uncertain and hostile world. It is not easy to hold the line amidst the panic. Whether in classrooms, schools or systems there is a renewed and urgent preoccupation with control. In the politics of education it is unwise to be caught using the 'soft' and 'romantic' language of the progressive seventies. Thus 'negotiation' has become 'making contracts' and 'writing to learn' translates to something like, 'increased use of extended prose in the content areas to promote intellectual rigour'.

'Language across the curriculum' as a slogan still surfaces from time to time, usually in the context of fears about the decline of language standards, but there are few schools which promote an inclusive school language policy of the kind that was promulgated in the UK in the early seventies.

'Language and learning' still has 'legs', as we say in Australia. It survives both as a slogan and as a strategy. The national Curriculum Development Centre has a language and learning management committee which has taken up the work of the former Language Development Project and is preparing a national statement on language development. While state-based language and learning units are all extinct, many of the people who were once part of them have moved into the system, usually at a higher-status level, and continue to promote the ideas through systems' guidelines, school improvement programmes, curriculum development policies and other special change initiatives, such as the nationwide Participation and Equity Program, which is a specific-purpose programme administered by my agency, the Commonwealth Schools Commission. I think you would be surprised to see how orthodox, at least in the rhetoric, many of the key tenets of language and learning theory have become in the official curriculum guidelines, often couched, of course, in subject-specific terms.

The Participation and Equity Program actually *requires* parents, teachers and students to work together in formulating and enacting plans for school improvement. Tasks set for participating schools included:

- engaging the whole school community in an investigation of the reasons for early school-leaving
- negotiating with students, staff and parents for appropriate changes in school organisation and curriculum
- organising professional development activities involving staff and parents at school level
- liaison with community groups, employment agencies and other education and training institutions [from *Participation and Equity in Australian Schools*, Commonwealth Schools Commission, March 1984].

Similarly, guidelines in mathematics will now emphasize the importance of small-group techniques for problem solving. They will discuss the special features of the language of mathematics and will emphasize teaching techniques which take account of and draw on the present conceptual frameworks and experiences of the learners. The national Curriculum Development Centre (part of the Schools Commission) currently has a Mathematics Curriculum and Teaching Project. This programme has translated principles of language and learning into an in-service model in mathematics. All courses in the project have these features:

- They all address issues of concern identified by classroom teachers.
- They take place as closely as possible to the teacher's own working environment.
- They take place over an extended period of time.
- The teachers have the support and participation of their colleagues and the administration.
- The programs provide opportunities for reflection and feedback.
- Participating teachers are able to feel a substantial degree of ownership.
- The programs involve a conscious commitment by the teachers participating [from Lovitt and Clark, 'The winds of change are sweeping through maths education', in *Curriculum Development in Australian Schools*, January 1987].

When you start to ask how this has come about you find many forces at work. First, there is the strong pressure being applied by students themselves. Teachers feel keenly the alienation and disaffection of students in mathematics. As more and more students stay on longer at secondary school, the mismatch between the mainstream mathematics courses and the interests and intentions of most students has been dramatized. At the same time economists are decrying the dearth of graduates in mathematics and the shortage of qualified mathematics teachers in schools. Something must be done, they say, to improve the image of mathematics and to attract more students to it. Into such a climate comes the UK research findings of the Cockcroft committee on the teaching of mathematics and our own studies on the role of language in the learning of mathematics, quite strongly influenced by language and learning theory, drawing attention to the need for more interactive, language-rich classrooms. Bolstering this drive is the work of those investigating the need to reform mathematics to make it hospitable and engaging for girls.

In the early years of primary school great advances have been made in the teaching of reading and writing. A nationally promoted early literacy in-service course has reached 20,000 teachers, supporting the notion of teacher-as-researcher, the use of conferencing techniques in the teaching of reading and writing and the role of expressive talk as a foundation for literacy. This early literacy project is based on materials developed in South Australia. It can be traced directly to the work of Marie Clay in New Zealand and to the work of many South Australian teachers with whom I worked in connection with the Language and Learning Unit and the national Language Development Project.

Australian primary-school teachers seeing these techniques work for them in the area of literacy are beginning to realize that similar principles can and should inform their teaching of mathematics. The Commonwealth Schools Commission-sponsored Basic Learning in Primary Schools Program has provided funds for investigative work in classrooms to test the applicability of language-teaching methods in the teaching of mathematics. Like the Participation and Equity Program, this programme is targeted on whole-school change and employs action–research methodology, putting teachers at the forefront of educational inquiry and action.

All this is to demonstrate that slogans and special language units have come and gone but key ideas remain and are working in the system at all levels. Concerted pushes across the curriculum from the 'language fraternity' in the seventies were resisted and seen as signs of incipient imperialism. A decade later the ideas, mediated in a variety of ways, are beginning to grip.

What I have said about mathematics holds also for science and social studies. Practitioners in these fields, I am sure, would not attribute advances in their understanding of learning to the 'language and learning' fraternity. They would see the ideas arising from, and growing in, their own practice and amplified through the work of networks and professional associations. This does not mean that the language and learning movement failed. Many of us who started out in this camp would like to feel that, by withdrawing a little, compromising and coming at the problem tangentially and more strategically, we have had increased influence. Good ideas prevail and grow.

Crucial to such strategy is the realization that we are not alone. There are many allies amongst minority groups, the women's movement, workers in Aboriginal education, those engaged in addressing the educational effects of poverty, and also those who seek improved quality in education, real intellectual bite rather than mindless exercise. An integral part of language and learning theory is a theory about power and enfranchisement. Many groups who might not necessarily connect with the language theory will connect with the drive to teach for personal and collective power towards a critical, productive society based on 'action knowledge'.

Such people, whether teachers, parents or educational administrators, while they would not group under a language banner, will recognize that each is dealing with the plight of the relatively powerless in the face of a regime which systematically discriminates in favour of certain sections of society. All are on about the liberation of students' minds; teaching the young how to think and act for themselves, confidently, personally and collectively.

When such groups confront the higher-order problems that face all of them, ideas about the role of language and learning can be introduced as enabling strategies without being seen as vested interests. It is also important to realize that there are allies not only at the grass roots. I am still learning how hegemony works, but I now know that top down/bottom up distinctions are dangerous and likely to be wrong. Ruling ideas from the ruling classes are not conducted smoothly through bureaucracies and systems. At all levels there is mess and contradiction which gives us all hope and opportunity.

My reading and understanding of Michel Foucault (1980) has been patchy and uncertain but I think he is saying that there are multiple and complex insurrections of new ideas in any system, each representing an upsurge of power, no matter how minuscule. Even when there is a major downsurge of hegemonic power, this is not necessarily unidirectional. Any manifestation of power contains the possibility of transformation or channelling into constructive purposes. Just as a yacht can advance against a head wind, so we can, by calculating vectors, use largely oppositional power to move forward, especially if we are also connected to networks of supportive insurrection. I suppose this is another way of describing compromise.

Let me give an example. Business and industry people in Australia, as represented by certain councils and associations, are dissatisfied with the products of schooling. They decry standards in literacy and numeracy, communication skills and knowledge of the world of work. They call for more rigour in national monitoring of standards and in public examinations and greater control over the quality of teachers. All this is seen to be in the interests of economic recovery. At the same time as they argue, with little corroborative evidence, for a return to the 'basics', they indicate the need for flexible, independent, cooperative and self-starting workers. They have considerable power, backed by the media, reinforced by key politicians in government and, in many quarters, applauded by the people. What they say is also endorsed by a goodly number of teachers and educators. There is strong hegemonic pressure on systems, schools and teachers to revert to a direct-instruction, transmission mode of operation.

How does one use this power creatively? In the first place, it is important to free oneself of the reification of 'business and industry'. If you can get to talk with some of the spokespersons, you find that there is a certain amount of bravado and bluster about the campaign: once the criticisms are levelled, there is not much hard evidence. Nor is there any certainty about how the desired ends are to be achieved. There is a hunch that the old methods will be the best methods, but really they are only interested in the results. It is up to the professionals to work out how to deliver the goods. It is also interesting to realize when you talk to these people that they have had very little conversation before with educators. You can actually talk to them seriously about some of the contradictions that exist in their demands. How can communication skills be promoted if students are not allowed to talk? Are not public examinations which require a good deal of rote memorization possibly destructive of creative problem-solving approaches to life? If we teach traditional academic mathematics and science courses, are we going to connect with the world of work and is this the kind of mathematics and science which workers in business and industry will need? Out of such discussion can come some compromises. We can agree on some common goals but remain tentative about how to achieve these goals. We can, perhaps, render the question of examinations and national testing problematic and offer alternative ways of checking on quality.

At the same time we can ally ourselves strongly with a drive to give greater national prominence to education, knowing that if education is not on the political agenda it will be hard to win resources. Education is our best investment. A well-functioning democracy depends on *all* its citizens being educated to as high a level as possible. We can complicate the world view of business and industry and not sell out on our principles.

The business-and-industry push destabilizes schools, opens up debate and to the vigilant progressive presents as many opportunities as threats.

Much of what critics outside education say about schools has some truth in it. We know many students are bored, alienated and working at low levels. We also know that to redress this we need to reform curriculum, credentialling and school structures while supporting teachers in dealing with such reforms. This requires additional resources and community support. Perhaps business and industry can be co-opted to join with us in this cause. It is a matter of delicate judgement just how far to go in such alliances.

To return to the yachting metaphor, it is also important for schools and teachers to know how to take advantage of a tail wind. Top-down interventions can interrupt schools in positive ways. In Australia, four years ago, the newly elected Labor government instituted the Participation and Equity Program, mentioned above, targeted on selected secondary schools across the nation. The programme, as I have said, required parent–teacher–student partnerships in addressing reforms which would increase equity and quality in learning. Funds were available to buy time for school communities to plan, carry out and reflect on changed practices. The programme got off to a rather bad start. Quite a few schools were not ready for it ideologically and so used the funds for spurious purposes, thus giving the initiative a bad name in some quarters. Other schools, or more correctly well-organized teachers in other schools, knew a promising force when they saw it. The programme was pressed into the service, to fuel reforms and changes which palpably increased student responsibility, decision making and purpose.

From my own experience within systems I can attest to the fact that all the good ideas do not emanate from the classroom. There are creative and skilful bureaucrats, well connected with the realities of schools, who know how to change structures and programmes to increase the power of schools and teachers, just as there are teachers who know how to empower children. There are also obstructive and cautious bureaucrats adept at freezing and denying.

An interesting top-down phenomenon at the moment in at least three states of Australia is a move to devolve more authority to schools and school councils. It could be seen as an act of negotiating the curriculum writ large. Some see it as a cynical move by governments to save money on the infrastructure by pushing more responsibility onto schools, at the same time as central superordinate controls on curriculum and assessment are brought down. Others see it as a commitment to increased quality through giving *ownership* to schools and their communities. Given the messiness and contradiction that I have already mentioned, the truth probably lies nowhere. My point is that, whatever the motives, it behoves schools, with due vigilance, to respond *as if* the intention is to enfranchise schools, teachers and parents.

What has all this to do with my report to you about the state of language and learning across the curriculum in 1987? I suppose it is to demonstrate how we are learning to work at all levels of the system at once, and how, at our best, we are abandoning labels in order to work with people of like mind, whose ideas have been generated in different ways, in different contexts, and are represented in slightly different language. We are also coming to understand that, to enable teachers to apply the kind of principles of language and learning that you have advocated, we need to change the ruling discourse and the containing structures of systems. This requires a sophisticated theory about systems and the way they work, as well as a learning theory.

Absolutely crucial to progress is the reform of student assessment and examinations. Examinations indicate what we value and how we intend to value it. Teachers are obliged, in the interests of their students, to teach what is valued. While there has been a movement to include more school-based assessment as a component of public examinations, it seems to me that, given the prevailing mood, there is little hope in the short term of doing away with examinations in most Australian states. It would seem, then, that the best compromise might be to change the kinds of assignments set in examinations, to require the application of principle, rather than the regurgitation of fact, to require exploratory problem solving and to allow extended time so that answers can be redrafted. There are promising signs of such reform.

Life in the classroom is hard, perhaps harder than it has ever been. It is not just a matter of reconciling teachers' intentions with students' intentions. Society and systems also have 'intentions', often unstated, often contradictory. These, as always, are given effect in promotion structures, examinations, textbooks, syllabuses, tertiary requirements, the media and public opinion. Finding constructive compromises between these intentions is a precarious business made even more complex by the increasing information that teachers have. They know much more than ever before about sexism, the need to offer inclusive curricula, the significance of technology in society and the demands of the economy. They know also that, in order to mobilize student intention, they must first establish enough order to allow attention. It is no secret that negotiating the curriculum and the application of enlightened language and learning techniques are easiest in well-ordered, middle-class schools. And yet many fine teachers are finding ways to engage and challenge children in the most unpromising of circumstances.

In summary, I'd say that, with your customary ten-year perspective, you would be well pleased with what teachers and schools are achieving in Australia. Powerful ideas have permeated the system across subject disciplines and levels and, indeed, have found their way into the rhetoric and practice of national and state system policy makers. This is not to say they are yet secure, but they are respectable. A pleasing point to make is that there are many more teachers as 'reflective spectators', action researchers, on the ground, with a theorized practice and practical theories about the art and craft of teaching.

Writing to you in this way has helped me count the gains. As for me, I'm less sure now than I was in 1978, but I'm a little wiser about the art of compromise. I wonder what advice you might have for me now?

Yours sincerely,

Garth

Teaching English as a Rehearsal of Politics
Martin Lightfoot

In the mid-seventies, as part of a spending appraisal, the elected members of the Inner London Education Authority were reminded that ever since anyone could remember the authority had been paying a handsome annual gratuity to the University of London, then amounting to some £200,000 annually. The arrangement was generous because, under the British system of education finance, universities are funded direct from central government and it is not regarded as in the least obligatory that a local education authority should contribute in this way to the funding of a university. The generosity was the more apparent because the payment was in return for no specific services. The authority promptly proposed to terminate this gratuity. A high-level delegation from the university – consisting, as one political wag had it, of 'three knights and an ordinary person' – failed to shift the members' resolve. The university was understandably dismayed by this decision, but perhaps more so by the grounds given for it. Over a decade in which the ILEA had been moving, against considerable political odds, towards the ending of selection at the age of eleven and the introduction of a comprehensive system of education, the ideology and commitment of the university's Institute of Education – the largest and most prestigious postgraduate teacher-training establishment in the country – appeared to rest largely with the old selective grammar schools.

The accusation was probably justified overall, but it was noticeably untrue of a small number of departments. Prominent among the exceptions was the Department of English, together with Sociology. It would have been an unjust or partial accusation, too, against Science. A minority of departments within the institute had indeed been active in developing appropriate curricula and involving students in a practical way in inner-city schools, and were actively nursing enlightened inner-city schools, both for teaching practice for students and as action research centres for research and development programmes.

Between such local controversies and the larger scene of educational change and development is a complex web of influences. Popular educational histories are built on large canvases and in primary colours: bold swatches of 'social climate' and 'social change', 'dominant ideologies', and the alleged overpowering influence of individual groups, such as 'teachers' or 'employers' or 'parents' or 'politicians'. Such histories have their mythological power and, once established, can become forces within the system in their own right, overlaying a mass of detail which, left to speak for itself, would tell a different but stuttering and uncertain story, the moral of which would be both difficult to interpret and difficult to discern. We tend to move onto a different level at this point, one in which, because interpretation of complex events and movements is difficult, we are dealing more with the pains and rewards associated with the adoption of different views of change, rather than any assessment of the change itself. It is in this sense that it becomes possible to speak of teaching as a rehearsal of politics, using 'politics' in its political science sense to mean 'those processes of discourse through which members of society seek to assert and ultimately reconcile their wishes' (Kogan, 1978).

Studies of professional groups, including teachers, do not encourage the thought that helpful generalizations can be made about subgroups within the culture, in spite of the strong intuitive perceptions about differentiations within the culture that are held within the culture itself. It seems from such studies of, for example, teachers or nurses that the differences between cultures are far more significant than those within it (see, for example, Jamieson and Lightfoot, 1982). That is to say, in considering 'English teachers' as a subgroup of 'teachers', it is unlikely that strong or striking differences could be discerned. It is likely to prove much more significant in outlining the culture that a person is a teacher than that he/she is an 'English teacher'. This is not to say that such differences do not exist, but that they are small by comparison with others.

Two examples of an attempt can be mentioned. Janet Emig (1983) outlines what she calls a 'tacit tradition' in writing and rhetoric research, which she argues is distinctive. It is a discipline, not in the sense of constituting a formal body of academic work, but in sharing language, a commonality of assumption about evidence and about 'root metaphors and governing paradigms'. Using Kuhn's concept of the 'paradigm' (a notoriously fluid formulation), she argues that the particular set of ancestries which has been built up by such inquirers constitutes, if not a paradigm in Kuhn's sense, at last a 'pre-paradigm', the essential conditions for the construction of one.[1] Such an argument can look strong in relation to the forming of an intellectual tradition, but it feels weaker when used to describe an entire professional grouping. Emig's 'pre-paradigm' applies more appropriately to the research community associated with English teaching rather than to English teachers as a whole. From a sociological standpoint, Ball (1985) argues that it is possible to disaggregate movements in English teaching into tendencies and schools, to highlight relationships (such as within institutions, or in co-authorship, or in 'discipleship') to provide a map of historical developments. Two major maps are offered, one placing F. R. Leavis at the centre, the other showing connections ranged around James Britton at the London Institute. Such exercises no doubt have their uses, but they compress too much into their frameworks and make no allowances for shifts in views and emphasis over time, for temporary alliances and genuine syntheses which cross classificatory lines. How odd in Ball's analysis, for example, to find James Britton in the linguists' camp and opposed to the promoters of literature.[2]

Nevertheless there are some distinctive features of English teachers which are likely to influence the way they operate within institutions and more generally within the larger educational and political systems. English teachers have contributed a great deal to our general understanding of human development and education; perhaps only the mathematicians have a stronger claim, and contributions from that quarter tend to be fragmentary. A former joint secretary of the Schools Council placed the National Association for the Teaching of English (NATE) alongside the Association for Science Education and a cluster of bodies concerned with school mathematics as the most 'effective' (Owen, 1973, quoted in Ball, 1985). And yet it would be difficult to ascribe distinctiveness in terms of the possession of a distinct *theory*. In their natural, routine mode, it is not obvious that English teachers need theory. Indeed, one strand of the culture within the UK specifically eschews it, at least in the formal sense: one has only to recall the classic exchange between Rene Wellek and F. R. Leavis on the appropriateness of 'philosophy' for literary criticism in the thirties (Leavis, 1952). In this sense the act of teaching English can be collecting and reflective, rather than structuring and theorizing, and, it seems safe to say, for much of the time for many English teachers it need be no more than that. The UK English teaching tradition can support a professional stance which is fiercely individualized, stressing 'freshness' of response, sensitivity and insight. One effect of this is that it can tend to make English teachers seem inward looking, in spite of the fact that English teachers are unusually well placed to see the educational process as a whole.

A substantial part of the grounds for this can be found in one distinctive feature of English teachers' history. At this distance it may seem strange to recall that the notion that there was such a thing as 'subject English' was not at all a natural one, and that the early years of this century in the UK were preoccupied with establishing a place on the curriculum for the study of the native language. Even when the case had been established, the arguments about the role of literature, as distinct from grammar, were long and bitter even when James Britton began teaching in the early thirties (quoted in Ball, 1985). The task of staking out specific expertise and the need for specific training for English teachers took even longer, and even by the time of the Bullock Report (1975) a substantial proportion of English teaching was not undertaken by trained specialists.

There is another important feature of English teaching that becomes particularly relevant in considering its political role within the system. Uniquely, there is a discontinuity between the subject as it is studied and understood in universities and the way it appears within schools. The discontinuity can be exaggerated, and there is little doubt that some of the values and judgements which are fostered in the university English departments leave a lasting impression. But the *task* of English teachers only relates closely to what is understood by the subject in universities at the top end of the secondary school, and then only with selected pupils. In seeking to make representations to government inquiries, to select committees of the House of Commons, sitting on examination boards or putting a case in the media, English teachers are hampered by this comparative lack of supportive voices from academic English. It would not be difficult for the Association of Teachers of Mathematics or the Association for Science Education to call on the support of an internationally distinguished academic from the mainstream of the university discipline in representing their case; it is almost impossible for the National Association for the Teaching of English to do so.

If there was a consensus in the universities in the thirties and forties, it was that graduates from an English department in a university should be equipped with a finely trained, discriminating sensibility, combined perhaps with wide reading in more than modern English and a developed sense of cultural history. The question of what happened to this finely trained sensibility when it encountered 5H on a Friday afternoon was not one which any university would have thought appropriate, even if it had been aware of the problem. Generations of graduates must have handled this problem somehow. But they were almost exclusively entering the grammar schools, and thereby joining the circle on the system which had educated them themselves. Some of the earliest attempts to think through the ways in which a continuity between university and schools could be effected stressed the same values of sensitivity and discrimination. F. R. Leavis's *Culture and Environment*, in collaboration with Denys Thompson, was published as early as 1933. The problem addressed by this little book was explicitly that of 'training taste and sensibility', and its preoccupation was with ways in which this could be done in a context in which 'multitudinous counter-influences – films, newspapers, advertising – indeed, the whole world outside the classroom' militated against it. This concept of the classroom as a haven of intellectual and cultural values, with its ultimate objective as the appreciation of literature, was widely held and underpinned Denys Thompson's magazine, *The Use of English*, in the fifties and sixties. Leavis himself was always sceptical about his influence, and yet it was common in the fifties to hear (admittedly as much in alarm as in impartial assessment) that his influence was greater in the grammar schools than in the universities.

Something of the flavour of *Culture and Environment* can be caught from the questions suggested for the use of the sympathetic teacher:

Do you know of any ugly building, furniture, tools, etc., before 1820? Account as far as you can for your findings.

Where can the use of machines be eliminated with advantage?

Estimate from one issue of the Sunday newspapers the annual average output of 'masterpieces' and 'great books'.

Why do we wince at the mentality that uses this idiom [Americanism]?

How does this pronouncement condemn itself? [Leavis and Thompson, 1933]

No open-ended questions here. At this distance the moral certitude and the extent to which the teacher is expected to lead the student are chilling. And yet at that time, and for some decades later, the approach and the ideology were a liberation from a stifling tradition of 'fine writing' and *belles lettres*. They remained so until well into the sixties, aided by Denys Thompson himself and *The Use of English*. And yet the attempt at replication across the ability range was problematic. Peter Medway has recalled:

deep commitment to literature as a source of values (certain literature, read in certain ways) reached down from Leavis's Cambridge via its graduates into the grammar schools; many of these grammar school teachers took their commitment into head of department posts in the new comprehensive schools; here however the sort of literature-based curriculum designed for the selected minority could not be straightforwardly replicated with the unselected majority; that particular stream of values and cultural concerns had to find another channel through which to flow [Medway, 1984].

The turning point in the sixties came when English teachers began to reconceive their activity. On this reinterpretation English teaching was less an attempt to mediate established values and canons, more a means of assisting the child's own linguistic development. The key symptom here was the teacher paying a great deal of attention to what children actually do in reading, writing, talking, telling stories. Various people contributed, including the late Brian Jackson and David Holbrook. But the key influence must surely be seen now as the London Institute, and especially the work of James Britton. Instead of seeing it as a problem of 'training' sensibility and of transmitting approved existing values, Britton argued that we should see the process of learning as a whole. It was necessary to ask what the function of language was in human development and to see language as itself a learning device, rather than as a tool which the child manipulated with greater or lesser skill. To do this required not just a minute attention to what children actually do, but the forging of a theoretical base which would see the development of language as a continuous process, from the first utterings of very young children through to the developed art of the poet. Britton's achievment in developing a coherent model was considerable and seminal, and very much a personal one. The historical accounts from both Ball (1985) and Emig (1983) quoted above acknowledge Britton's central-ity. Drawing on a very varied set of sources – Jakobson, Polanyi, Sapir, Whorf, D. W. Harding, but especially the Russian school of psychologists such as Vygotsky and Luria – he managed to develop a taxonomy of language which could be used to account for what language was doing for the people who used it, and also to provide some models of development. Beginning with its application to the assessment of composition, Britton and his collaborators moved on to seeing how the model could be extended to provide a detailed map of writing development.

With this perspective it was possible to develop a conception of the purpose of English teaching which, largely for the first time, could be applied throughout the spectrum of abilities. It redirected the teacher's energies and provided a more integrated conception of the child's linguistic activity. It placed less stress on *hierarchies* of linguistic forms, so that it was possible to see that, almost universally, teachers were turning their backs on what ought to be one of the most important aspects of linguistic develop-ment, that of talk. And it extended the emphasis on developing the child's own creative abilities more plausibly by drawing attention to the inherently creative learning opportunities offered by anecdote, stories, talk within groups, while stressing that growing skills in using a *variety* of linguistic forms and testing them against different audiences were essential to nurture the skills of a mature, communicating adult.

It is at this point that it is possible to see a political agenda emerging, though few involved would have conceived it in that way. The recognition of the centrality of the child's own language production pushed the child's own activity into the centre of the stage and required a greater degree of responsibility on the children's part for their own learning. The identification of the role of talk and of group learning had implications for the organization of classrooms and the style of interaction that occurred within the classroom. Spelling and grammar, though still important, had to be seen in the context of meaning, appropriateness and audience. It was possible to propose a continuity between children's linguistic production and the great works of the university syllabus, and hence to diminish the sense of an elite canon. Moreover, where close attention to what children actually do became important, in an important sense every teacher became his/her own researcher. The natural conclusion from the analysis was to place the focus very much on the child's entire language output, giving rise to a compaign for a 'language policy across the curriculum'. English teachers proselytized for modification to the way other teachers went about their business.[3]

Not an easy task, and made more difficult by the political position which English teachers had forged for themselves. By breaking with the literary tradition within the university, they had cut themselves off from an important source of authentication. (At the London Institute itself, so rudely disinherited by the Inner London Education Authority, the English Department was criticized for having forsaken literature, an ironic charge in the light of Britton's evident commitment to literature.) The direction of their inquiries suggested alliance with the linguists and developmental psychologists. And yet here there were hazards of behaviourism and reductionism to be charted, and in this company the inherently humane and liberal origins of the endeavour were likely to be at risk. At the same time English teachers were at risk of relinquishing popular and parental support, by appearing to denigrate solid traditional virtues like 'correct' English. In seeking to steer between these obstacles it was perhaps inevitable that for many the maintenance of an independent tradition was untenable, and 'media studies' or 'communication' or 'social studies' enticed many.

It is notoriously dangerous to generalize about educational movements and the degree to which their effects are evident in actual classrooms (Barnes and Barnes, 1984), but it seems clear that an independent tradition is what it has become. Through the London Association for the Teaching of English, out through the National Association, the regenerative power of the revised role for the teacher and the broader view which the ideas gave about education in general were sufficient to build a group which was committed, if somewhat inward looking. The early stages of this process – for example, in the London Association's annual conferences – were dynamic. It is possible to chart the current situation in terms of an apparent paradox: a group of committed teachers who are at one and the same time isolated from potential power sources and yet highly influential in ways which have meant that the recognition of potential pressure points of influence and the consequent growth in confidence have been slow.

The UK educational system is devolved. Something is known about such systems in general (for example, House, 1974; Kogan, 1978; Archer, 1984), but the precise way in which they operate in individual circumstances is nevertheless difficult to disentangle. Dislocations can occur, but fundamentally such systems involve a delicate balance of influence between the central (and those responsible in formal terms) and the local, which may be the local education authority or individual headteachers or individual teachers. In devolved systems new initiatives are constantly being generated at the local level, while the centre is constantly trying to reassert its authority. The political condition for such reassertion will determine how far the centre is able to imbue the system with its values and chosen procedures. Without such political conditions, the centre will find itself at the mercy of disparate movements and measures which, cumulatively, will threaten its formal role. It must move in these circumstances, both to correct what it may see as aberrations in what is happening and to reaffirm its technical control of the system. The problem for reformers is therefore to seek change without threatening (or being seen to threaten) the fundamental structure of the system.

The question of the influence of NATE, and through it of English teachers as a whole, is more than a matter of securing a large number of members, well spread over different educational sectors, more than a matter of credible representation. There are distinctive qualities necessary to the organization operating in this context and for this purpose. It has been, first, a matter of establishing expertise. It is another characteristic of devolved systems of education that, in its struggle to assert its position, the centre rarely has the expertise to match its ambitions. It will constantly need the assistance, or at least the connivance, of those who are closer to the actual delivery of the system. Influence then will involve not just the willingness to participate in the system as it is, but a confident assertion of knowledge and skills, which, if not exactly esoteric, at least depend critically on proximity to the processes of education. This in turn depends on a willingness to master technical skills of a kind which can achieve credibility in the company of those deployed by other academic disciplines. In these respects NATE grew in influence during the sixties and seventies: prominent NATE members were influential in the Schools Council, on the

Assessment of Performance Unit (set up by the government to monitor school achievement on a sampling basis), on the examination boards, on the Bullock inquiry into English teaching, and the research record is an impressive one. (If these points seem obvious ones to non-UK observers, it is important to stress how novel they are in relation to the traditional literary culture.)

But there were other requirements. The association needed a coherent persistence in pushing its case. The natural, fragmented and individualized tendency of the culture had in some way to be bound around a core of beliefs. On the face of it, this might seem easy, but there were several points at which it seemed that minority interests (from sociology, from the literary tradition, from instrumentalist concerns) could fragment the movement. Beyond this, it was necessary to move to a position of confidence and mutual trust where public utterance could be safely delegated, for fast and cogent response. Early moves in this – again very obvious – direction were fraught with caution and ill-concealed distrust.

In the UK educational system subjects rule. It is difficult to say how far this is more true of the UK than of other educational systems, but the legacy of the old university-dominated examination system means that the public debate on education is very largely framed in terms of traditional subject disciplines. The growth of specialist advisers in English within local education authorities, sometimes cited as an achievement of NATE in enhancing its position within the system, is at best an ambiguous development. It has certainly created space for some very able people, most of NATE persuasion if not actually members, to pursue their interests in collaboration with classroom teachers. However, this development has been at the cost of the marginalization of the subject specialists within the local authority management teams. With the centre in English education becoming increasingly strident and interventionist, there has been a tendency for the intermediate management of local authorities to distance itself from direct curriculum involvement by using specialist advisers. This in turn has meant that local authority management concentrates on resource allocation, logistics, employment policies and, above all and overwhelmingly in the seventies and eighties, on the *structure* of the system. The autonomy gained by the specialist advisers is therefore severely limited by restricted access to the policy-making process and to resources. By the same process, educational administrators in local authorities have relinquished responsibility for distinctively curriculum matters, and the old style of committed adminis- trators – in the mould perhaps of Alec Clegg in the West Riding or Henry Morris in Cambridgeshire – are scarcely anywhere in evidence. There are

indications that the possibilities for what might be called 'heroic management' are stronger in other English-speaking countries (see, for example,
the articles by Rutledge and Boomer in this volume).

In spite of this growing confidence and a growing coherence in public
positions, it is clear that, as one former chairman of NATE has put it, 'we
had to learn a language of political communication' (Adams, 1984). The
difficulties in finding the right kind of public voice are apparent in NATE's
evidence to the Education Select Committee in 1981. In its written submission the association, conscious of the political climate of the time, was
defensive about its achievements and the activities of English teachers.
Although it was familiar with the criticisms made, it felt that they were
misguided, and that better results could be achieved with more resources.
Moreover, it was dismissive about instrumental functions: conventions in
written language were referred to as 'minutiae', spelling, punctuation and
grammar were called 'decencies', 'matters of important courtesy and convention rather than of status and prestige.'[4]

It seems safe to say that some Members of Parliament did not have to
read any further. In the oral session one MP described the passage about
formal language attributes as 'thrown away with a happy little laugh';
another adduced letters from his constituency as indicating a massive
decline in standards; another (in a bold spirit of compromise) attempted to
get the NATE spokesperson to say that all these points were justified, but
that it was all a question of timing, a matter of what stage formal teaching of
language should be undertaken. NATE fought back with adroitness, but it
was on losing ground against such entrenched positions.[5]

There is a contrast between the 1981 Select Committee and the evidence
which NATE presented to the Kingman Committee in 1987. The assertions
here are confident, secure in intellectual and research corroboration, international consensus and the support of its membership:

Over the past 20 years we have developed a coherent school of practice firmly
founded in theory and forged in the testing conditions of the classroom.

It has won us an international reputation. Its leading exponents are in demand all
over the world. We are not short of productive ideas; support and dissemination are
another matter.

Since the committee of enquiry does not include anyone who has contributed
significantly to this development, we must do our utmost to see that our case is put
and that the argument does not go by default [*Evidence to the Kingman Commission*,
NATE, 1987].

The point about confidence is not to do with intellectual quality or
drafting ability – or rather, those may come into it, but they are not the

salient issues. It is to do with the degree to which a sectional group can operate positively in a political environment. The values of this environment, its language, mythologies and the terms of engagement which it is capable of imposing need not, should not, diminish that capacity to rehearse that politics from which all influence in a democratic society is ultimately derived. In a renewed attempt to assert central authority, and with a populist determination to resist the professional consensus about English teaching, the British Government has set up a further national committee to report on English teaching, just twelve years after the Bullock Committee. No other subject has been subjected to two such major inquiries in such a short space of time. In declining to appoint a single member of NATE to the Kingman Committee, the government has declared its sympathies and its determination to uncover or weld an alternative paradigm to that developed by James Britton and his collaborators in the seventies and eighties. It will not be easy.

Notes

1. Kuhn proposes two conditions for a paradigm: first, that it should be 'sufficiently unprecedented to attract an enduring group of adherents away from competing modes of scientific activity'; second, that is it 'sufficiently open-ended to leave all sorts of problems for the redefined group of practitioners to resolve' (Kuhn, 1972, p. 10).
2. This may be an appropriate place to correct some of the inaccuracies in Ball's article. In his chart of influences, with Britton shown at the centre, on p. 68, the following corrections should be noted: Connie Rosen did not hold an appointment at the London Institute; neither Basil Bernstein nor Michael Halliday has ever been involved in NATE, though both have spoken at conferences; for 'Williamson' read 'Wilkinson'. In the chart showing Leavis at the centre on p. 66, neither Raymond Williams nor David Holbrook were pupils of Leavis, though both were influenced; Leavis's PhD was supervised by Quiller-Couch. I am grateful to Douglas Barnes and Nancy Martin for help with some of these points.
3. See Torbe (1986) for an illuminating account of this process.
4. House of Commons (1981), Education Science and Arts Committee, *The Secondary School Curriculum and Examinations: with special reference to the 14 to 16 age group*, vol. 2, Minutes of Evidence, pp. 149–53. HC 116–II. Select committees of the British House of Commons are similar to congressional committees under the US system. They are entirely composed of 'backbenchers' who do not hold office either in the government or in the official

opposition, and the representation on them reflects (roughly) the balance of the political parties as a whole. In 1977 the system was dramatically expanded by the introduction of a select committee to shadow every major department of state.

5. ibid., pp. 171–3.

Annexe   For Jimmy Britton, for the Record

This book has been planned to stand on its own. It looks at the concerns developed in *Language and Learning* in a contemporary context and in relation to current research and preoccupations, including the political perspectives which teachers internationally need to interpret and negotiate. In doing so, we believe that it reaffirms the importance of the issues raised in *Language and Learning* and pays an implicit tribute to the original formulation.

Something of the nature of Jimmy Britton's contribution certainly emerges from the preceding sections, and perhaps especially from the contributions from Don Rutledge and Garth Boomer in Section Four. Yet as the range of it stands thus far the book leaves a gap in terms of some kind of recognition of the range of Jimmy Britton's overall influence on English teaching, on education in general and his international role, especially since his retirement. For *that*, one needs to look at things like the networking of like-minded people, to personal style, to the contribution made to larger institutional frameworks, to other countries and to other academic disciplines.

For a number of reasons we cannot devote the book to a purpose of this kind, but we cannot leave it out either. This Annexe contains reminiscences and analyses which constitute a modest attempt to reflect the scope of Jimmy Britton's contribution. It is, at least in part, an index of how much could be done in this way that we have had to restrict both the number of items in this section and their length. These all too brief contributions must stand for those of many others who have been taught, helped and made to understand a bit more.

For Jimmy Britton, for the record.

Starting a School: Learning with Jimmy Britton

In 1902 Laurence Housman wrote:

> Hendon, and further out afield
> Low water meads are in his ken,
> And lonely pools by Harrow Weald.

By 1933 things had changed as the area was covered by mock-Tudor villas to house Londoners socially escaping into 'metroland' and Scots, Welsh and Northerners escaping from the industrial depression.

It was all neat, tidy, clean, but lacking in roots, neighbourliness and tradition. It all grew so rapidly that it lacked schools, but, following the May Report the proposed twelve new schools for Middlesex were cut to one – Harrow Weald County School, which opened in September 1933.

I was far too young in the beginning to know or care about teaching methods, but we were aware that we were pioneering a new school. I belonged to nothing else outside my family and increasingly I cared about the developing institution which accepted and absorbed each year new pupils and new staff. I was not untypical. The school as a community was what mattered.

We learned with each other in an environment led by a headmaster who often talked of 'standards'. I have heard that word since and winced, but what E. Barlow Butlin meant was different and was epitomized for me by the motto he chose for the school – 'Valiant for Truth'.

With that as a lodestone there was no need for any transient short-term ideology and, guided by it, he united a diverse group of staff and pupils at a time when secondary education for all was just beginning.

We read books, acted in plays, swam, ran, played cricket and football. We debated; I stood as the Labour candidate, and lost, in the mock General Election of 1935.

It was to this new school that the young J. N. Britton came in 1933 as senior English master. Barlow wrote later of his 'original and brilliant methods of teaching English'. Increasingly as pupils we knew this and sampled them, but we knew also that Jimmy treated us differently from others. As adults? Perhaps. As equals? Yes, in a certain sense. The phrase eludes me, but it is something to do with lack of condescension. There was no soppy friendliness, and in retrospect there could never have been from him for he is nothing if not sharp in his approach to people and things.

The first time I recall noticing this was the morning after the invasion of the Rhineland (or somewhere). It was not what he said but the way he said it; it was a questioning of the incident, in the gym of all places, and it remained with me long afterwards. He made us think. The quasi-adult relationship which he forged with so many of us, however, made the transition to real friendship later on in life with both Jimmy and Robert all the easier; we did not have to start again.

What we understood from the beginning was his enthusiasm for all the activities of the school, particularly for the school camp which he started and where we mixed and saw different sides of each other; for the school plays (one of which he wrote) which involved us in droves – acting, painting, prompting as well as acting – and for the school magazine which he pioneered.

Jimmy Britton played a major part in pointing the direction in which the new county school should go. It was still there when I returned to teach in the school in the late forties; it is still there in the sixth-form college that has evolved. It added up to creating the spirit of a questioning community; it was forged in the beginning and it lasts.

It mattered to Jimmy Britton as, from his family background, he brought and transmogrified a spirit of service to a fledgling community. It was not a matter of imposing a tradition from older generations of schools; it was creation of a tradition for a new type of school, for different sorts of people, living in a different environment.

When Jimmy left the school in 1938 to move into educational publishing he wrote in the school magazine that he had founded – and for me not surprisingly – on the theme of the community:

The great point about a community, it seems to me, is that everybody in it knows everybody else's business – in the right way, I mean. It's only when you get this state of affairs that a community can really act as a community at all – only then that every thrust and kick of the lively societies and subsections does actually result in some forward movement of the whole school.

That was the Harrow Weald I knew: a community concerned about today but looking to the future. So there was an ideology after all, but arising out of a plural community incorporating varied attitudes from staff and pupils with different backgrounds. There was no one way of thinking; there was much to question.

It was in that new school that we all learned with each other, and with Jimmy Britton.

Merlyn Rees

Books of Verse and Books of Stories

> There is no frigate like a book
> To take us lands away,
> Nor any coursers like a page
> of prancing poetry
> Emily Dickinson

In 1957 the four slim *Oxford Books of Verse for Juniors* were published, imaginatively commissioned by a former student of James Britton at the London Institute of Education. In the briefest of introductions to the reader J.B. writes:

I think a book of poems is more like a children's picture-book than any other kind of book. You may turn over the pages of a picture book often and always enjoy seeing the pictures again. You may turn over the pages of this book and read the poems often, and still enjoy reading them or listening to them. Of course there will be some poems in it that you don't like: but not many, I hope.

The anthologies are no longer in print. Fashions in publishing are ephemeral. Much that is currently offered to children has to have an instant appeal and design styles are more assertive. But, hidden away in primary school stock cupboards there may be stacks of these quietly elegant anthologies and I suggest that anyone reading this piece with legitimate access to a junior school scouts around. For the anthologies are classics and should be in the library of anyone who loves literature for children. Most important, give any extra copies you rescue to the children you know.

Here is verse to read and return to, ponder and delight in, gloat over and savour. There is a pervading singing quality, a sense of rhythm and proportion, a clarity of language. They are poems to read aloud and to *hear*.

Certain themes recur: wind and weather, birdsong and flowers, tides and sea voyages, smugglers, ghosts and small domestic mysteries. The voices that speak most strongly focus on intense moments of experience or precise observation of a natural happening – like Ruth Pitter's thrush singing in the elder ('Stormcock in the Elder') and John Walsh's child searching a haven for a bunch of wilting flowers ('Ann's Flowers'). These poets savour the passing moment and shape their experience so that we can share their pleasures, a theme to return to again and again.

The anthologies were seminal in several important ways. The poems are all. There are no questions, no comments, no overt divisions into topics.

The printer (and it was the printer; there was then no design department in OUP) designed the books with a border of printers' flowers around each page. There are no illustrations. Each reader creates the imagery in the head, subtly different at every hearing. Many of the poets were then new or rare in primary classrooms: Charlotte Mew, Emily Dickinson, Robert Graves, James Reeves, Ian Serraillier, James Stephens and Auden, Frost, Sassoon, Thomas. There were ambitious choices for children from Herrick, Hopkins and Yeats, with a reassuring leavening of ballads and old favourites. Icicles hang by the wall/The splendour falls on castle walls/The hag is astride/The tide rises, the tide falls/Old Meg plaits her basket of rushes/The fiddler fiddles on in Dooney.

A balance of classical legends and extracts from contemporary children's stories is the hallmark of the three *Oxford Books of Stories for Juniors* which came out nearly ten years later. (If we are to chronicle the history of Jimmy Britton's influence on school books there should be a passing reference to his part in the development of *Reflections*, 1963.) His choice of narratives derives from many cultures; there is a lot of magic, adventures of heroines and heroes and a fair sprinkling from the American Mid-west. The stories are linked by an unobtrusive commentary that speaks warmly and personally out of the page and nudges the reader to speculate and wonder and imagine what might happen next. This too was an original approach in 1966: to free pupil and teacher from the expected barrage of questions.

There is something more important still for the development of literature in classrooms and perhaps also for teachers' perceptions of what children can do with language. Among the narratives are pieces by Graham and Pauline and June and other anonymous ten-year-olds. Just as many of the poems in the *Books of Verse* celebrate moments of experience, so these prose pieces make satisfying shapes from the amorphous flow of daily life, and enrich us all as they do. Maybe this is the most valuable legacy of the Britton anthologies of the fifties and sixties.

Mary Worrall

James Britton and Poetry

I was a colleague of Jimmy Britton's before the war in a new co-ed school on the edge of London. It was, incidentally, the school in which Miss Robertson – later to become Roberta Britton – taught art. I remember walking in the woods near the school with Jimmy and playing the poetry game. You quote a line of a poem and the other player has to think of a line which begins with the last word in your quote; then you take up with a line beginning with the last word in his, and so on. As our repertoire became exhausted we found we were beginning to invent our own lines. More seriously, I found for the first time in my life I was living in a climate where poems were a continuing part of conversation and action. (I might add that grammar was part of this climate too; Jimmy was writing a book on grammar and composition.) All this was disrupted by the war.

And I remember him coming, at the end of the war, to the Institute of Education to lecture to the English Department, but what he did was to read poems to us – always lyrics and always recent or contemporary ones, Ezra Pound, Frost, Auden, Wallace Stevens, Carlos Williams, Nemerov. The Institute English Department always had a place for poetry and when he left John Murray's and joined us it was like someone who belonged coming home.

He used to talk a lot about 'negative capability' – a willingness to suspend judgement because you believe in the existence of things you do not easily understand; poetry acknowledges a sense of experience you cannot share in any other way. I remember too all the talk that went on round Michael Oakshott's 'The Voice of Poetry in the Conversation of Mankind'. Oakshott says that the voice of poetry is fading in our conversation, but we can always recapture it by going back to childhood; what is a total picture in childhood is a returnable picture (in part) in adulthood. For a grandchild (and himself) James wrote,

June

'Cool now,' says the warm earth, and sighs.
'Quiet now,' say the trees with barely a murmur
Rustling their leaves.
Small now, under a single sheet,
    Quiet.
    Cool.

He thinks that poems communicate a structuring and exchange of feeling otherwise incommunicable. He values the poems he writes for this and thinks it is only secondarily to do with publishing, though some of his poems will have found an audience by being published and others may yet do so. What matters, he says, is that they have been written and shared. Now that retrospect looms larger than prospect, poems assume a greater significance in their function of shaping and logicalizing memory. In an unpublished poem he wrote,

> The physiognomies of the young speak.
> On our faces who are older
> The message is blurred.

Nancy Martin

James Britton at the London Institute of Education

In January 1963 I had the good fortune to get leave of absence from my school for a year to concentrate on research. In those days full-time researchers were extremely rare, almost unknown, at the institute, and it was not even clear whether I was eligible to join the senior commonroom. I could easily have become lonely and isolated, but instead I was immediately adopted as a colleague by James Britton and Nancy Martin, met them for coffee in the senior commonroom, and frequently for lunch in the Red Bar at the old Imperial Hotel.

Apart from the purely social benefit of this contact, James influenced me in a number of important ways. First, I was introduced to the splendid custom of drinking beer at lunchtime; second, I was exposed to other aspects of the culture of the English Department, which ranged from the Russian psychologists to folk singers and discussions of such television programmes as 'That Was the Week That Was'. I found that English at the institute was far from being a narrow, restricted discipline. One of the activities I got involved in was the Friday afternoon session for PGCE students (of all departments) which I think was called 'Art, Music and

Literature'. Outside performers came, introduced their topic and engaged in lively discussions with the students. I do not remember much about the content of those sessions, but I have a lasting recollection of the enthusiasm generated. It was a splendid way for PGCE students to end the week. I forget now why the programme was eventually abandoned – probably the victim of the cuts which began in the late 1960s.

James's work also had direct influence on my own research into social class and language. I attended his course of lectures on language development and this threw a good deal of light on some of the problems of language differences that I was trying to grapple with. Vygotsky and Piaget came to life in the context of examples provided by James from English children – including some I suspect from his own children. I was flattered when he asked me to contribute a short piece to the collection he so sensitively put together and edited – *Talking and Writing* (1967) – a book which, incidentally, provides many of the answers to questions currently being asked by the Kingman Committee.

I also remember being involved in the selection of students for the PGCE course in the English Department. Recently the Secretary of State for Education has built into the 'CATE criteria' recommendations for improving the selection of potential teachers, such as the involvement of practising teachers. Back in the 1960s James Britton and his colleagues in the English Department had already moved away from the half-hour interview as a means of selecting PGCE students. I took part in a complex screening session involving face-to-face interaction, group discussions and a variety of other activities designed to draw out the existence of the sympathetic qualities being sought. There was never any difficulty in gaining the cooperation of practising teachers: James Britton and his colleagues were active members of the London Association for the Teaching of English (LATE), which provided them with a network of good, professional colleagues, working in local schools, some of them ex-students, others simply those who shared the ideals and high standards of James and the department.

I also remember James for the fact that, although he was deeply involved in his own department, he was never one who sheltered behind departmental barriers. He was an institute person, bringing a bit of sanity to committees and working parties when it was most needed. He was also a regular contributor to social functions and semi-social events such as the annual staff weekends at Beatrice Webb House. It was a great loss to the department and to the institute when James decided to accept the offer of a Chair in Education at Goldsmiths' College. At that time there was no Chair in the Teaching of English (Mother Tongue) at the institute, and so the Goldsmiths' Chair was an attractive post – less administrative work and more time for writing. It was a sad loss to the institute but good for the university as a whole.

I do not suppose he remembers, but on the way back from one of our lunches in the Red Bar he quoted a passage from Martin Buber's *I and Thou*, which I have never forgotten. I am sure that all his colleagues and students would have similar episodes which they could report. The qualities which I remember most are the tremendous respect he had for his students and the way in which he clearly enjoyed his work. He possessed a love of poetry which came across unobtrusively in his discussions with students; he not only understood poetry, but also understood how children reacted to poetic language and used it themselves. Above all else Jimmy is a splendid teacher.

Denis Lawton

Jimmy Britton and NATE

More than forty years ago, when I was teaching English in Dover (75 miles from London) I became the first 'associate' member of the London Association for the Teaching of English. Still with a somewhat struggling membership, LATE was closely identified with the London Institute of Education. That meant, above all, Jimmy Britton and Nancy Martin and fascinating weekend conferences at Beatrice Webb House deep in the Surrey woods in bluebell time.

It now seems extraordinary that English teachers had no common voice. There were, it is true, small associations with limited objectives and influence, but Jimmy, from his vantage point as educational editor at John Murray's (which published the influential *School Science Review*) saw the need for some comparable publication for English teachers and in 1947 transformed Percy Gurrey's loose organization of Institute of Education past English students into the London Association for the Teaching of English to provide a forum for all London teachers. Its modes of work – study groups which reported to the association or published, annual conferences which always took the development of theory as a major part of the weekend's work and always included some sessions for reading literature, and an officer entitled 'Secretary of Studies' – came largely from Jimmy and were influential sixteen years later when the National Association came to be founded (1963). With the founding of NATE many people and groups concerned with English teaching drew together, and Jimmy was among those who contributed significantly in various ways.

Inevitably relationships between the new National Association and the many local groups persuaded to coalesce in it raised problems of organization and administrative arrangements. Such problems were naturally more acute in negotiating with London than with other regions. By then LATE, largely through Jimmy's efforts, was the best-established and the biggest group. It could not be expected to surrender any of its strength to a nominally nationwide but newborn body (literally a neo-NATE). On the other hand, it recognized the need for English to take its place (belatedly) alongside other subject associations. The solution of our problems and the consequent excellent cooperation now prevailing between London and the rest has owed a great deal to Jimmy's personal role and his unobtrusive guidance.

In due course he took his turn as chairman of the association, and his period of office was memorable for the first international conference of English teachers at York in 1971. Outside NATE there was his influence on the Bullock Report and the English Committee of the Schools Council, and their repercussions could be found in much of the Association's work.

Recently it dawned upon us, as it should have done long before, that there was a danger that Jimmy's work for the cause of English might be inadequately recognized in Britain, perhaps just because, with his inexhaustible energies, he had made himself indispensible in many diverse ways; LATE, NATE, the London Institute, and international liaison with Australia, Canada, New Zealand and the USA through what came to be called IFTE (International Federation of Teachers of English) would not have been the same without him. So, belatedly, NATE is trying to make amends for taking him for granted by sponsoring this book in his honour.

For me, friendship with Jimmy has meant constant reminders that 'English' is an enormous single phenomenon, that language and literature interweave, that drama and microcomputers are not disparate, that the spoken and written and indeed the examined word are inseparable, and so on. He alerted me to the big thinkers who must not be overlooked – to Polanyi and Susanne Langer, George Kelly and James Moffett *et alii, et alii*. For those things and, of course, for his own most thoughtful and penetrating writings, I am as grateful as all teachers of English must be.

Bill Mittins

Jimmy Britton and Linguistics

To write about linguistics in relation to Jimmy Britton's work is at once a challenge and an occasion for some rather chastened reflections. On the one hand, it is clear that his own work has always seen the centrality of language in human development and thus in the educational enterprise; on the other, one could say that linguistics has both failed to offer him what he sought and failed either to acknowledge or to take advantage of what he has had to offer.

I see three strands crystallizing in Britton's publications of the 1960s as his views began to be more fully articulated: that a philosophy of English education must not only refer to, but actually be rooted in, a theoretically well-informed observation and interpretation of children's language development; that language acquisition and development do not, and could not, take place in other than a social context, a context in which real people use language for genuine (not necessarily simple) purposes; and, following from these, that in the years of formal education, language development, intellectual and cognitive development, and social and moral development are all so closely interrelated and interdependent that to isolate any one for the sake of discussion, or analysis, or extrapolation to pedagogy, is to distort.

Such a series of realizations, I suppose, must have sent Britton frequently to linguistics to look for generalizations that would help to underpin his own theorizing. It is in this context that, as an academic linguist, I start to feel chastened. In *Language and Learning*, where his philosophy of education is first fully articulated, one can see the clear evidence of an unsuccessful search: occasional references to works which were seminal in their own time, but which would hardly have figured on an undergraduate's reading list for a linguistics course in 1970, at least in North America (Hockett, Firth, Sapir, Whorf); reference to Russian developmental psychologists in whose work language development is important (Luria and Vygotsky, of course, but also Chukovsky); then a number of American authors whose presence is indirectly a testimony to how different Britton's concerns were from the excitement in academic linguistics over Chomsky's innateness hypothesis – experimental and clinical psycholinguists such as Roger Brown, Ursula Bellugi, Erich Lenneberg; and, finally, a great linguist, one whose views of the centrality of social contexts in language development and use were largely consonant with Britton's views, but whose interests were so far removed from the current preoccupations of most other academic linguists that he too might well not have appeared on an American undergraduate's reading list at that time: Michael Halliday.

I do not mean to suggest that the work of any of these people is trivial. On the contrary, what I do want to stress is that all were, in different ways, remote from the mainstream linguistics of the late 1960s. Britton took from what must have been much wider reading in linguistics whatever was useful in the synthesis he was developing. But what he needed most could nowhere be found in current academic linguistics, and so he had to invent it. Most of the chapter headings in *Language and Learning* take up concerns that linguistics needed to address; most of them have yet to be taken up by linguists in what is now clearly the mainstream of academic linguistics.

It is, of course, easy to mock the narrowness and apparent sterility of academic linguistics as it has developed since 1970. Harold Rosen is particularly good at this, but Jimmy has got in a few good licks as well. I do not want to be a party to this enterprise either; in my view, the importance of what has happened in academic linguistics since the publication of Chomsky's *Syntactic Structures* in 1957 cannot be overestimated. None the less, linguistics has hardly responded to the challenge posed by the publication of *Language and Learning*. Seeking in that work to develop a theory in which language is seen to be centrally important in education, Britton also pointed to an urgent need for a broader theory in linguistics, a theory of performance perhaps. Not finding it in linguistics, Britton himself sketched the outlines of a possible theory. Few have followed his lead. With the outstanding exception, once again, of Halliday and his former students, linguists on the whole are still not comfortable with the notion that language is important as a social semiotic. With not many exceptions, linguists have barely begun to come to terms with the centrality of meaning in language acquisition and development, and almost without exception linguists have not gone anywhere near a theory of language development that could inform a philosophy of mother-tongue education.

Ironically, even where Britton's work has had an influence on developments in academic linguistics, that influence is hardly ever recognized, let alone acknowledged. For example, Britton's early work with Barnes, Rosen, Martin and Medway on classroom discourse undoubtedly had an enormous influence on what is now a recognizable speciality within academic linguistics, the field of discourse analysis. Of about a dozen introductory works on this subject in my library, all treat classroom discourse at some length, and in almost all the direct influence of Britton is apparent, but he is not mentioned in the index of a single one.

Linguistics, then, was a subject whose potential importance Britton saw very early, but it was not in a position to give him much of what he sought. As a result he offered quite a lot to linguistics; much of this has yet to be fully appreciated by linguists.

Ian Pringle

Dartmouth

Among the participants at the Dartmouth Conference (1966) were a fairish number of charismatic subjects, people whose past accomplishments allowed them to assert their authority to speak definitely on the matter at hand; viz. the nature of the school and college subject 'English'. Some of these self-confessed authorities spoke wistfully and at length, in rather Leavisite measure, giving literature a central function in English as a humanizing, sensitizing experience. Others, more ploddingly, found the meaning and value of English grammar, defining or rationalizing their position by asserting that, since control of Standard English is a necessary prerequisite to access to jobs, full membership of the polity and so forth, English teachers must be seen to have the duty, nay, the right to teach grammar to children and young people.

Conditions at the Dartmouth seminar were such that discussion could very easily have ended up being dominated or at least shaped by those two sterile and sterilizing concepts. First, there were the representatives from the United States, fresh from several years of trying to prune English of the various socially useful activities that had come to be attached to it. They were full of notions like the tripod of English, the sequential and cumulative curriculum, the spiral curriculum. With those notions went a feeling – not always well concealed – that real progress had been made. If English hadn't yet been sorted out, it soon would be. Then, second, among both English and Americans there were people who seemed to believe sincerely and trustingly in literary works as purveyors of truths and values. They craved received lists and were anxious to choose the best for their charges.

I think the conference was saved – the word may be too strong – from the imbroglios that might have ensued from the mixing of so many attitudes, values and personalities. And this was done by Britton's comment, in the first day's discussion, on Kitzhaber's plenary paper 'What is English?', which somehow came out sounding like 'What English is'. In effect, Kitzhaber said flatly, 'English is knowledge about language, literature, and, in the form of rhetoric, knowledge about composition.' To this more than positive statement, Britton responded by correcting the question. Properly, he said, it should have been, 'What do English teachers do?'

Of course, that question is open to the simple answer that English teachers teach about language, literature and composition/rhetoric. I dare say that some of those listening to Britton supposed that nothing much had been changed by the reformulation of the problem Kitzhaber addressed. The basic issues were still basic, English was still English, and a curriculum was still out there, separate from both teachers and children, just waiting to be put together by what were called 'subject-matter specialists'. Such a fancy could have been enjoyed only by someone unaware of the rich tradition in philosophical linguistics that lay behind Britton's quip. (It was, I think, the 'out-there-ness' of the Kitzhaber programme that above all prompted Britton to look for a formulation in terms of observable – active and interactive – behaviour.)

Following the tradition contributed to by Sapir, Cassirer, Langer and, I suppose, Coleridge, Britton held that language is the means by which human beings create the world for themselves and themselves in the world. What English teachers 'do', then, is find reasons and occasions for young children and young people to extend their experience, at first hand and through books, so that there will be a concomitant development of their linguistic resources. The idea is important because it requires teachers to shift their interest and attention from what they (and their textbooks) know, and which children must study – generally on the excuse that some day, in some future situation imagined by curriculum designers, that knowledge will prove its usefulness. With his question Britton asked teachers to look at children realistically, not as mere objects of instruction but as developing human beings who will go on learning. As the Bullock Report has put it, 'Thus in a very real sense the classroom and its extensions can constitute a language environment, with experience extending language, and language in turn interpreting experience' (p. 62).

W. W. Douglas

A Community of Inquiry: James Britton and Educational Research

To acknowledge the vast reach of James Britton's influence upon educational research across the English-speaking world in what, essentially, is a long note is of course not possible. Simply to appreciate in their full subtlety and power such conceptual contributions as the *expressive/poetic/transactional* or *spectator/participant* distinctions or the role of intention in speaking and writing requires essays of the generosity and scope found earlier in this collection.

Even more pervasive and influential than these may be perhaps an attitude, a set of beliefs about what educational research is, about who does it, in what kinds of human arrangements, about the language in which it discovers its meaning, and, indeed, about why we do it, to what ends. Central here are the roles of teachers in such inquiries.

Perhaps because he was a practising teacher for so many years, James Britton, earlier than almost anyone else anywhere, recognized two logical and obvious facts about these roles. One, teachers are a primary source – like imagine! the children themselves – of insights into how children learn in school. Two, because they are the ones who possess, in the full Polanyian sense, that personal knowledge, teachers must become active members in any community of inquiry. From its initial call for student scripts the London Schools Council Project engaged the talents and participation of teachers. And in the richness that followed – the books, the booklets, the policy statements, the curricula, the subsequent research – teachers stayed steadily participating and openly honoured members of the community of inquiry. Aware too that the purpose of such research was to make a difference in how classes and schools were conducted, this community from the outset followed a conscious policy of writing in grounded, richly exampled, non-jargoned English, in recognition of who their audience needed to be.

The United States has come late but fervently to believe in communities of inquiry, late because, even thirty years after Chomsky's devastation of Skinner's *Verbal Behavior*, many North American departments of psychology remain white-coated, laboratoried, rodented and, assiduously, childless. Also, unlike social studies research in the UK, American graduate education emanated from a Teutonic model, with the policies of tenure and promotion still rewarding solitary egos pursuing solitary tasks with solitary passion – preferably, grimly. In this lone eagle approach to research, collaboration in too many American universities still connotes the Second

World War or, worse, an anti-capitalistic statement: however will we know what individual to reward singly if we don't know who precisely did what?

But once, of course, a concept is embraced, it is embraced fervently. Now teacher-centered and teacher-directed research represent perhaps our liveliest branch of inquiry. It has taken five major forms: (a) journal articles about successful classroom experiments, such as Margaret Quinlan's 'Teachers as researchers?' in the April 1987 issue of *The English Journal*; (b) full-length accounts by brilliant teachers teaching, such as Nanci Atwell's *In the Middle*, Lucy Calkin's *Lessons from a Child* and Tom Romano's *Clearing the Way*; (c) guidebooks for teachers wanting to conduct their own research – *Reclaiming the Classroom*, edited by Dixie Goswami and Peter Skilman, Miles Myers's *The Teacher-Researchers: How to Study Writing in the Classroom*; (d) ingenious patterns of teachers networking, such as those sponsored by the National Writing Project and the Bread Loaf School of English; and (e) most recently, the bold and research-supported recommendations issued by the sixty elementary, secondary and college teachers who participated in the coalition on the future of English teaching, held in July 1987 in the state of Maryland.

The current leadership of our two countries – ever tender, ever alert – rightly regard the empowering of teachers as a political threat. Any anti-hierarchical action is profoundly threatening to groups with their own agendas for controlling education, which means of course controlling access by certain portions of the population to language and literacy in their fullest dimensions. Happily, the international community of inquiry into language learning and teaching, which James Britton so helped form, is now a banyan tree, with too many roots to be deracinated. Indeed, this community of inquiry may well become one of the most powerful forms of democratic action in the educational world.

Janet Emig

Teachers Learning about Learning

I am sure that all teachers who care about the job they are trying to do in their schools, in their classrooms, with pupils, will steadily change their practice in their efforts to provide effective education as weeks become months and months turn into years. The last thing such teachers need is a list of fatuously impositional statements, utterly divorced from their own experience, purporting to tell them what to aim for.

But sometimes teachers, including me, have the great good fortune of working for a time with someone truly wise. I do not use that word lightly; for me, Jimmy Britton was exactly that. In the gentlest and most modest way he turned me around from thinking as a teacher, to thinking as a learner again. It is thanks to him that everything I have tried to do for nearly ten years now in my job as an English adviser has been focused on learning – for teachers as well as for their pupils – and, of course, for me too.

Jimmy helped me to understand that language is a powerful human *activity* – not merely a great mass of words outside our heads, but a generative mental process which enables all of us (five or fifty) to shape meaning and to try to make sense.

Thanks to his perceptions, our 'Learning about Learning' residential weeks took shape – offering teachers an opportunity to rediscover together how that rich mixture of verbal, visual and kinetic representation takes all learners, young and old, forward to fresh opportunities in the shared context of their own classrooms.

We have just celebrated the launch of fifteen booklets produced by practising teachers in the Wiltshire/Somerset 'Write to Learn Project', which describe their efforts to offer both talking and writing to children as modes of expression which encourage these young talkers and writers to reach for further understanding.

The teachers are excited by the responses of their pupils to many areas of the curriculum – art, maths and science as well as the reshaping of personal experiences, through their talk and through their words on paper – especially the teachers who are working with five- and six-year-olds. They are discovering and celebrating children's determination and confidence to shape meaning from the moment that they come to school. They recognize, because they have created fresh possibilities for self-expression, that five- and six-year-olds can take a powerful hold on written language as well as speech if they are given the encouragement and the opportunities to do so.

Similarly, teachers in our project who work with older pupils are discovering the value of students' learning logs as a way of mapping progress, which can also involve genuine self-assessment. Such discoveries are going to be very important for current GCSE and TVEI developments. Thanks to James Britton, we have been offered a constructive sense of direction.

Pat D'Arcy

And Gladly Learn

Recently I have written forewords to three books by teachers which the Australian Association for the Teaching of English is publishing. They are books which have grown out of our research policy, a policy which encourages teachers to take on the role of researchers in their own classrooms: to be pragmatic theorists, seeking a better language and learning environment for their students, believing that their discoveries are worth reflecting on and sharing with others.

A sociologist might argue that this action-research model suits our reputed national temperament: a race of individualists and pragmatists, not given to suffering fools – or theorists – gladly. (Who else would produce a language arts book entitled *This Works for Me?*) I want to reflect on a different shaping influence. If you like, to rewrite the first paragraph in different words.

James Britton's contribution to English teaching in Australia can be discerned in the profession's understanding of research in language and learning, its belief in the centrality of the classroom teacher's role in achieving this, and its acknowledgement that we belong to a community – an *international* community – willing to learn from each other and to celebrate what we learn. But it has been the demonstrated consistency of Britton's teaching role, what is preached *and* what is practised, which has been critical.

'Teachers teach most profoundly what they are at the core,' says Garth Boomer (1982a). 'The lasting lesson is the demonstration of the self as it handles its authority and those under its authority.'

In 1972 Unesco funded a watershed seminar in Sydney, the starting point for the first national curriculum project in English, and Britton's first visit to Australia. His opening address was entitled 'The Present State of Theory and Knowledge Relating to English Teaching'. It summarized participant/spectator language functions and the implications of these for learning. It outlined some of the findings of the Schools Council Writing Research Project, then in its final year. The view of language and learning which was presented shaped the theoretical framework of the subsequent national Language Development Project. But the *teaching* demonstration was equally generative: 'I shall select those areas where it seems to me that currently fruitful problems exist' (Britton, 1973a). Not a static, state-of-the-art speech, but a Kellyian inquiry. One teacher to another. An invitation to think.

In 1977 Britton returned for a longer visit, to direct a state-wide, in-service project in Victoria, focusing on language and learning across the curriculum. He worked with a team of young teachers and consultants. He might have chosen a university base from which to lecture. In fact he travelled to teachers' centres and schools across the state. Teachers who had spent their lives in isolated rural areas joined workshops and looked afresh, or for the first time, at their teaching and their students' learning. They discovered a renewed belief in the importance of their work.

By now you may have guessed my conclusion. In 1980 James Britton presented the opening address, again in Sydney, of the Third International Conference for the Teaching of English. He concluded by proposing a toast to the 1980s as the age of the classroom teacher:

As we have developed our view of learning as interactive, and that of the curriculum as negotiable; as we have recognised the dramatic effect of intentions upon perform-ance, by teachers as well as by students; as it has become clear that teaching consists of moment-by-moment interactive behaviour, behaviour that can only spring from inner conviction – I think we are, perhaps for the first time, ready to admit that what the teacher can't do in the classroom can't be achieved by any other means [1982a].

Notice the collaborative and empowering 'we', so hospitable to teachers' intentions, and thus turning a vast lecture hall into a classroom. It is that demonstration above all which has made possible Britton's incalculable contribution to Australian English teaching.

Margaret Gill

A Centre of Influence

Interweaving strands of our lives are marked by episodes highlighted by persons. At relevant moments the mind releases selected memories of past events to be re-examined through new eyes and reflected on through a changed perspective. This experience transforms both event and individual, and the future as well. I am at such a moment now.

I first met James Britton in 1966. He had come from Vancouver for a day to talk to teachers at the first 'English Institute' held in Calgary. The next summer he returned to teach at the institute. Thus began the strand of a continuing association which later included his spending a term as visiting professor here. Three years later *Language and Learning* appeared; it became an important influence in my professional life.

For the classroom Jimmy reintegrated language and child within the context of world and society. His emphasis on learning as a prime characteristic of humankind and language as its main instrument gave a new focus to the learning process. By his model of modes and roles he created a unified framework for examining and understanding language development and use. In drawing upon other areas of knowledge he confirmed the need for an interdisciplinary approach in language studies in education. The structure of his view was accommodating to new knowledge. Ultimately he provided new perspectives on language and intimated new directions for research. The relevance continues.

Over the next two decades *Language and Learning*, as well as Jimmy's continuing publications, was a central influence in the research and projects of the students/teachers with whom I worked. Complementing this influence were the contributions of many others working in the area of language. Collectively, the students' studies of classroom language extend across the range of school levels, examine not only learning in English, but in art, music, social studies, science and mathematics also, and may constitute an extensive body of data of children's talk, reading and writing. These explorations of language altered the perspectives of the explorers themselves and gave new directions for their work. The result was a close network of teachers who had not only translated theory into practice in their own classrooms but also influenced policy and practice within their schools, jurisdictions, the province and beyond.

Of necessity some of the pervasive confirmations and intimations of these studies can be limned only briefly and too categorically here. Children engage in collaborative learning easily and profitably when they are recognized as learners with intentions. Expressive language is their common currency, both for melding the group and for exploring ideas. In all subjects spectator role is an important complement to that of participant. The students' frequent and often sustained shifts into spectator-role narrative talk enable them to bring to bear on a topic their own experiences in a familiar language form. Consistently it is the spectator episodes which most frequently project students into generalization and other higher levels of abstraction. Out of such episodes also usually emerge their first intentions for further related work in writing. Within the exploring collaborative group individual intentions interplay towards creating an intention in common; in the end, however, basic individual intentions and views remain, though often subtly extended and refined. Personal constructs appear to be determinants of intention. Their expression may be activated by affective components of analogous past experiences triggered within memory by items in the ongoing talk. Within group talk students at various ages demonstrate their capacities as learners, often with strategies of unusual relevance and power.

Implicit in this brief interview are contexts beyond the immediate context. The teachers engaged in the research, many of whom Jimmy came to know, discovered in the man and his ideas new directions and a renewed vitality for their work in schools. The concept of language and learning restored individuality to children and confirmed personal knowledge as a means to power and growth, not only for students but for teachers as well. Within their classrooms they could be continuing researchers and learners in relation to their teaching.

To this point I have shared reflections which are personal and local. However, Jimmy's influence transcends place and time. In this country the Calgary Connection is one of a number of networks of teachers who value his ideas and practise them in their work. There is other evidence of his influence in Canada: in the language arts curricula of half the provinces, in new textbooks in English, in conferences of provincial teachers' associations and of the Canadian Council of Teachers of English, which is part of an international network with shared perspectives and aspirations for children and their learning.

I am aware that these instances still constitute but a strong cutting edge; however, it seems time to stop short of further qualification. Within the context of time and circumstance what has been achieved in Canada and other countries is already impressive. If extensive change should be slow and require continued effort, it may also ensure more responsible and lasting results.

James Britton has been at the heart of this change, not only through the force of his ideas, but equally by his constant commitment to teachers and their work, his imaginative actions for the growth of national and international networks. By embodying those qualities of teacher and learner which he proposes and by living what he professes, he has made a difference.

Merron Chorny

Notes on Contributors

Arthur Applebee is Professor of Education, State University of New York at Albany.

Douglas Barnes is Reader in Education at the University of Leeds School of Education. He is co-author of *Language, the Learner and the School, Versions of English* and *Communication and Learning in Small Groups*, and author of *From Communication to Curriculum*.

Myra Barrs is Warden of the Centre for Language in Primary Education, Inner London Education Authority.

Garth Boomer is Chairman of the Commonwealth Schools Commission in Canberra. He is co-author of *The Spitting Image* and author of *Fair Dinkum Teaching and Learning*.

Amanda Branscombe is currently a doctoral student at Auburn University, Alabama.

Tony Burgess is Senior Lecturer in English at the University of London Institute of Education and co-author of *Language and Dialects of London Schoolchildren*.

Courtney Cazden is Professor of Education at Harvard University, and editor of *Classroom Discourse: The Language of Teaching and Learning*.

Merron Chorny is Emeritus Professor of English Education, University of Alberta at Calgary.

Pat D'Arcy is County English Adviser for Wiltshire. She is co-author of *Writing and Learning across the Curriculum* and author of *Reading for Meaning*.

Henrietta Dombey is Principal Lecturer in the Primary Education Department at Brighton Polytechnic, and currently Chair of the National Association for the Teaching of English.

Wallace Douglas was formerly Professor of English at Northwestern University.

Janet Emig is Professor of Education at Rutgers University and currently Chair of the National Council for the Teaching of English.

Margaret Gill is Lecturer in Charge of English Education at Victoria College of Advanced Education (Rusden Campus). She is President of the Australian Association for the Teaching of English and currently Chair of the International Federation for the Teaching of English.

Denis Lawton is Director of the University of London Institute of Education. He is author of *Social Class, Language and Education* and of a number of books on the curriculum.

Martin Lightfoot is Director of the Centre for the Study of Community and Race Relations and Co-Director of the Education Policy Centre at Brunel University. He is co-author of *Schools and Industry*.

Nancy Martin is an Education Consultant, working chiefly in North America, and was formerly Reader in Education at the University of London Institute of Education. She is co-author of *Writing and Learning across the Curriculum*, and author of *Mostly about Writing*.

Peter Medway is Senior Research Fellow, National Evaluation of TVEI Curriculum, University of Leeds. He is co-author of *The Climate for Learning* and author of *Finding a Language*.

Margaret Meek (Spencer) is Senior Lecturer in English at the University of London Institute of Education and Book Reviews Editor of *The School Librarian*. She is co-editor of *Changing English: Essays for Harold Rosen* and editor of *The Cool Web* and *Achieving Literacy*.

Bill Mittins was formerly Senior Lecturer in Education at the University of Newcastle-upon-Tyne.

Gordon Pradl is Professor of English Education in the School of Education at New York University and an Editor of *English Education*. He is co-author of *Learning to Write/Writing to Learn* and editor of *Prospect and Retrospect: Essays by James Britton*.

Ian Pringle is Professor of English and Linguistics at Carleton University, Ottawa. He has edited *Re-Inventing the Rhetorical Tradition* and is the author of *A Comparative Study of Writing Abilities in Two Modes*. He was President of the International Federation of English Teachers, 1985–87.

The Right Hon. **Merlyn Rees,** PC, MP, is the Labour Member of Parliament for Morley and South Leeds and previously taught history and economics at Harrow Weald Grammar School. He has been Secretary of State for Northern Ireland and Home Secretary in the British Cabinet, and is the author of *The Public Sector in a Mixed Economy* and *Northern Ireland: A Personal Perspective.*

Harold Rosen is Emeritus Professor, Department of English and Media Studies, University of London Institute of Education. He is co-author of *The Language of Primary School Children* and *The Language and Dialects of London Schoolchildren* and author of *The Language Monitors* and *Stones and Meanings.*

Don Rutledge is Associate Director of Education – Program for the Toronto Board of Education.

Janet Taylor is Associate Professor of Early Childhood Education, Auburn University, Alabama.

Mike Torbe is General Adviser for English with Coventry local education authority. He is co-author of *Language, the Learner and the School, The Climate for Learning* and *A Framework for Reading* and author of *Teaching Spelling.*

Claire Woods is Superintendent of Studies for the Education Department of South Australia. She is co-author of *Two Pathways to Literacy.*

Mary Worrall is a Managing Editor at Oxford University Press.

References

Adams, T. (1984), in N. Martin (ed.), *NATE – The First Twenty-One Years*. Sheffield: NATE.

Applebee, A. N. (1986), 'Problems in process approaches: toward a reconceptualization of process instruction', in A. Petrovsky and D. Bartholomew (eds.), *The Teaching of Writing*. Eighty-fifth Yearbook of the National Society for the Study of Education. Chicago: NSSE.

Applebee, A. N., and Langer, J. A. (1983), 'Instructional scaffolding: reading and writing as natural language activities', *Language Arts*, 60, pp. 168–75.

Archer, M. (1984), *Social Origins of Educational Systems*. London: Sage.

Atkinson, P., and Delamont, S. (1976), 'Mock-ups and cock-ups: the stage management of guided discovery instruction', in M. Hammersley and P. Woods (eds.), *The Process of Schooling*. Milton Keynes: Open University Press.

Auden, W. H. (1963), 'Making, knowing, judging', in *The Dyer's Hand and Other Essays*. London: Faber.

Bailey, C. (1986), 'The characterisation, justification and content of liberal education', in R. Gibson (ed.), *Liberal Education Today?*. Cambridge: Cambridge Institute of Education.

Baird, J., and White, R. (1982), 'A case study of learning styles in biology', *European Journal of Science Education*, 4, pp. 325–37.

Bakhtin, M. N. (1981), *The Dialogic Imagination*. Austin: University of Texas Press.

Bakhtin, M. N. (1986), *Speech Genres and Other Late Essays*. Austin: University of Texas Press.

Ball, S. J. (1985), 'English for the English since 1906', in I. F. Goodson (ed.), *Social Histories of the Secondary Curriculum: Subjects for Study*. London and Philadelphia: Falmer Press.

Barnes, D. (1976), *From Communication to Curriculum*. London: Penguin.

Barnes, D., and Barnes, D. (1984), 'English and the "Real World"', in M. Meek and J. Miller (eds.), *Changing English*. London: Heinemann.

Barnes, D., and Barnes, D. (1986), 'English in action', *English in Australia*, 78 (December), pp. 3–14.

Barnes, D., Barnes, D., and Clarke, S. (1984), *Versions of English*. London: Heinemann.

Barnes, D., Britton, J., and Torbe, M. (1986), *Language, the Learner and the School*, 3rd edn. London: Penguin.

Barrs, M. (1983), 'The new orthodoxy about writing: confusing process and pedagogy', *Language Arts*, 60 (7), October 1983.

Barrs, M. (in press), 'Maps of play', in M. Meek and C. Mills (eds.), *Language and Literacy in the Primary School*. Brighton: Falmer Press.

Barthes, R. (1967), *Writing Degree Zero*. London: Cape.

Barthes, R. (1975a), *S/Z* (translated by R. Miller). New York: Hill & Wang.

Barthes, R. (1975b), 'An introduction to the structural analysis of narrative' (translated by S. Heath), *New Literary History*, 6, pp. 237–72.

Bartlett, F. (1932), *Remembering*. Cambridge: Cambridge University Press.

Bauman, R. (1986), *Story, Performance and Event*. Cambridge: Cambridge University Press.

Berlak, A., and Berlak, H. (1981), *Dilemmas of Schooling: Teaching and Social Change*. London: Methuen.

Bernstein, B. (1971), 'Schools cannot compensate for society', in *Class, Codes and Control*. London: Routledge & Kegan Paul.

Bissex, G. (1980), *Gnys at Wrk: A Child Learns to Write and Read*. Cambridge, Mass.: Harvard University Press.

Bond, D., Keogh, R., and Walker, D. (1985) (eds.), *Reflection: Turning Experience into Learning*. London: Kogan Page.

Boomer, G. (1982a), 'Struggling in English', *English in Australia*, 59 (March), p. 3.

Boomer, G. (ed.) (1982b), *Negotiating the Curriculum*. Sydney: Ashton Scholastic.

Boomer, G. (1987), 'What the teacher saw: an experiment in poetry teaching and action research', address to the Canadian Council of Teachers of English, Winnipeg, May.

Booth, W. (1984), 'Narrative as the mold of character', in *Telling Exchange*, report of the conference on Narrative held to mark the retirement of Harold Rosen. London: University of London Institute of Education.

Britton, J. (1967), *Talking and Writing*. London: Methuen.

Britton, J. (1970), *Language and Learning*. London: Allen Lane.

Britton, J. (1971), Introduction to A. R. Luria, *Speech and the Development of Mental Processes in the Child*. London: Penguin.

Britton, J. (1973a), 'The present state of theory and knowledge relating to English teaching', in *The Teaching of English: Australian UNESCO Seminar*. Canberra: Australian Government Publishing Service.

Britton, J. (1973b), 'How we got here', in N. Bagnall (ed.), *New Movements in the Teaching of English*. London: Temple-Smith.

Britton, J. (1977), 'Language and the nature of learning: an individual perspective', in *The Teaching of English*, National Society for the Study of Education Year Book, Part 1, 76th Year, p. 138.

Britton, J. (1978), 'I'm listening', *Journal of the Canadian Association for Young Children*, 4 (1), pp. 33–6.

Britton, J. (1982a), 'English teaching: prospect and retrospect', in R. D. Eagleson (ed.), *English in the Eighties*. Australian Association for the Teaching of English.

Britton, J. (1982b), *Prospect and Retrospect: Selected Essays of James Britton* (ed. G. Pradl). London: Heinemann.

Britton, J. (1983), 'Writing and the story world', in B. M. Kroll and G. Wells (eds.), *Explorations in the Development of Writing*. New York: John Wiley.

Britton, J. (1986), 'Attempting to clarify our objectives for teaching English', *English Education*, 18 (3), pp. 153–8.

Britton, J. (1987), 'Call it an experiment: what can we expect our reading to do for our writing', *English Education*, 19 (2), pp. 83–92.

Britton, J., Burgess, T., Martin, N., McLeod, A., and Rosen, H. (1975), *The Development of Writing Abilities, 11–18*. London: Macmillan.

Brown, A., and Palincsar, A. S. (in press), in L. Resnick (ed.), *Cognition and Instruction: Issues and Agendas*. Hillsdale, NJ: Erlbaum.

Brown, G. (1977), *Listening to Spoken English*. London: Longman.

Brown, R. L., and Herndl, C. G. (1986), 'An ethnographic study of corporate writing: job status as reflected in written text', in B. Couture (ed.), *Functional Approaches to Writing: Research Perspectives*. London: Francis Pinter.

Brumfit, C., Ellis, R., and Levine, J. (eds.) (1985), *ESL in the UK: Educational and Linguistic Perspectives*, ELT Document 121. Oxford: Pergamon.

Bruner, J. S. (1966), *Towards a Theory of Instruction*. Cambridge, Mass.: Harvard University Press.

Bruner, J. S. (1986), *Actual Minds, Possible Worlds*. Cambridge, Mass.: Harvard University Press.

Bullock Report (1975), *A Language for Life*. London: HMSO.

Burgess, T. (1984), 'Diverse melodies', in J. Miller (ed.), *Eccentric Propositions*. London: Routledge & Kegan Paul.

Burgess, T. (1985), 'The Question of English', in M. Meek and J. Miller (eds.), *Changing English: Essays for Harold Rosen*. London: Heinemann.

Burlend, R., and Burlend, E. (1987 [1848]), *A True Picture of Emigration*. Lincoln, Neb.: University of Nebraska Press.

Cameron, D. (1985), *Feminism and Linguistic Theory*. London: Macmillan.

Carr, W., and Kemmis, S. (1986), *Becoming Critical: Knowing through Action Research*. Deakin University.

de Castell, S., Luke, A., and Egan, K. (1986), 'On defining literacy', in S. de Castell, A. Luke and K. Egan (eds.), *Literacy, School and Schooling*. Cambridge: Cambridge University Press.

Cazden, C. B. (1980), 'Peekaboo as an instructional model: discourse development at home and at school', in *Papers and Reports in Child Development*, 17.

Cazden, C. B. (in press), *Classroom Discourse: The Language of Teaching and Learning*. Portsmouth, NH: Heinemann.

Cazden, C. B., *et al.* (1979), ' "You all gonna hafta listen": peer teaching in a primary classroom', in W. A. Collins (ed.), *Children's Language and Communication*, Twelfth Annual Minnesota Symposium on Child Development. Hillsdale, NJ: Erlbaum.

Cazden, C., John, V., and Hymes, D. (eds.) (1972), *Functions of Language in the Classroom*. New York: Teacher's College Press.

de Certeau, M. (1980), 'On the oppositional practices of everyday life', *Social Texts*, 1 (3).

Chambers, R. (1984), *Story and Situation*. Minneapolis: University of Minnesota Press.

Chatman, S. (1978), *Story and Discourse*. Ithaca, NY: Cornell University Press.

Chomsky, C. (1979), 'Approaching reading through invented spellings', in L. Resnick and P. Weaver (eds.), *Theory and Practice of Early Reading*, vol. 2. Hillsdale, NJ: Erlbaum.

Christie, F. (1985), 'Language and schooling', in S. N. Tchudi (ed.), *Language, Schooling and Society*. Upper Montclair, NJ: Boynton/Cook.

Clay, M. M. (1975), *What Did I Write?* Auckland: Heinemann.

Clay, M. M. (1985), *The Early Detection of Reading Difficulties*, 3rd edn. Auckland and Portsmouth, NH: Heinemann.

Cochran-Smith, M. (1983), 'Reading stories to children: a review critique', in *Advances in Reading/Language: A Research Annual*, Vol. 2. Greenwich, Conn.: JAI Press.

Cochran-Smith, M. (1984), *The Making of a Reader*. Norwood, NJ: Ablex.

Coggan, J., and Foster, V. (1985), *But My Biro Won't Work ... : Literacy and Learning in the Secondary School Classroom – An Action Research Study*. Australian Association for the Teaching of English.

Cook-Gumperz, J. (1986), 'Literacy and schooling: an unchanging equation?' in J. Cook-Gumperz (ed.), *The Social Construction of Literacy*. Cambridge: Cambridge University Press.

Connell, R. W., *et al.* (1982), *Making the Difference*. London: Allen & Unwin.

Creber, J. W. P. (1987), 'Some lessons from a short story', *English Journal*, 76 (2), 1987, pp. 82–95.

Crystal, D. (1987), *Child Language, Learning and Linguistics*, 2nd edn. London: Arnold.

Culler, J. (1976), *Saussure*. London: Fontana.

Culler, J. (1977), *Structuralist Poetics*. London: Routledge & Kegan Paul.

Delamont, S. (1983), *Interaction in the Classroom*, 2nd edn. London: Methuen.

Doise, W., and Mugny, G. (1984), *The Social Development of the Intellect* (translated by A. St James-Emler and N. Emler). New York: Pergamon.

Dore, R. (1986), *The Diploma Disease*. London: Allen & Unwin.

Douglas, M. (1987), *How Institutions Think*. London: Routledge & Kegan Paul.

Doughty, P., Pearce, J., and Thornton, G. (1971), *Language in Use*. London: Arnold.

Driver, R., Guesne, E., and Tiberghien, A. (1985), *Children's Ideas in Science*. Milton Keynes: Open University Press.

Dyson, A. (1983), 'Young children as composers', *Language Arts*, 20 (4).

Dyson, A. (1984), 'Learning to write/learning to do school: emergent writers' interpretations of school literacy tasks', *Research in the Teaching of English*, 18, pp. 233–64.

Dyson, A. (1986a), 'Children's early interpretations of writing: expanding research perspectives', in D. Yaden and S. Templeton (eds.), *Metalinguistic Awareness and Beginning Literacy*. Portsmouth, NH: Heinemann.

Dyson, A. (1986b), 'Transitions and tensions: interrelationships between the drawing, talking and dictating of young children', *Research in English*, 20.

Edwards, A. D., and Furlong, V. J. (1978), *The Language of Teaching*. London: Heinemann.

Edwards, D., and Maybin, J. (1987), *The Development of Understanding in the Classroom*. Milton Keynes: Open University Press. (EH207, Communication and Education.)

Edwards, D., and Mercer, N. (1986), 'Context and continuity: classroom discourse and the development of shared knowledge', in K. Durkin (ed.), *Language Development in the School Years*. London: Croom Helm.

Edwards, D., and Mercer, N. (1987), *Common Knowledge: The Development of Understanding in the Classroom*. London: Methuen.

Emerson, C. (1981), 'Outer world and inner speech: Bakhtin, Vygotsky, and the internalization of language', in G. S. Morson (ed.), *Bakhtin: Essays and Dialogues on His Work*. Chicago: University of Chicago Press.

Emig, J. (1983), *The Web of Meaning: Essays on Writing, Teaching, Learning and Thinking*. Upper Montclair, NJ: Boynton/Cook.

Feinburg, S. (1976), 'Combat in child's art', in J. S. Bruner, Jolly and K. Sylva (eds.), *Play*. London: Penguin.

Ferriero, E. (1984), 'The underlying logic of literacy development', in H. Goelman, A. Oberg and F. Smith (eds.), *Awakening to Literacy*. Portsmouth, NH: Heinemann.

Ferriero, E., and Teberosky, A. (1982), *Literacy before Schooling*. Portsmouth, NH: Heinemann.

Fischer, K. W., and Bullock, D. (1984), 'Cognitive development in school-age children', in W. A. Collins (ed.), *Development During Middle Childhood: The Years From Six to Twelve*. Washington, DC: National Academy Press.

Foucault, M. (1980), *Power/Knowledge* (ed. C. Gordon). Brighton: Harvester.

Friedenberg, E. Z. (1965), *The Dignity of Youth and Other Atavisms*. New York: Beacon Press.

Fulwiler, T. (1986), *Teaching Writing*. Upper Montclair, NJ: Boynton/Cook.

Gannon, P., and Czerniewska, P. (1980), *Using Linguistics*. London: Edward Arnold.

Gardner, H. (1980), *Artful Scribbles*. London: Jill Norman.

Genette, G. (1980), *Narrative Discourse* (translated by J. Lewin). Oxford: Basil Blackwell.

Giacobbe, M. A. (1981), 'Who says children can't write the first week of school?' in R. D. Walsh (ed.), *Donald Graves in Australia: 'Children Want to Write . . .'*. Rozelle, Australia: Primary English Teaching Association.

Gilbert, J. (1984), 'Reflections on a process approach to learning art and design, based on the experience of teaching in a primary school in a London borough', unpublished MA thesis, Royal College of Art.

Goelman, H., Oberg, A. A., and Smith, F. (eds.) (1982), *Awakening to Literacy*. Portsmouth, NH: Heinemann.

Goodman, K. (1973), 'Psycholinguistics universals in the reading process', in F. Smith (ed.), *Psycholinguistics and Reading*. New York: Holt, Rinehart & Winston.

Goodman, Y. (1968), 'A psycholinguistic description of observed oral reading phenomena in selected young beginning readers', unpublished PhD thesis, Wayne State University.

Goodman, Y. (1984), 'The development of initial literacy', in H. Goelman, A. Oberg and F. Smith (eds.), *Awakening to Literacy*. Portsmouth, NH: Heinemann.

Goodson, I. F. (1984), 'Subjects for study: towards a social history of the curriculum', in I. F. Goodson and S. J. Ball (eds.), *Defining the Curriculum*. Brighton: Falmer Press.

Goody, J. (1977), 'Classroom interaction in the multiracial school', *English in Education*, 11 (1).

Gough, N. (1985), *Curriculum Programs for Practical Learning*. Melbourne: Education Department of Victoria, Australia, Curriculum Branch.

Graves, D., and Hansen, J. (1983), 'The author's chair', *Language Arts*, 60, pp. 176–83.

Grice, H. P. (1975), 'Logic and conversation', in P. Cole and J. L. Morgan (eds.), *Syntax and Semantics*, vol. 3: *Speech Acts*. New York: Academic Press.

Groen, G. J., and Resnick, L. B. (1977), 'Can preschool children invent arithmetic algorithms?', *Journal of Educational Psychology*, 69, pp. 562–645.

Gundara, J., Jones, C., and Kimberley, K. (eds.) (1986), *Racism, Diversity and Education*. London: Hodder & Stoughton.

Gundlach, R. (1982), 'Children as writers: the beginnings of learning to write', in M. Nystrand (ed.), *What Writers Know*. London: Academic Press.

Halliday, M. A. K. (1969), 'Relevant models of language', *Educational Review*, 22 (7), pp. 26–34.

Halsey, A. H. (1972), *Educational Priority*, vol. 1. London: HMSO.

Hammerston, M. (1984), 'Language and the learning of practical skills', in M. Meek and J. Miller (eds.), *Changing English*. London: Heinemann.

Harding, D. W. (1962), *Experience into Words*, London: Chatto.

Hammersley, M. (1974), 'The organisation of pupil participation', in A. Hargreaves and P. Woods (eds.), *Classrooms and Staffrooms*. Milton Keynes: Open University Press.

Hammersley, M. (1977), *Teacher Perspectives*. Milton Keynes: Open University Press. (E202, Schooling and Society.)

Hardcastle, J. (1985), 'Classrooms as sites for cultural making', *English in Education*, 19 (3).

Hargreaves, D. H. (1982), *The Challenge for the Comprehensive School*. London: Routledge & Kegan Paul.

Harste, J. C., Woodward, J. A., and Burke, C. L. (1984), *Language Stories and Literacy Lessons*. Portsmouth, NH: Heinemann.

Heath, S. B. (1982), 'Protean shapes in literary events: ever-shifting oral and literate traditions', in D. Tanne (ed.), *Spoken and Written Language*. Norwood, NJ: Ablex.

Heath, S. B. (1983), *Ways with Words*. Cambridge: Cambridge University Press.

Heath, S. B. (1986), 'The functions and uses of literacy', in S. de Castell, A. Luke and K. Egan (eds.), *Literacy, School and Schooling: A Reader*. Cambridge: Cambridge University Press.

Hicks, D. (1984), 'Geography', in A. Craft and G. Bardell (eds.), *Curriculum Opportunities in a Multicultural Society*. London: Harper & Row.

Hills, G. (1983), 'Misconceptions misconceived: using conceptual change to understand some of the problems pupils have in learning science', in H. Helm and J. D. Novak (eds.) *Misconceptions in Science and Mathematics*. Proceedings of the International Seminar.

Holdaway, D. (1979), *The Foundations of Literacy*. Sydney: Ashton Scholastic.

Hong Kingston, M. (1975), *The Woman Warrior*. London: Picador.

House, E. (1974), *The Politics of Educational Innovation*. Berkeley: McCutchan.

Hull, C. (1984), 'Marking: a critical alternative', *Journal of Curriculum Studies*, 16 (2), pp. 155–64.

Hughes, T. (1976), 'Myth and education', in G. Fox, G. Hammond, T. Jones, F. Smith and K. Sterck (eds.), *Writers, Critics and Children*. London: Heinemann.

Hymes, D. (1981), *In Vain I Tried to Tell You*. Philadelphia: University of Pennsylvania Press.

ILEA English Centre (1981), *Languages*. London: ILEA.

ILEA English Centre (1979), *Our Lives*. London: ILEA.

Inglis, F. (1987), 'The condition of English in England', *English in Education*, 21 (3), Autumn 1987.

Iser, W. (1978), *The Art of Reading*. Baltimore: Johns Hopkins University Press.

Jamieson, I., and Lightfoot, M. (1982), *Schools and Industry*. London: Methuen.

Jones, A., and Mulford, J. (eds.) (1971), *Children Using Language*. Oxford: Oxford University Press.

Jones, C. (1986), 'Racism in society and schools', in J. Gundara, C. Jones and K. Kimberley (eds.), *Racism, Diversity and Education*. London: Hodder & Stoughton.

Kamii, C. (1985), 'Leading primary education towards excellence – beyond worksheets and drill', *Young Children*, 40, pp. 3–9.

Kelly, A. V. (1986), *Knowledge and Curriculum Planning*. London: Harper & Row.

Kelly, G. (1955), *The Psychology of Personal Constructs*, 2 vols. New York: Norton.

Kelly, G. (1963), *A Theory of Personality*. New York: Norton.

Kierkegaard, S. (1962), *The Point of View for My Work as an Author: A Report to History*. New York: Harper & Row.

Kilbourn, B. (1985), 'Science, society and the general level student', Ontario Institute for the Study of Education (unpublished).

Kogan, M. (1978). *The Politics of Educational Change*. London: Fontana.

Kozulin, A. (1987), 'Vygotsky in context', in L. Vygotsky, *Thought and Language*, rev. edn. Cambridge, Mass.: MIT Press.

Kuhn, T. S. (1972), *The Structure of Scientific Revolutions*, rev. edn. Chicago: Chicago University Press.

Labov, W. (1972), *Language in the Inner City: Studies in the Black English Vernacular*. Philadelphia: University of Philadelphia Press.

Labov, W., and Waletsky, J. (1967), 'Narrative analysis: oral versions of personal experience', in J. Helen (ed.), *Essays in the Verbal and Visual Arts*. Washington DC: American Ethnological Society.

Lacan, J. (1977), *Ecrits: A Selection* (translated by A. Sheridan). London: Tavistock.

Langer, J. A. (1984), 'Literacy instruction in American schools: problems and perspectives', *American Journal of Education*, 93 (1), pp. 107–32.

Langer, J. A., and Applebee, A. W. (1986), 'Reading and writing instruction: toward a theory of teaching and learning', in E. Rothkopf (ed.), *Review of Research in Education*, 13, pp. 171–94.

Langer, J. A., and Applebee, A. N. (1987), 'Language learning and interaction: a framework for the teaching of writing', in A. N. Applebee (ed.), *Contexts for Learning to Write*. Norwood, NJ: Ablex.

Lave, J., Murtaugh, M., and de la Roche, O. (1984), 'The dialectic of arithmetic in grocery shopping', in B. Rogoff and J. Lave (eds.), *Everyday Cognition: Its Development in Social Context*. Cambridge, Mass.: Harvard University Press.

Layton, D. (1973), *Science for the People*. London: Allen & Unwin.

Leach, M. (1986), 'TVEI will fail', *Times Educational Supplement*, 31 October 1986.

Leavis, F. R. (1952), 'Literary criticism and philosophy', in *The Common Pursuit*. London: Chatto & Windus.

Leavis, F. R., and Thompson, D. (1933), *Culture and Environment*. London: Chatto & Windus.

Leont'ev, A. N. (1981), 'The problem of activity in psychology', in J. V. Wertsch (ed.), *The Concept of Activity in Soviet Psychology*. Armonk, NY: M. E. Sharpe.

Levine, J. (1981), 'Developing pedagogies in multilingual classrooms', *English in Education*, 13 (3).

Little, G. (1987), 'The happiest days of your life', *Meanjin* (Autobiography and Childhood), 46 (1).

Lodge, D. (1981), *Working with Structuralism: Essays and Reviews on Nineteenth and Twentieth Century Literature*. London: Routledge & Kegan Paul.

Lomax, J. (1979), 'Interest in books and stories', in M. Clark and W. Cheney (eds.), *Studies in Pre-School Education*. London: Hodder & Stoughton for the Scottish Council for Research in Education.

Lundgren, U. P. (1977), *Model Analysis of Pedagogical Processes*. Stockholm, Sweden: Stockholm Institute of Education, Department of Educational Research.

Luria, A. R. (1983), 'The development of writing in the child', in M. Martlew (ed.), *The Psychology of Written Language*. New York: John Wiley.

Mandler, J. M. (1984), *Stories, Scripts and Scenes: Aspects of Schema Theory*. Hillsdale, NJ: Erlbaum.

Martin, N. (ed.) (1984), *NATE – The First Twenty-One Years*. Sheffield: NATE.

Mason, J. (1981), *Pre-Reading: A Developmental Perspective*, Technical Report no. 198. Urbana: University of Illinois, Center for the Study of Reading.

Mayher, J., Lester, N., and Pradl, G. (1985), *Learning to Write/Writing to Learn*. Upper Montclair, NJ: Boynton/Cook.

McNeil, L. M. (1981), 'Negotiating classroom knowledge: beyond achievement and socialisation', *Journal of Curriculum Studies*, 13 (4), pp. 313–28.

Medway, P. (1980), *Finding a Language*. London: Chameleon.

Medway, P. (1984), 'Doing teaching English', in M. Meek and J. Miller (eds.), *Changing English: Essays for Harold Rosen*. London: Heinemann.

Medway, P. (1986), 'What counts as English: selections from language and reality in a school subject', unpublished PhD thesis, University of Leeds.

Meek, M. (ed.) (1983), *Opening Moves* (Bedford Way Papers no. 17). London: University of London Institute of Education.

Meek, M., Armstrong, S., Austerfield, V., Graham, J. and Plackett, E. (1983), *Achieving Literacy*. London: Routledge & Kegan Paul.

Meek, M., and Miller, J. (eds.) (1984), *Changing English: Essays for Harold Rosen*. London: Heinemann.

Mercer, N. (ed.) (1981), *Language in School and Community*. London: Edward Arnold.

Michaels, S. (1981), '"Sharing Time": children's narrative styles and differential access to literacy', *Language in Society*, 10, pp. 423–42.

Michaels, S. (in press), *Text and Context: A New Approach to the Study of Writing*. Discourse Processes.

Miller, J. (1983), *Many Voices: Bilingualism, Culture and Education*. London: Routledge & Kegan Paul.

Miller, J. (ed.) (1984), *Eccentric Propositions*. London: Routledge & Kegan Paul.

Miller, J. (1985), *Women Writing about Men*. London: Virago.

National Writing Project (1987), *Work Experience*. Hampshire Writing Project.

Neisser, U. (1976), 'General, academic and artificial intelligence', in L. B. Resnick (ed.), *The Nature of Intelligence*. Hillsdale, NJ: Erlbaum.

Newman, D. (1986), 'The role of mental knowledge in the development of perspective taking', *Developmental Review*, 6, pp. 122–45.

Ninio, A., and Bruner, J. S. (1978), 'The achievement and antecedents of labeling', *Journal of Child Language*, 5, pp. 1–15.

Olson, D. R. (1977), 'Oral and written language and the cognitive processes of children', *Journal of Communication*, 27 (3), pp. 10–26.

Olson, D. R., and Bruner, J. S. (1974), 'Learning through experience and learning through media', in D. R. Olson (ed.), *Media and Symbols: The Forms of Expression, Communication and Education*. Chicago: University of Chicago Press.

Owen, J. (1973), *The Management of Curriculum Development*. Cambridge: Cambridge University Press.

Paley, V. (1985), *Boys and Girls: Superheroes in the Doll Corner*. Chicago: University of Chicago Press.

Palincsar, A. S. (1986), 'The role of dialogue in providing scaffolded instruction', *Educational Psychologist*, 21, pp. 73–98.

Payton, S. (1984), *Developing Awareness of Print*. Educational Review, Offset Publications no. 2, University of Birmingham.

Pearson, D. P., and Gallagher, M. C. (1983), 'The instruction of reading comprehension', *Contemporary Educational Psychology*, 8, pp. 317–44.

Perera, K. (1984), *Children's Writing and Reading*. Oxford: Blackwell.

Polanyi, L. (1982), 'Literary complexity in everyday storytelling', in D. Tannen (ed.), *Spoken and Written Language*. Norwood, NJ: Ablex.

Polanyi, M. (1958), *Personal Knowledge*. London: Routledge.

Postman, N., and Weingartner, C. (1966), *Linguistics: A Revolution in Teaching*. New York: Dell.

Pradl, G. (1987), 'Close encounters of the first kind: teaching the poem at the point of utterance', *English Journal*, 76 (2), pp. 66–9.

Prince, G. (1982), *Narratology*. Berlin: Mouton.

Quine, W. V. (1960), *Word and Object*. Cambridge, Mass.: MIT Press.

Ratner, N., and Bruner, J. S. (1978), 'Games, social exchange and the acquisition of language', *Journal of Child Language*, 5, pp. 391–401.

Read, C. (1971), 'Preschool children's knowledge of English phonology', *Harvard Educational Review*, 41, pp. 1–34.

Resnick, L. B. (1985), 'Cognition and instruction: recent theories of human competence and how it is acquired', in B. L. Hammond (ed.), *Psychology and Learning: The Masser Lecture Series*, vol. 4. Washington, DC: American Psychological Association.

Richards, J. W. (1978), *Classroom Language: What Sort?* London: Allen & Unwin.

Rogers, C. (1967), *On Becoming a Person*. London: Constable.

Rosen, B. (1988), *And None of It Was Nonsense*. London: Scholastic/Mary Glasgow.

Rosen, H. (1972), *Language and Class*. Bristol: Falling Wall Press.

Rosen, H. (1984), *Stories and Meanings*. Sheffield: National Association for the Teaching of English.

Rosen, H., and Burgess, T. (1981), *The Language and Dialects of London Schoolchildren: An Investigation*. London: Ward Lock.

Rosenblatt, L. (1978), *The Reader, the Text, the Poem*. Carbondale, Ill.: Southern Illinois University Press.

Rowlands, S. (1984), *The Enquiring Classroom*. Brighton: Falmer Press.

Rumelhart, D. (1976), *Toward an Interactive Model of Reading*, Technical Report no. 56. San Diego: San Diego Center for Human Information Processing, University of California at San Diego.

Said, E. (1978), *Orientalism*. London: Routledge & Kegan Paul.

Sapir, E. (1961), *Culture, Language and Personality*, Berkeley: University of California Press.

Sartre, J. P. (1964), *Words*. London: Braziller.

Saunders, M. (1979), 'Locality and the curriculum: towards a positive critique', *Comparative Education*, 15 (2), pp. 217–30.

Saunders, M. (1982), 'Productive activity in the curriculum: changing the literate bias of secondary schools in Tanzania', *British Journal of the Sociology of Education*, 3 (1).

Schilling, M. (1986), 'Knowledge and liberal education: a critique of Paul Hirst', *Journal of Curriculum Studies*, 18 (1).

Scholes, R. (1987), 'Textuality: power and pleasure', *English Education*, 19 (2), pp. 69–82.

Schon, D. A. (1983), *The Reflective Practitioner: How Professionals Think in Action.* London: Temple-Smith.

Schutz, A., and Luckmann, T. (1973), *The Structures of the Life World.* London: Heinemann.

Schwab, J. J. (1970), 'The practical: a language for curriculum', in I. Westbury and N. J. Wilkof (eds.), *Science, Curriculum and Liberal Education.* Chicago: University of Chicago Press.

Scribner, S., and Cole, M. (1981), *The Psychology of Literacy.* Cambridge, Mass.: Harvard University Press.

Searle, D. (1984), 'Scaffolding: who's building whose building', *Language Arts*, 61, pp. 480–83.

Searle, J. R. (1979), *Expression and Meaning: Studies in the Theory of Speech Acts.* Cambridge: Cambridge University Press.

Sinclair, J. M., and Coulthard, M. (1975), *Towards an Analysis of Discourse.* London: Oxford University Press.

Smith, B. H. (1981), 'Afterthoughts on narrative', in W. J. T. Mitchell (ed.), *On Narrative.* Chicago: Chicago University Press.

Smith, F. (1982), 'The creative achievement of literacy', in H. Goelman, A. A. Oberg and F. Smith (eds.), *Awakening to Literacy.* London: Heinemann.

Snow, C. E. (1977), 'The development of conversation between mothers and babies', *Journal of Child Language*, 4, pp. 1–22.

Soloman, J. (1983), 'Learning about energy: how pupils think in two domains', *European Journal of Science Education*, 5 (1), pp. 49–59.

South Australian Education Department (1987), *The Connecting Conversation: Literacy, Language and Learning in the English Classroom.* Adelaide: South Australia Education Department.

Stahl, S. (1977), 'The oral personal narrative in its generic context', *Fabula*, 18, pp. 18–39.

Stahl, S. (1983), 'Personal experience stories', in R. M. Dorson (ed.), *Handbook of American Folklore.* Bloomington, Ind.: University of Indiana Press.

Steiner, G. (1975), *After Babel.* Oxford: Oxford University Press.

Stern, D. N. (1985), *The Interpersonal World of the Infant: A View from Psychoanalysis and Developmental Psychology.* New York: Basic Books.

Street, B. V. (1984), *Literacy in Theory and Practice.* Cambridge: Cambridge University Press.

Stubbs, M. (1983), *Discourse Analysis: The Sociolinguistic Analysis of Natural Language.* Oxford: Basil Blackwell.

Stubbs, M. (ed.) (1985a), *The Other Languages of England.* The Linguistic Minorities Project. London: Routledge & Kegan Paul.

Stubbs, M. (1985b), *Educational Linguistics.* Oxford: Basil Blackwell.

Tannen, D. (1984), 'What's in a frame? Surface evidence for underlying expectations', in R. Freedle (ed.), *Directions in Discourse Processing.* Norwood, NJ: Ablex.

Taylor, J. B. (1984), 'Shared writing experience', paper presented at the Alabama Department of Education, Early Childhood Workshop, Montgomery, Alabama.

Tizard, B., and Hughes, M. (1984), *Young Children Learning.* London: Fontana.

Todorov, T. (1977), *The Poetics of Prose.* Oxford: Blackwell.

Torbe, M. (1978), *Teaching Spelling.* London: Ward Lock Educational.

Torbe, M. (1986), 'Language across the curriculum: policies and practice', in D. Barnes, J. Britton and M. Torbe, *Language, The Learner and the School,* 3rd edn. London: Penguin.

Tough, J. (1979), *Talk for Teaching and Learning.* London: Ward Lock.

Volosinov, (1986 [1973]), *Marxism and the Philosophy of Language.* Cambridge, Mass.: Harvard University Press.

Vygotsky, L. (1962), *Thought and Language.* Cambridge, Mass.: MIT Press.

Vygotsky, L. (1978), *Mind in Society.* Cambridge, Mass.: Harvard University Press.

Wagner, R. K., and Sternberg, R. J. (1986), 'Tacit knowledge and intelligence in the everyday world', in R. K. Wagner and R. J. Sternberg (eds.), *Practical Intelligence.* Cambridge: Cambridge University Press.

Walkerdine, V. (1982), 'From context to text: a psychosemiotic approach to abstract thought', in M. Beveridge (ed.), *Children Thinking through Language.* London: Edward Arnold.

Watzlawick, P., Beavin, J. H., and Jackson, D. D. (1967), *Pragmatics of Human Communication: A Study of Interactional Patterns, Anthologies and Paradoxes.* New York: Norton.

Wells, C. G. (1981), 'Some antecedents of early childhood attainment', *British Journal of Educational Sociology,* 2 (2), pp. 180–200.

Wertheimer, M. (1959), *Productive Thinking,* enlarged edn. New York: Harper & Row.

Wertsch, J. V. (1984), 'The zone of proximal development: some conceptual issues', in B. Rogoff and J. V. Wertsch (eds.), *Children's Learning in the 'Zone of Proximal Development'.* New Directions for Child Development, 23.

Wertsch, J. V. (1985), *Vygotsky and the Social Formation of Mind.* Cambridge, Mass.: Harvard University Press.

Wertsch, J. V., and Stone, C. A. (1985), 'The concept of internalization in Vygotsky's account of the genesis of higher mental functions', in J. V. Wertsch (ed.), *Culture, Communication and Cognition: Vygotskian Perspectives*. Cambridge: Cambridge University Press.

Whitty, G. (1985), *Sociology and School Knowledge*. London: Methuen.

Williams, J. T. (1977), *Learning to Write or Writing to Learn*. Slough: National Foundation for Educational Research.

Winkley, D. (1985), *Diplomats and Detectives: LEA Advisers at Work*. London: Robert Royce.

Witkin, H. A., Moore, C. A., Goodenough, D. R., and Cox, P. W. (1977), 'Field-dependent and field-independent cognitive styles and their educational implications', *Review of Educational Research*, 47 (1), pp. 1–64.

Wood, D., Bruner, J. S., and Ross, G. (1976), 'The role of tutoring in problem solving', *Journal of Child Psychology and Psychiatry*, 17, pp. 89–100.

Wood, D., McMahon, L., and Cranstoun, Y. (1980), *Working with Under-Fives*. London: Grant McIntyre.

Young, M. F. D. (1971), 'An approach to the study of curricula as socially organised knowledge', in M. F. D. Young (ed.), *Knowledge and Control*. London: Collier Macmillan.

Zipes, J. (1983), *Fairy Tales and the Art of Subversion*. London: Heinemann.

Index

Polakon, V., 205
Polanyi, L., 200
Polanyi, M., 184, 185, 231, 247, 262, 266
Postman, N. and Weingartner, C., 21
Pradl, G., xiv, 2, 154n
Prince, G., 195
problem-solving, 17
Progressive Education Association, 210
Project English, 210
proximal development *see* zone of psychology, 158, 176

Quinlan, M., 266

Ratner, N. and Bruner, J. S., 5
Read, C., 108, 109
Reading Recovery Programme, 8
Resnick, L. B., 3, 4, 6, 10, 13n
Richards, I. A., 157
Richards, J. W., 28
Rogers, C., 40
Romano, T., 266
Rosen, B., 205
Rosen, C., 252n
Rosen, H., 104, 135, 168n, 200, 263
Rosen, H. and Burgess, T., 167n
Rosenblatt, L., xiv
Rowlands, S., 26
Rukeyser, M., 145
Rumelhart, D., 75
Ruskin, J., 71
Rutledge, D., 217, 218, 254

Sapir, E., 225, 247, 262, 265
Sartre, J. P., 83, 84
Saunders, M., 15, 22
Saussure, F., 163
shared journals, 107
scaffold
    as model for instruction, 8, 49, 215
    in school, 6
    in science, 13
    social interaction as, 1, 4, 5, 12
Schilling, M., 24
Scholes, R., 152, 178, 179
Schon, D., 26
Schools Council, 159

Schutz, A. and Luckman, T., 15
Schwab, J. J., 22
Scott, W., 211
science, 13, 23, 27, 29, 145, 151, 153, 236, 238, 270
Scribner, S. and Cole, M., 19
Searle, D., 12, 42
Select Committee on Education, Science and Arts, House of Commons, 251
Sendak, M., 72, 92, 144
Seuss, Dr, 71
Shakespeare, W., 93, 196, 211
shaping at the point of utterance, 44, 148, 184
Sinclair, J. M. and Coulthard, M., 78
skills, 184, 208
Skinner, B., 266
Smith, B. H., 200
Smith, F., 62, 69, 82, 92
Snow, C. E., 4, 38
sociality corollary, 39
social studies, 152, 172, 236
sociology, 158
Solomon, J., 16
South Australia Education Department, 140, 141, 172
spectator role, xvi, 34, 69, 147, 176, 266, 270
spelling, 183, 193, 208, 248, 251
Stahl, S., 197, 200
Stern, D., 35
Stevens, W., 45
stories, x, 42, 69, 71, 95, 145, 161, 195
Strauss, R., 173
Street, B. V., 19, 187
Stubbs, M., 78, 167, 168n
system belief, 220

talk, 2, 248, 271
Tannen, D., 200, 201
Taylor, J., 107
teacher–education, 206, 245
teacher–pupil interaction, 6
teching
    as listening, xiv
    critical, 2
    reciprocal, 8, 10